5.00
W9-ARI-323

RACE: A Study in Superstition

BOOKS BY JACQUES BARZUN

HISTORY

The French Race, 1932
Race, a Study in Superstition, 1937; (TORCHBOOKS, 1965)
Darwin, Marx, Wagner, 1941; (ANCHOR BOOKS, 1958)
Classic, Romantic, and Modern, 1943; (ANCHOR BOOKS, 1961)
Berlioz and the Romantic Century, 1950; (MERIDIAN BOOKS, 1956)
The Modern Researcher (with Henry F. Graff), 1957; (HARBINGER BOOKS, 1962)

CRITICISM

Of Human Freedom, 1939; (REV. ED. LIPPINCOTT, 1964)
Teacher in America, 1945; (ANCHOR BOOKS, 1954)
God's Country and Mine, 1954; (VINTAGE BOOKS, 1959)
Music in American Life, 1956; (MIDLAND BOOKS, 1962)
The Energies of Art, 1956; (VINTAGE BOOKS, 1962)
John Jay Chapman: Writings, 1957; (ANCHOR BOOKS, 1959)
The House of Intellect, 1959; (TORCHBOOKS, 1961)
Science: The Glorious Entertainment, 1964; (TORCHBOOKS, 1965)

TRANSLATIONS

Becque's La Parisienne, 1949
Pleasures of Music, 1951; (CAMPUS BOOKS, 1960)
Diderot's Rameau's Nephew, 1952; (ANCHOR BOOKS, 1956)
Mirbeau's The Epidemic, 1952
Musset's Fantasio, 1955
Flaubert's Dictionary of Accepted Ideas, 1954
New Letters of Berlioz, 1954
Berlioz's Evenings with the Orchestra, 1956
Four Plays by Courteline, 1958-1960
Beaumarchais' Figaro's Marriage, 1961

TO THE MEMORY OF
GEORGE RUSSELL SHAW
(1848—1937)

It's a wise child that knows its own father.

WISDOM OF THE NATIONS

La recherche de la paternité est interdite.

CODE NAPOLÉON

572
B

Jacques Barzun

RACE:
A Study in Superstition

Revised, with a new Preface

HARPER & ROW, PUBLISHERS
New York, Evanston, and London

WINGATE COLLEGE LIBRARY
WINGATE, N. C.

This is a revised edition of a work previously entitled *Race: A Study in Modern Superstition.*

RACE: A STUDY IN SUPERSTITION. *Copyright © 1937, 1965 by Jacques Barzun. Printed in the United States of America. All rights reserved. No part of this book may be used or reproduced in any manner whatsoever without written permission except in the case of brief quotations embodied in critical articles and reviews. For information address Harper & Row, Publishers, Incorporated, 49 East 33rd Street, New York 16, N. Y.*

LIBRARY OF CONGRESS CATALOG CARD NUMBER: 64-25106

M-O

CONTENTS

30140

Preface to the Second Edition

RACISM TODAY

THIS BOOK IS COMING back into print because the idea it treats of, although repeatedly killed, is nevertheless undying. As long as people permit themselves to think of human groups without the vivid sense that groups consist of individuals and that individuals display the full range of human differences, the tendency which twenty-eight years ago I named "race-thinking" will persist. Suppose a group of thirty to forty fairly congenial people working together in an office or factory: they observe common ways and achieve mutual understanding: they think of themselves as one entity—"the sixth floor" or "Wing B" or "the department of such-and-such." Now divide them at random into two parts and move one or the other half to another floor or building, but maintain intermittent relations through their work. Shortly, "cultural" differences will develop. Old habits and tolerances will break down, friction and resentment will arise. Soon each group will tend to ascribe unpleasant characteristics to all the members of the other group. It will be a more or less open conflict of "We" and "They"—They being those impossible people on the tenth floor, who never do what they should and always what they shouldn't. The cultural differences of divergent habits will have become "race" differences.

As an operation of the mind, race-thinking rests on abstraction—singling out certain traits that are observed, accurately or not, in one or more individuals, and making of these traits a composite character which is then assumed to be uniform, or at least prevailing, throughout the group. This product of thought is properly speaking a superstition—literally, an idea that "stands over" the facts, presumably to explain them or make them coherent and memorable. All that is needed to make the superstition permanent and powerful is the presence of some easily noted feature—color of skin or hair, striking appearance of face or body, unusual mode of speech or dress. The fusion of the visual sign and the expected behavior is all the more rapid and unshakable that it satisfies a need common in complex societies—the need to give body to vague hostility, to find excuses for what goes wrong, to fear aliens or neighbors and curse them, while enjoying self-approval from within the shelter of one's own group.

This urge is reinforced, in civilized communities, by the desire to explain through theory and system the facts of class distinction, of difference in temperament or ability, of variation in bodily features and mental habits. Political science, sociology, psychology, and physical anthropology have often helped to feed this desire. Thus on top of spontaneous race-thinking we find race-theorizing, which tries to make the haphazard abstractions of the people rational and even scientific. The present book deals with this astonishing enterprise of super-superstition.

I became interested in it, as I mention later, when studying the works of the great liberal philosopher, Montesquieu, in whose pages I came across the protracted dispute about the "race" of the nobility and of the bourgeoisie in France before the Revolution. I retraced the meanders of that long quarrel in a first book, ironically entitled *The French Race*. After the Revolution, race-theorizing in Europe expressed the struggle between nations, political parties, religious faiths, and social groups. A crisscrossing of economic and cultural differences added to the confusion and aggravated the fears and hatreds. The elaborate intellectual rationalizations I discuss no doubt betray a sense of guilt for these aggressive emotions. But whatever its source, the urge to build theories in order to justify collective hostility is strong, as the Nazi regime proved in Germany and as Communist literature continues to prove. Not merely Marxist propaganda but Marxist doctrine at its purest is in form and effect racist thought. Indeed, the class struggle is but the old race antagonism of French nobles and commoners writ large and made ruthless. Marx's bourgeois is not a human being with individual traits, but a social abstraction, a creature devoid of virtue or free will and without the right to live.

I am aware that to elucidate the racial conflicts of our time by condemning false abstraction is not usual or popular. Most social critics prefer to argue the case concretely about a particular group: are the Negroes, the Arabs, the Puerto Ricans, the equals of the French, the Israelis, the Irish? To which the enlightened reader, seeing tables of IQs and recognizing the cultural handicaps of submerged groups, dutifully answers "Yes!" I have no objection to this procedure, except that it proposes to establish an ill-defined "equality" by a long series of separate proofs and leaves the moral and intellectual question of racism where it was before. Nor do tests and tables work with practical effect to abate prejudice and stop violence. Other books, also based on research, "prove" the opposite and find sponsors in the scientific community and the United States Senate.

The issue of equality is in fact irrelevant and unmeaning. Equality is neither provable nor disprovable. This is so for groups and individuals alike. Equality is not a scientific but a political idea, and it is valid only when one *assumes* it, as do the Declaration of Independence and the French Declaration of the Rights of Man. All men are *declared* equal in the sight of God and under the laws of a free society; after which anyone may claim his equal right by establishing his identity as a man.

Men as men, groups as wholes, are strictly incommensurable. A society, by its laws and customs, favors the traits or types it thinks useful. It measures (very roughly) fitness for the role of governor, astronaut, or public accountant, and gives each different wages and honors. But even this hierarchy is not absolute: it gives two governors different amounts of influence or respect. But in what is called a free society all are equal as citizens without proof. Therefore, once a people chooses a free constitution and recognizes it as the law of the land, there is nothing to prove or disprove about races as such, there is no issue to debate except the honest administration of the law.

In short, scientific discussions of heredity, of the incidence of disease or of the distribution of talent, are beside the point. To enlist genetics for or against the "grounds of prejudice"—as if prejudice needed grounds—only serves to embroil the layman in doubts and technicalities he is not trained to handle. The main impression he is left with is that here is a complicated problem he cannot quite grasp and solve for himself. To be sure, the misuse of science must be countered, and since people insist on bolstering their fears and hatreds with reasons drawn from science and history, learning must come to the rescue. What does genetics actually show about race? It shows by statistics that genes recur in predictable linkages that permit certain physical characteristics to endure in successive generations. This in turn makes for noticeable likenesses within what is technically called a population, that is, a delimited intermarrying group. But, still according to genetics, the transmission of the factors called genes does not automatically determine the human traits that the racist and the anti-racist fight about. Genes will help account for so-called white skin, not for socialism, genius, dipsomania, or delinquency.

The attempt at historical demonstration is as futile as the scientific. Can anyone believe that the tension in, say, South Africa is going to be lessened by arguing against the White

Supremacist that the Bushmen and Hottentots were first in possession of the land? Has it stopped the Arab-Israeli struggle to establish either group as "really" the oldest settlers? Could anything be more useless than to try to stop border raids by appealing to ancient linguistic and cultural connections? Since when have family quarrels been stopped by common descent or a single mode of life?

To ask these questions is to answer them. Peace springs only from the desire for peace and the use of reason in removing grievances. The practical settlement of modern race conflicts can come only from a combination of these forces. And the desire for peace, as we can see in the present situation in the United States, is strengthened by the existence of a law of equal rights. For it is clear that although the American Negroes' struggle for equal treatment has been marred by violence on both sides, there is no comparison between what has happened here since the beginning of integration by force of law and what we see happening in the rest of the world whenever passions flare up and groups clash: the death toll in those older or younger nations is at the rate of dozens a day—or thousands, as occurred on the liberation of India. Our conduct of the transition is indeed far from ideal, but by comparative standards it has been remarkably restrained—restrained by the force and the *influence* of a law of equal rights.

Such a law, moreover, has the astonishing power of proving its truth in proportion as it is carried out. Give people roughly equal treatment and in the end they will prove themselves equally worthy of it, again roughly speaking. For it is only race-thinking that imagines all whites to be industrious and intelligent and clean and law-abiding, while their Negro (or Irish or Spanish) neighbors are the reverse. Such a generality is but a translation of the fundamental racist thought that only the nobility (or the rich or the poor or the workers or the artists) have virtue. And this means, too, that sentimental or indignant reversals of the racist proposition are false and dangerous. The victims of oppression do not turn into angels by being emancipated. This theoretical point is in the end the most practical. It undercuts the whole paraphernalia of "scientific proof" which cloaks stubborn hate and fear. Race-thinking is bad thinking and that is all.

It can of course be argued that in the present struggles between white and black, yellow and white, black and black, Moslem and Hindu, Arab and Israeli, communist and capitalist, all pretense at right reason has been given up: the war is one of naked self-interests. Hence it is a waste of time to point out the fallacies by which science and history have attempted to justify aggression. The truth is that we hear less about scientific and other pretexts only because the battle is on. Race theories are a peacetime occupation. But race-thinking has not thereby decreased. On the contrary, it has gained a firmer grip on all minds because of the new conflicts, which are indeed for material ends, but which assume the moral and cultural and genetic uniformity of the warring groups. So, once again, the image of the enemy clan, the hostile race, must be blotted out; and this can best be done by uprooting the old theories that have become buried assumptions. We must learn to see and to believe that generalities about groups, even when true, tell us nothing about the individual, and that it is the individual we must judge. If we want social peace, this restriction on judgment must become a moral imperative; it must be taught as we teach "Thou shalt not steal" and "Thou shalt not kill." Part of the common upbringing must consist in showing the danger and the folly of thinking that groups are made up of identically hateful or identically lovable people.

Childhood is the time to strike, for children are the worst abstractionists. They seek security in a puzzling world by assuring themselves that all like things are wholly alike and that any one thing is all of a piece. The good kings and bad kings of the child's history book answer this requirement, leaving no room for the idea of comparatively good and bad. All the more reason, then, for the discipline of judging only individuals and thus limiting harm by limiting error. To see this parallel between judging groups and judging naïvely is also to see that race-thinking in adults is but childish abstraction eked out with pedantic reasons.

The resolve to pass no judgment without at least imagining individuals is also the guarantee against the mere turning of prejudice upside down that I spoke of a moment ago. When injustice is redressed, the hitherto outcast and maligned group must not benefit in reverse from the racism they justly complained of. They do not suddenly possess, as a group, the virtues they were formerly denied, and it is no sign of wisdom in the former oppressors to affect a contrite preference for those they once abused. Some years ago a student of mine studying in Paris on a Fulbright grant wrote to me that he had just attended in the Latin Quarter a memorable celebration. French artists and writers, all whites, led by Negro writers and by students both French and American, had solemnly burned the white race in effigy. This simulated lynching of the white by Negroes, encouraged by "enlightened" whites, is but an emblem of suicide for both. And no demonstration is needed to show that to change the supremacy of one "race" for that of another leaves social justice as much violated as before.

Again, the principle of judging individual cases, not empty abstractions, must apply whenever a group, thinking racially, feels attacked through a tendentious representation of one of their members in a work of art. The repeated attempts to have *The Merchant of Venice* banned and *Huckleberry Finn* removed from library shelves proceed from the same associative tendency which the interested group should on the contrary combat. To want Shylock and the slave Jim kept from public sight does not of course mean that Negroes and Jews recognize themselves at all in those fictions, but that they fear the public's inability to imagine better traits than the ones shown—for example, a kindly Jew, an educated Negro. That being the point, the effort should not be to suppress by group power but to enlighten by stressing the difference between an individual and a social group—and by making clear what literature is. The children in school must not be protected from reading about Mark Twain's lovable creation but from thinking that Negroes are born slaves and fated illiterates.

This anxious wrangling which goes on about books and plays seems at times trivial but is in fact fundamental. If democratic culture yields on this point, no prospect lies ahead but that of increasing animosity among pressure groups. A dozen years ago a Broadway play was picketed by a union of domestic servants because the maid in the play was made fun of. The race of housemaids was generically insulted by this unmerited ridicule which, I suppose, only lack of power and daring kept from being avenged in blood. Perhaps a world-wide congress of races and nations and unions and professional groups could ultimately force playwrights to put on the stage either characters entirely flawless and adorable or else divested of every social attribute—neither maids nor bankers, neither foreign nor native, neither parents nor children—and of no particular sex either, for in these analytic days each sex and its variants tends to think of itself as a victimized minority.

It is clear that in the absence of such limitations on race-thinking and group solidarity as I am suggesting, every self-conscious group will have to engage in raucous self-defense and self-praise or risk being slandered and abused by a more powerful group or cartel of groups. In social and cultural relations the law rarely intervenes effectively; the protection of rights and feelings only comes from decency and self-restraint. This is a generality that physicians might well ponder when in hospitals or medical schools they carry on against dentists a systematically hostile discrimination, a "race war" whose cruel incidents occasionally pass belief.

In urging these views against misdirected passions and wrongheaded remedies, I am not under the illusion that changing habits and emotions is easy. Even when one has been persuaded by reason and swears off the practice of race-thinking, one must be continually on guard against betrayal by words and especially by thought-clichés. The power of a superstition is that it speaks in the tones of common sense. Yet the possibility of destroying superstition can be historically shown. We now laugh and shudder at the belief in witches, not because the symptoms of what used to be called witchcraft have disappeared but because we no longer have the abstraction with which to lump together diverse individuals: eccentric old women, lascivious young ones, and variously "possessed" personalities—hysterical or otherwise deranged. Because we judge each individual as such, and if diseased classify him only for the sake of cure, it has become impossible to think "witch," and witch-thinking has disappeared from our midst.

The advantage of neutralizing a false abstraction by the equally abstract but more adequate principle that in social judgments the mind's eye must vividly see a crowd of diverse persons is not merely its simplicity as a moral principle, as a clear guide to the decency one wants to observe, whether watched by a policeman or not: that principle has value also in its power to diversify one's aggressive feelings, to scatter them in small fragments, and thus to restore the emotional freedom that democracy and liberalism allow. How ridiculous (and even offensive) to be told that one must love one's fellow man because the geneticist tells one to—via UNESCO—or because the historian can show reasons and the user of intelligence tests "results." The point is not to love one's fellow man but to be fair to him; it is not to show that social groups, previously despised, are all good companions and budding geniuses who will shortly reinvent the electric light. The point is to render absurd (not to say obscene) the hostile *or friendly* attribution of qualities to men otherwise than as individuals. One may of course speak of the collective achievements of a nation; one may criticize institutions, parties, tendencies; these aggregates have a place as shorthand terms in the well-stocked mind, but such judgments cannot without harm be carried over into daily life and action, where likes and dislikes have a right to exist provided they are exercised with decency and upon direct knowledge of individuals. Exclusion and rejection are here not only inevitable—one cannot know everybody and be in favor of everything—but even prejudice becomes proper when one acknowledges it as an infirmity and peaceably takes the consequences, that is, by excluding oneself from the activities and acquaintances that one dislikes.

Despite modern cant, there is no duty to "get to know" the members of an alien group toward which one is not attracted, no obligation to like foreign food, art, or manners, provided one is content to let them be. Forced encounters and even voluntarily acquired knowledge of other peoples do not guarantee friendship. It is foolish to suppose that if we could but exchange multitudinous visits with foreign nations we should all be smitten with one another. With the known or the unknown the right to quarrel must not be denied. Only, the moral man's quarrel is always with some aspect of reality. Race-quarrels are with a phantom which will not let men sleep and which ultimately imbrues them in blood. The moral remedy, imperfect but aimed at the heart of the problem, is to uproot the habit of hating and despising en masse on the basis of imputed traits.

The new race-antagonisms within the democracies of Western Europe show that the old superstition is close under the skin. To travel in France during the late Algerian troubles and hear vintage liberals say confidentially *"Je suis raciste"* is an experience that shocks only those unfamiliar with mankind's latent readiness for race-thinking—the easy, vulgar method for dealing abstractly with a threat to comfort or pocketbook. If in the teeth of such an old reflex there is to be any hope of averting riot or civil war, it lies in turning group antagonisms into consciously economic or political struggles by removing their racist covering. For there are established ways of coping with the conflicts of political and economic groups, and there are none for racial strife. In that respect race is like ancient religions: it utters a blind commandment to shed blood.

But the reader of this book would be left with an incomplete idea of the subject if he were so struck by the negative racism, born of fear and hate, that he failed to notice the secondary or positive role of race-theories. The elaborate systems constructed in Europe and America during the past three hundred years often had another purpose than vindictiveness. Particularly since 1850, when industrialization broke traditional bonds and detached man from his native soil without affording him new loyalties, the idea of race has been put forward as a principle of political and emotional union. The empire builder Cecil Rhodes was only one of many who had visions of global brotherhood and dominion for "their race." Hitler was borrowing a well-worn notion when he tried to unite the still separatist portions of Germanic Europe by preaching the sanctity of the blood bond. The same idea, as this book shows, had currency in other lands. Its appeal is twofold: it satisfies the starved sense of kinship and it promises a vast supernational community. We are witnessing a new effort of the same kind in the doctrine of *Négritude,* which the President of the Republic of Senegal, Léopold Senghor, is propounding to the West Africans. Like all race-theories, Négritude is a mixture of vagueness and pedantry. It proposes to weld a people together in the usual way of marking it off from all others. A difference—however defined—is first strongly asserted and then its "cause" is shown as something permanent, ineradicable, beyond man's will. Whether the advocates know it or not, such doctrines war against freedom by denying individuality its rights: race denies the citizen any cultural choice—he is bound by Négritude or Nordicism or some other principle of "blood" determinism. And race presumes that the nation or people forms a single group having but one mind and living solely for a political purpose. It negates alike the purpose of the various groups that do exist and that of a people which adopts various groupings for various purposes. Perhaps the new nations require this artificial welding, but they will regret its costly efficacy when it leads, as it must, to mutual massacre.

How can a civilized community get rid of this fatal superstition, supposing that it cannot afford to wait for the slow results of training the young with playground and schoolroom examples? I have no answer. The present book attempted a modest beginning of persuasion, having in view the adult educated reader to whom it showed in some detail the inconsistent racial fantasies developed in civilized Europe during the last 180 years. Men of good will, men of honor, scholars and scientists in the several branches of learning, have been the authors of these theories and the apologists of this superstition. They have argued on every conceivable premise of physique, language, temperament, moral character, coloring, shape of skull, and political belief, to establish the reality and the ranking of dozens, of hundreds, of supposed races. To each race they have ascribed traits that explained why the world was as it was and whither it was going. They have struggled to gloss over stubborn facts or to dismiss them; they have argued with the fanatics of rival theories or despised them. Encased in verbal armor, they have fought sham fights with real emotions and on real issues within and across national boundaries. Their labor has been great, and in the aggregate self-destructive, for their "facts" cancel one another and their habits of thought only prove to the detached observer that here are men of one culture, cast in the same intellectual mold, and unfortunately not graced with simple judgment.

It was my hope that the spectacle of this waste of intellect would illustrate for the reader the propositions I have now reexpressed. I expected that the recital might so irritate and, in the end, bore the said reader that he would be inoculated against race-thinking. He would conclude that the superstition of race need not be uprooted point by point, but that it can be swept away as a single repeating fallacy. Except perhaps for the chapter on the generally misunderstood Gobineau, the contents of this book are thus unique in being offered by the author as something to read and *forget*. If this is done in the light of the principle implied in my title, I am confident that what will not easily be forgotten is my point.

Since the first publication of this book in 1937 I have had no opportunity to correct the errors which I noted almost as soon as it appeared. I have felt particularly badly about the opening sentence of the Preface, originally enclosed in inverted commas, which somehow disappeared in the editing and made of my quotation from Coleridge a piece of involuntary plagiarism. A similar cause garbled some Greek and Latin terms. All these formal mistakes I believe I have now caught, as well as others more substantial. I have also docked the title of one needless adjective, straightened out sentences for clarity, and shortened paragraphs out of compassion for the reader who is asked to absorb in quoted form so much dogmatic nonsense. But I have not tried to replace the contemporary illustrations in the last chapter by more modern ones, which would have confused the reader and spoiled such artistic unity as the book possesses.

Besides the reviewers and other readers who drew my attention to misstatements, I should like to thank persons I associate with the making of this book and remember with particularly grateful feeling: in the forefront, Carleton J. H. Hayes, who taught me method and encouraged me to write this essay; the officers of the American Council of Learned Societies, and particularly Mr. Donald Young, who awarded me a two-year fellowship for study abroad in 1933-34; the librarians at Dresden, Berlin, and Frankfurt-am-Main—unknown to me by name—who facilitated, in spite of Nazism, researches of which they knew the bearing; and finally the late Reginald Reynolds, who when finishing his little classic, *Cleanliness and Godliness,* engaged me in correspondence and enshrined in his work a reference to the egregious Dr. Bérillon, whose tragicomic researches Reynolds had come across in my ninth chapter.

J. B.

September 1, 1964

PREFACE TO THE FIRST EDITION (1937)

"AN AUTHOR HAS three points to settle: To what sort his work belongs, for what description of readers it is intended, and the particular end or object that it is to answer." To meet these points in order, it must be said that this book undertakes to give a critical history of the Idea of Race in recent times. Though based on research, it is intended for the general educated reader, and the particular end or object of the work is to show how equally ill-founded are the commonplace and the learned views of race.

Although the task of research and writing was completed nearly a year ago, certain motives of diffidence kept the author from putting the final touches to the manuscript and preparing it for the press. As Aldous Huxley once remarked, modern writers seem to do little else than tell the rest of the world how it should think and behave. To add even a modest volume to the pile of hortatory literature seemed an act that deserved thinking over twice. Two factors overcame this hesitancy. One was the author's gratitude to the American Council of Learned Societies for generously subsidizing eighteen months of travel and reading in Europe at the beginning of this study. The other was the repeated experience encountered in reading or in conversation with friends and students, of being in possession of facts that seemed to be overlooked in the arguments both for and against race-beliefs and in the history of modern race-prejudice. The possession of such facts was felt as a burden and a responsibility.

One word more, concerning the scholarly apparatus. The European practice of limiting footnotes, quotations, and bibliography to a strict minimum has been followed, out of deliberate choice. No increase of the accessories can dispel mistrust, and the wish to confirm an author's truthfulness is baffled rather than served by the discovery that what he says is indeed to be found on such and such a page of such and such a book. Good scholarship has always been the joint work of diligence, honesty, and art, and these are qualities not to be measured by the amount of scaffolding left lying about in the finished product. To conclude ironically by violating this precept, a quotation from Emerson's Journals sums the matter up by placing the responsibility where it belongs: "I hate quotations. Tell me what you know."

J. B.

Chapter I

RACE: FACT OR FICTION?

I

Proudly they learn all mankind to contemn;
And all their race are true-born Englishmen.

* * *

A true-born Englishman's a contradiction,
In speech an irony, in fact a fiction;
A banter made to be a test of fools,
Which those that use it justly ridicules;
A metaphor invented to express
A man akin to all the universe.

—DANIEL DEFOE, 1701

AMONG THE WORDS that can be all things to all men, the word "Race" has a fair claim to being the most common, the most ambiguous, and the most explosive. No one today would deny that it is one of the great catchwords about which ink and blood are spilled in reckless quantities. Yet no agreement seems to exist about what Race means. Race seems to embody a fact as simple and obvious as the noonday sun, but if that is really so, why the endless wrangling about the idea and the facts of race? Why is it that every writer and nearly every man, literate or illiterate, differs from every other on the questions: What is a race? How can it be recognized? Who constitute the several races? Which are superior? Which nearest the ape and which nearest the image of the Creator?

These questions are not the playthings of academic minds. Today no argument is needed to prove that race and the feelings connected with race are one of the powers shaping the world. One European nation of seventy million inhabitants is governed by men whose main policies involve certain hard-and-fast race-beliefs. Another European nation not long since found it useful to whip up animosity against black-skinned men to help justify an imperialistic war.[1] In the Balkans, in Turkey, in Persia, in Scandinavia, in Holland, sizable groups of the population work with or without government backing to boost their own "racial type" at the expense of all the others. "Oppressed nationalities" in Catalonia, Brittany, Ireland, Alsace-Lorraine, and Palestine throw race into the balance of their economic and political grievances as an important makeweight. Immigrants from the various countries of Europe have spread the virulent germs of modern race-feeling into other parts of the world, notably the United States, where the older antagonism of whites against all other colored races has had a long history of prejudice and violence. Race may indeed be a mere pretext or it may be the aegis of a sincere fanaticism. In either case it is a reality in the minds of millions who hold the lives and fortunes of their neighbors in their hands. The sequel to the termination of the Gentlemen's Agreement between the United States and Japan in 1924 shows how dangerous it is to tamper with this reality on any grounds, political, social, or intellectual. The very vagueness of the notion of race adds to its protean power, for to the racist and to his victims the "facts of race" are a scientific truth as well as a belief satisfying a deep emotional impulse.

This threat to social peace is no less strong in the intellectual realm. To consolidate political unity, certain national cultures

[1] Written in 1936. The allusions are to Nazi Germany and the Italian war against Ethiopia, respectively.

seek to exclude one another on the ground of the racial incompatibility of minds. The idea of race makes easy the transition from cultural to political ill-feeling, and when we want to condemn some course of national action in our neighbors, race provides the universal joint that holds together the aliens' ignoble traditions, their present shameful course, and their innate perversity. This pattern of judgment is familiar to contemporaries of the First World War, in which a sincere belief in the wickedness of Kant, Hegel, and Nietzsche—"cultural poisons"—proved as strong as the hatred of the enemy, and as useful to the Cause as money or matériel.

Within national boundaries, race as a basis of judgment in matters of art and thought helps carry on the critics' war. It nourishes self-approval, stiffens factions, and decides among imponderables. Russian music, jazz, atonality, and other live issues are discussed by critics as conservative as Ernest Newman and Olin Downes in terms of "barbarian races," "racial strain," "Celtic melancholy," and "Afro-American harmonic elements." In mathematics and philosophy, which might be thought abstract and passionless subjects, "races" are discovered by ingenious scholars—not all of them Germans by any means—and "threats" or "dangers" to the national culture are staved off by the usual discriminatory means. The sincerity of the partisans can hardly be doubted when, as in Germany, the elite of the nation goes in bodily for this form of ideologic warfare.

Such manifestations of the race-spirit have led observers of the ever-spreading intolerance to believe that it originated exclusively in Germany, more particularly in Nazi Germany. It is quite true that the Third Reich has been the most blatant apostle of racism in the modern world, but the movement has deeper roots than that regime. The race-propaganda and "scholarship" in Germany show that it used words and ideas by no means novel in Western culture, and that its ammunition was largely borrowed from the European science, art, and history-writing of the past century, without distinction of nationality—or race.

Equally important, though generally overlooked, is the fact that articulate minorities in other countries than Germany have been as deeply engaged in thinking and talking about race. The only difference is that no other government has yet gone as far as the Nazi regime in adopting race as a popular slogan, despite its obvious value as a means of diverting attention from economic problems and as a satisfaction of the ever-latent zest to persecute. But read attentively the press and political literature of the modern period in England, France, Italy, and the United States; in Mexico, Turkey, Rumania, and Scandinavia: you will not read very far before you are told or left to infer that the whites are unquestionably superior to the colored races; that the Asiatic Peril is a race-peril; that the Japanese are deemed so exceedingly yellow-perilous that the Chinese become white brothers in comparison (and vice versa); that the great American problem is to keep the Anglo-Saxon race pure from the contamination of Negro (or Southern European, or Jewish) "blood." The quarrel about race and blood comes even closer home when we are told that among the whites the tall blond Nordics are a superior breed destined to rule the world and that brown-eyed, round-headed Latins, whether in Europe or in South America, are a degenerate, revolutionary lot. They have no sense of race-discrimination and are incapable of governing themselves, probably because they live under a hot (and blue) southern sky.

But alas! even among Anglo-Saxons, there seem to be impassable barriers of race. Few are the consistent believers in the Nordic unity of Anglo-Saxons and Germans; for the Germans are Teutons, a people notoriously refractory to civilization, as is conclusively shown by the Roman historians and the burning of the Library of Louvain in 1914. Of course, the Aryans among us are willing to patch up a good many contradictions if only we can be made to unite against the dreaded Semite with his international ideas, decadent passion for the arts, and intolerable financial ability. The Semite himself is race-conscious and, given his chance, just as scornful and prejudiced as the Aryan who would oppress him. Needless to add, every one of the foregoing statements can be found refuted, modified, or twisted into strange compounds of incoherent animus. And yet these are but the cruder ways of race-prejudice: they form the common, casual superstition. When we rise into higher spheres and glance at learned papers on the race of fossil remains, or the proportion of Celtic blood in Shakespeare, we can measure the subtle spread and unlimited power of racist thought.

Within the babble of fanatics and theorists one can distinguish voices shouting that the notion of race is a myth which all intelligent people should discard. Yet the quarrel about race is certainly not between the uneducated, on the one hand, and the cultured elite on the other. Intelligence and education do not prevent a man from holding fast to race-prejudice. A British Foreign Secretary with a biblical surname feels it necessary to dispel doubts about his race. "I am not a Jew," says Sir John Simon, recklessly adding, "I am just an ordinary Briton of Aryan stock." The well-known scientist, Sir Arthur Keith, spends a great deal of time and energy stressing the value of race-prejudice in modern life and urging the necessity of conflict among races as a means of improving the species. It is not the German professors alone who publish treatises proving that the authors and their friends are Nordics, heirs of the Greeks, and creators of all that is good, true, and beautiful. In France, where it is often thought that race-ideas can take no hold, the most impenitent form of race-superstition thrives, namely, that which is unaware of itself. Indeed, race-controversies raged in France long before they became a constant preoccupation in the rest of Europe. In seventeenth- and eighteenth-century France, race was already a weapon in the struggle between absolutism, aristocracy, and the middle class. The warfare spread to the arts and philosophy in the nineteenth century, by which time independent shoots in other cultures had also borne fruit, leaving the grand harvesting on a world-wide scale to our generation.

Viewed in the light of such facts, the race-question appears a much bigger affair than a trumped-up excuse for local persecution. It becomes rather a mode of thought endemic in Western civilization. As I shall show, the greatest, as well as the weakest, minds of the past century and a half have yielded to its lure. Other outstanding forces of the epoch—Romanticism, Nationalism, Political Democracy, Imperialism, and Science—have reinforced the power of race-thinking in popular as well as educated opinion. It adorns or defaces, as one chooses, every type of mental activity—history, art, politics, science, and social reform.

The following chapters will therefore consider racism as a Western phenomenon, with a special emphasis on the course of race-doctrines in modern France. The reason for stressing French ideas will become obvious. France has produced some of the most powerful myths and personalities in the field—Montesquieu, Gobineau, Thierry, Renan, and Taine, to mention only the geniuses: without these there would have been no Hitler as we know him, and a very different Third Reich. France, moreover, has always been deemed free from race-prejudice in spite of her large contributions to doctrine. Hence, in examining a culture in which race-theories are so numerous and diverse as to have permitted no single national dogma to emerge, the fury of assertions and contradictions will be most illuminating. It follows also that by showing the causes and effects of race-thinking in France, more violent manifestations of the same phobia elsewhere cannot be held exceptional and temporary aberrations. In this instance, proving the least is the best way of proving the most. For the race-theorizing of no country and of no man is entirely original. Gobineau may have had a hint from Klemm, as Nietzsche had one from Gobineau. Buffon came before Blumenbach who came before Thurnam. Thierry and Guizot owe much to Boulainvilliers and Montesquieu, and all of them to the Roman Tactitus who, if anyone, must be credited with starting the powerful race-dogma of Nordic superiority.

Since 1850 race-thinking is international, though it is much less like a stream with numerous tributaries than like an impenetrable jungle ever sprouting more luxuriantly. To follow any one path is to be enmeshed at once in a tangle of quarrels, a confusion of claims, a knot of facts and fictions that revolt the intellect and daunt the courage of the most persistent. In its mazes, race-thinking is its own best refutation. If logic and consistency are the marks of truth, not a single system of race-classification can be true. Indeed, speaking in a mood of paradox, one could say that the only logical argument in favor of the diversity of races would be that no one race could possibly have been gifted with such a capacity for nonsense as the literature of the subject affords.

II

What race do you belong to? A white citizen of France is of French race and French nationality.

—UNITED STATES APPLICATION FORM FOR CITIZENSHIP PAPERS (1933)

SUPPOSE FOR A MOMENT that the word and concept "Race" were wholly alien to our thought and vocabulary, and that someone to whom it was familiar were trying to tell us what it meant. How could he go about it? He might begin by saying that a race was a group of people of all ages and sexes who were found in one place and resembled one another. We should certainly object to the definition as being too vague. How large is "one place" and what does "resemblance" mean? In some ways all men resemble one another; but in another way, no two individuals are alike. Even supposing that our interlocutor mentioned a white skin and light hair as the signs denoting a given race, we should find it difficult to agree on the precise point where white skin ends and dark begins among individuals. The Berbers of North Africa are blue-eyed and lighter-skinned than the Sicilians, and as Shaw has pointed out, a really *white* man would be a horrible sight. The same difficulty would arise about light hair or brown eyes; indeed, all the characteristics of the human body that might be named as criteria would be found in actuality to merge into a finely graded series which one can break up into groups only by being arbitrary and saying, "I shall call this man white, and that one, a shade darker, black." Moreover, we should find that, contrary to common opinion, no set of fixed characteristics occurs in human beings as a constant distinguishing mark of race. So-called Nordics have long skulls, but so have many so-called Negroes, the Eskimos, and the anthropoid apes. The "Mongolian" birth-spot occurs among the whites, and the Ainos of Japan frequently show features that should class them as "Nordics."

This lack of uniformity is bad enough but we could also stump our informant with another query. What if the striking differences of skin and hair and eyes were more striking than significant? A knowledge of the normal life of men in society suggests that a Japanese scientist is in many ways more like an American scientist than either is like a manual laborer of his own color. In other words, it is fallacious to consider human beings as mere arrangements of organs, apart from their functions, their habits, and their minds.

If we voiced this objection, the word "Mind" would probably recall to our friend the great differences among the shapes of the human skull, thought to be related to mental differences, and expressible in index numbers. But if we forced him to be a little clearer about what is meant by *dolichocephalic* and *brachycephalic* and what can be inferred from this classification of skulls (as we ourselves shall do in Chapter VII) we should soon find ourselves in a maze of contradictions fit to make us despair of discovering a reliable token of race.

True, another word than Mind is for many people the clue to race. That word is Blood. For the French and German racists "blood" is an infallible oracle giving answers to all questions. Conversations with intelligent Nazis convinces one that for them the phrase *"Mein Blut spricht"* is no figure of speech. In their minds, blood is synonymous with race, with conscience, with honesty, with artistic judgment, and with a sense of their own superiority. To more prosaic minds blood is merely a tissue which is carried in a serous fluid and which circulates through the body. The blood of neither parent is directly communicated to the offspring and the properties of any individual's blood are not ascertainable without fairly complicated tests, which, according to competent serologists, have nothing to do with determining race. It seems difficult to form a clear idea of what the world is talking about when it says "Race." What next? Well, one might frame a definition by borrowing from animal husbandry: a race is the total number of descendants from common ancestors, that is, all the offspring from one pair of progenitors. Adam and Eve are the traditional human pair in Christendom, but they hardly help if one is looking for distinct races in mankind. One pair of ancestors would obviously make us all of one race. How account for the "striking differences" that caught our attention earlier? It is not usual for "white" parents to give birth to "Hindu" children. The divergence between a supposed original pair of ancestors and their offspring must have occurred somewhere. The influence of environment readily suggests itself as a cause of modification. In other words, we arrive naturally at the climate-theory of races, which has had a long and troubled history. It includes all explanations from accounting for a dark skin by the heat of the sun to interpreting German philosophy as a result of fog and heavy annual rainfall. At this juncture two questions arise: How do "striking characters" get transmitted from parent to progeny? and What are the results of mixing strikingly different groups? The answer to the first question is the subject of a whole science, Genetics, and its most competent students are the most hesitant to give categorical answers. Some of the facts of heredity are known, but these are few compared to the questions that one could ask. This is not the place and I have not the competence to deal with the technical problems of heredity. What few general remarks can be made will be found further on, together with the simple conclusion that the idea of race as it is used in politics and social life will not be tenable until we know something definite about the transmission of non-physical traits. To build racial anthropologies without a comprehensive genetics is like starting a house with the roof. This self-evident proposition has, nevertheless, not deterred even the best scientific minds of this and the preceding century. That is why we cannot stop the discussion of race here, but must show in detail how absurd and unsubstantial its manifold dogmas are.

We are no nearer finding out what a race is by asking biology than we are by measuring skulls or judging at sight on the basis of pigmentation. The remaining methods are even less promising. First comes history. We can arbitrarily go back to the time of the Germanic invasions in the fourth and fifth centuries A.D. and find in the struggle of peoples after the Fall of Rome the origin of modern races. We shall then juggle with the names of Celts, Gauls, Iberians, Ligurians, Helvetii, Belgae, Brythons, Latins, Franks, Normans, Saxons, Goths, Angles, Jutes, Lombards, and Burgundians. But when it comes to determining who these were, where they lived, whether they survived, what they looked like, and whether in our day the French writer, Rémy de Gourmont, is a Gaul or a Norman[2]—one man's guess is nearly as good as another's. Next we can try nationalism. We can assert, with Sir Arthur Keith, that a race and a nation are synonymous; that several hundred years of a common history and a common way of life have welded people of divergent physiques into one race. That definition hardly defines. Under it, the "renegade Englishman," Houston Stewart Chamberlain, who elected Germany as his Fatherland, would be of German

[2] This typical "problem" is drawn from Havelock Ellis, who explains Gourmont by his Norman blood, blue eyes, "with the golden glow of an autumn leaf," his Viking race, etc. *From Rousseau to Proust,* 1935, 307, 309, 312, 314, and 322 n.

race. The language spoken is an equally unsatisfactory criterion. By that token Henry James and Joseph Conrad would be of the same race, though one was born in New York and the other in the Ukraine. Some people are bilingual, and the race of a head-waiter would be beyond conjecture.

As for "centuries of common history," that is a familiar metaphor, but it is inexact as a statement of fact. No human being lives through centuries of common "history" and what anyone picks up of the past through education or common report varies with social class, education, and intelligence. The "common way of life" is equally fallacious, except in self-contained, one-class communities; and this is true in spite of the tremendous power over mass emotions which the press, the cinema, and the radio have acquired in recent times. They are powerful agents of assimilation but they have not yet created distinct breeds of men. The fact that one can make all Western Europeans believe for a time in atrocity stories or flying saucers is no test of their belonging to the same race. It only proves them to be men by proving them to be gullible. We are still far from our original goal, which was to understand what the separate, unmixable races of men might be.

But if we give up the pursuit on our own account, we must still see what men who have written about race think it is. Their ideas form, not a definition of race, for they disagree among themselves, but a mode of thought to which I give the name race-thinking and which is easily recognizable.

III

> *. . . the new importance that has been attached for the last half-century to the idea of common descent as opposed to that of mere artificial nationality has made a word necessary. "Racial" is not* the *word that might have been ornamental as well as useful; but it is too well established to be now up-rooted.*
>
> —H. W. AND F. G. FOWLER in *The King's English,* 1906

RACE-THINKING does not consist merely in believing a particular theory about human races, and to refute the believer in Aryan or Nordic supremacy would not suffice to show up the error that underlies the notion of a Nordic or Aryan race. It would only let the disillusioned racist fall into the arms of the Celticist, the Yellow-Peril fanatic, or the dolichocephalic anthropologist. What must be uprooted is the passion for labeling and classifying groups on insufficient evidence. The remarkable wish to generalize and impute individual traits to masses of people with whom we have no acquaintance is an everyday occurrence. "The Japanese are a crafty and imitative race." "Isn't that typically American?" "That is a Jewish trait." "Nordic self-control." Why do we all feel an inward satisfaction in mouthing these groundless platitudes? Why does it take conscious restraint to keep from doing it? Some answers will be suggested throughout this book. At this point it is needful only to note that if one cliché or theory is destroyed by facts, the mind that entertained it is not proof against adopting another. The strength or weakness of the notion does not affect the liability of the mind to repeating its error. In short, race-thinking is a habit. It is not confined to the anthropologists and ethnologists, the historians and publicists who make up systems or preach discrimination; race-thinking occurs whenever someone, in a casual or considered remark, implies the truth of any of the following propositions:

1. That mankind is divided into unchanging natural types, recognizable by physical features, which are transmitted "through the blood" and that permit distinctions to be made between "pure" and "mixed" races.

Example: "The races amongst whom the Greeks planted themselves were in some cases on a similar level of culture. Where the natives were still backward or barbarous, they came of a stock either closely related to the Greek or at least separated from it by no great physical differences. Amalgamation with the native races was easy and it involved neither physical nor intellectual degeneracy as its consequence. Of the races with which the Greeks came in contact the Thracian was far from the highest in the scale of culture; yet two of the greatest names in the Great Age of Athens are those of men who had Thracian blood in their veins, Cimon and the historian Thucydides." (E. M. Walker, *Encyclopaedia Britannica,* 14th ed., X, 766.)

2. That the mental and moral behavior of human beings can be related to physical structure, and that knowledge of the structure or of the racial label which denotes it provides a satisfactory account of the behavior.

Example: "In March last [the book] was subjected to a brief but pungent critique by Du Bois-Reymond, the celebrated Perpetual Secretary of the Academy of Sciences in Berlin. . . . He thus exposes himself to the suspicion—which, unhappily, is not weakened by his other writings—that the fiery Celtic blood of his country occasionally runs away with him, converting him for the time into a scientific Chauvin." (John Tyndall, *Fragments of Science*, I, 385.)

3. That individual personality, ideas, and capacities, as well as national culture, politics, and morals, are the products of social entities variously termed race, nation, class, family, whose causative force is clear without further definition or inquiry into the connection between the group and the spiritual "product."

Example: "Yet there is in Celtdom a certain literary feeling which does not exist in Anglo-Saxondom. It is diffused, no doubt, and appreciative rather than creative, and lacking in the sterner critical spirit which is so necessary to all creative work; still it is there, and it is delighted with the rolling sound of the noble phrase. . . . So far then, as a man three-parts Celt, I was by nature inclined to the work of words." (Arthur Machen, *Far Off Things*, 86.)

WINGATE COLLEGE LIBRARY
WINGATE, N. C.

These three types of race-thinking naturally merge into one another. Few writers limit themselves to any one type, and mankind at large uses all three with equal readiness according to the occasion. The formal rejection of the fallacy in one guise does not protect against its other guises. When race seems inappropriate, nation does the same work, and from nation the shift is easy to the family, class, college, or vague "tradition." We thus get not only the Celtic or the Jewish mind, but the German or the Greek mind, and also the bourgeois and the Harvard mind, and beyond this (as we find in biographies, novels, and plays), the X-, Y-, or Z-family mind which is made to account for the hero's personality, achievements, and failings.[3]

This critique of a common practice may seem a denial of the obvious fact that people who belong to the same family, nation, climate, class, or "race" have a tendency to think alike, perhaps even to look alike. No such denial is made or implied. What is asserted and implied is that *these similarities, if they exist, must be shown.* They must not be merely presumed. The particular individual of whom the group quality is predicated must be studied in his own person and in his relation to the group before the "explanatory" label can be affixed. The need to do this is obvious. The mind's tendency is to assume greater simplicity and regularity in nature than actually exists. Possibly, if we could study environment, descent, nation, climate, and class like natural objects, and if they stayed put, again like natural objects, we might draw tenable conclusions about their role in shaping human character. But we are nowhere near this stage of investigation, and the race-thinker, whatever his affiliation, does not even conceive the lack. He takes ready-made the names by which we refer to the supposed factors and from the name deduces arbitrarily what he wishes to find: the Mongo-

[3] "Race" or "stock" is often substituted for "mind" in these senses. For examples, see in Meredith's *Beauchamp's Career,* the character of Everard; and again, this time in art criticism, the treatment of Ravel, Rabelais, and Berlioz in P. Rosenfeld, *Musical Portraits,* quoted on pp. 78-79 of this book.

lians are crafty; the Dutch have no sense of humor; brachycephalic people are excitable; the Aryan is a born leader. Finally, persuaded by his own glibness, the race believer comes to see only those instances that seem to bear out his preconceived notion. He may not consciously suppress evidence against his thesis, but he becomes blind to its existence and immune to its presentation by others.

The race-formula is applied to groups and individuals and to the quick and the dead. As a classical scholar has pointed out in treating of the familiar "character" of ancient peoples—Greek equipoise, Roman gravity, and so forth: "Our reverence for scientific method has made us the more prone to pick out a single characteristic of a people as a convenient label for a pigeon-hole and then ignore other possible descriptions. We talk glibly of the Greek mind, the medieval mind, and the like—as if there has ever been more than one kind of mind—and we forget that it is merely environment that emphasizes one fashion at a given time, in thought as in dress, without, however, obliterating other fashions. Certainly the prevailing temper or trait is illuminating, but it must not so focus our attention upon itself as to exclude other attitudes or traits which in their aggregate may be more significant." (M. Hadas, *Classical Journal*, Oct., 1935, 18.)

The connection between race-thinking and scientific method is especially paradoxical. One would think that the so-called scientific habit of thought would encourage care in dealing with details and differences. It should seem as though the object under consideration, be it a man or a group, would be looked at from all sides, seen as it really is. The very opposite has happened. The inclination is to lump individuals together on the most superficial, unverified grounds of similarity and describe them en masse. We class, as it were, all white powders as bicarbonate of soda and dispense them on that convenient principle. When such a mode of thought becomes quasi-universal, sinks out of the conscious mind to reappear in everybody's mouth as the most obvious of truths, then it is no exaggeration to term it a superstition on a par with the belief in witchcraft and horoscopes.

To sum up: a satisfactory definition of race is not to be had. The formulas in common use do not really define or do not accord with the facts, so that a prudent man will suspend judgment until genetics can offer a more complete body of knowledge. But to expect prudence in thinking about subjects charged with political emotion is folly too; and so we find the racists of the past 150 years leaping over the initial obstacle to race-theorizing, making assumptions to suit their object and failing to define their terms, just like the man in the street who borrows their language without questioning its validity.

Chapter II

THE NORDIC MYTH

1

The outstanding trait of the German character is that it has no need of prestige, domination or precedence; that it is sufficient unto itself.

—BISMARCK

MODERN GERMANY HAS taught the world at least one lesson, namely, that race-theories generally have a practical political purpose. That purpose is not peculiar to Hitlerite doctrine. Although in Homer there is no racial feeling of Greek versus Barbarian, it is present in Herodotus, who makes the Athenians speak to the Spartans of their common Greek brotherhood as an argument for joining forces against the Medes (VIII, c. 144). Still it is but a subsidiary reason, which crops up here and there only fitfully among historians until the first century of our era.

It was in that century, very probably in the year 98, that Tacitus composed his short essay on the Germans which contains so many of the beliefs and feelings that animate modern racism. Tacitus wrote as traveler, historian, and moralist, but especially as an embittered foe of the Imperial tyranny. Hence his eulogy of the Germanic race is systematic and politically pointed. According to him, the Germans are an indigenous race; they are virtuous, individualistic, freedom-loving, and jealous of their racial purity; physically they are tall and blond, brave and tough, they live frugally, and are adventurous rather than toilsome. "What is very remarkable in such prodigious numbers, a family likeness obtains throughout the nation."

Almost every line of the 30-page pamphlet contains some assertion that holds a germ of later Nordicism, and the piece as a whole is the model of all political race-theories; that is, it combines physical criteria, mental qualities, and an implied or expressed superiority. It is noteworthy that a re-edition of Tacitus's *Germania* by Lathom in 1851 created a stir in European intellectual circles, but it is not true that modern political racism had to go back to A.D. 98 for its ammunition. Tacitus and his tract had already been used in France to meet a similar situation in the seventeenth and eighteenth centuries. Leaning on the *Germania* for a description of the special gifts and institutions of the Frankish or Germanic race, the Count Henri de Boulainvilliers (1658-1722) evolved the still lively notion that all political freedom comes from the Germanic strain. Hence, he argued, Louis XIV's absolute monarchy, based on the Roman idea of the imperium, was a government fit only for slaves. Boulainvilliers wanted the nobles of his day to revolt against slavish institutions and restore the aristocratic freedom of the German forest.[1]

Boulainvilliers's theories did not fall on deaf ears. He split educated opinion and political thinkers in France into two camps—the Germanists and the Romanists—and opened a breach which has not yet been healed between the partisans of the two "races" that stand for divergent ideals. Gobineau in the nineteenth century was a modern Boulainvilliers, as were in the

[1] For an account of the growth of these ideas from Tacitus to the French Revolution, see: Jacques Barzun, *The French Race, Theories of Its Origins and Their Social and Political Implications,* Columbia University Press, N.Y., 1932.

early twentieth many members of the *Action Française*. In the eighteenth century, the distinguished littérateur Abbé Dubos was the champion of the Romanist cause. But he was crushed in debate by Montesquieu who, for his own Anglophile purposes, was delighted to find that the "beautiful system" of freedom embodied in the English Parliament had been "invented in the forests of Germany." Mably, the Marquis d'Argenson, and Abbé Sieyès were defenders of the Gallo-Romans, while the Duc de Saint-Simon and Mademoiselle de Lézardière (the first woman historian of France) were rather inclined to be Germanists. Only two men—the two greatest of the century—stayed out of the fray: Rousseau, because he was essentially a political realist, knew that these capriciously built-up appeals to an uncertain past were but the cloak of present ambition for power; Voltaire, because he was essentially a humorist, was sure that retrospective history based on racial descent was farcical. "I have but lately read a book," he writes, "beginning, 'The Franks, from whom we are descended . . .' Halloo, my friend, who told you that you were descended in a straight line from a Frank?" (*Œuvres,* Beuchot ed., 29, 471.)

Boulainvilliers was widely read in England, not only because of his historical ideas, but also because of his connection with the important movement of Freemasonry. The result was that the doctrine of Germanic freedom and individualism, of race conflict as the explanation of governmental institutions, was kept alive across the Channel, to emerge again incubated in the historians of the mid-nineteenth century—Carlyle, Kemble, Freeman, Stubbs, John Richard Green—until by the end of the period it became a commonplace in the mouths of the entire "Anglo-Saxon" populace.

In nineteenth-century France the inheritance of this politico-racial doctrine involving Nordic superiority was complicated by the political realignments of the Revolutionary and Napoleonic periods. Just before the French Revolution the Abbé Sieyès, the rousing pamphleteer of *What Is the Third Estate?* had tried to settle the race-issue for all time. The nobility, said Sieyès, claims that its political rights are based on the inheritance by blood of the privileges won in the Frankish conquest. "Very well. We, the Gallo-Roman plebs, will now conquer the nobility by expelling or annihilating them. Our rights will supersede theirs on exactly the principle they invoke." This *reductio ad absurdum* of the conquest argument worked very well in its day, for the leaders of the French Revolution were eager to substitute the natural Rights of Man for the haphazard rights conferred by history—or race. But with the accession of Napoleon, the restoration of monarchy, and the return of the émigrés, the race-issue revived in a new and more complicated form.

Sieyès, by simplifying everything, had unwittingly confused everything. Under the old regime, Boulainvilliers and Montesquieu as aristocrats had wanted freedom from the centralized monarchy. They had appealed to old Germanic rights and customs but had failed to obtain any "aristocratic freedom" under the monarchy. Instead, the bourgeoisie had overthrown both the monarchy and the aristocracy and had lumped the two, through the voice of Sieyès, into one Germanic tyranny. "Freedom" had thereby changed camps, from the Franks to the Gallo-Romans. This is the first change made in the Nordic myth of freedom found in Tacitus.

The second complication is due to the rise of Celticism, which will be discussed elsewhere in this book. In this new theory, the Gauls and Romans were no longer thought of together in opposition to the Franks, but came to represent two racial characters. Napoleon reflected this attitude when he preferred to consider himself the heir of both Caesar (the Roman) and Charlemagne (the German) and despised the French for their Gallic (Celtic) failings: "Our frivolity, our inconsequence come from the remote past. We are still Gauls. . . . Credulity and loitering are the national character of the French since the time of the Gauls." (*Maximes et Pensées de Bonaparte,* 193-95.)

This view of the racial division of France into Franks, Gauls, and Romans was not adhered to in every later instance of politico-racial animus, but it played a part in the antagonism between what has been called the two Frances,[2] that is, the familiar parties of the Right and the Left, which have divided the country since the French Revolution. The Right is Catholic, conservative, frequently monarchical or fascist. The Left is liberal, anticlerical, frequently socialist or communist. Some historians, it is true, find the division to be older than 1789. They make it go back to the Reformation and even to the heresies and disaffections of peasant and serf during the Middle Ages. It was with the momentum of these conflicts behind it that the Nordic race-issue, hopefully buried by Sieyès, surged up again at the beginning of the nineteenth century.

II

The mystical belief in race, which has played almost no part in France . . .

—E. SEILLIÈRE, 1911

AFTER THE FALL of Napoleon in 1815, the restored Bourbons not only brought back the most reactionary of the émigrés, but also created a public for works of history and political theory designed to blot out those of the French Revolution. The Revolution had theoretically leveled all men, had legislated into existence the eighteenth-century rationalist idea of Man, in whom without distinction of rank, creed, or race certain rights were inherent. The task of the reactionary theorists consisted chiefly in showing that there is no such thing as Man, that only men exist, and that therefore laws, constitutions, and social hierarchies must be made to suit particular types, that is, races of

[2] Michelet seems to have coined the term. See Paul Seippel's book of that title, Lausanne-Paris, 1905.

men. Moreover, the natural inequality of men being a necessary principle and hierarchy a stabilizing force, it follows that the aristocracy, the middle, and the lower classes must transmit their several characteristics by process of generation; in other words, they too are races. Such was the teaching of the greatest political theorists of the Reaction, Joseph de Maistre and Louis de Bonald. The former, a diplomat, traveler, and wit, is a mystic when it comes to the rights of race: "There has never been a ruling family to whom a plebeian origin could be assigned. If this phenomenon occurred, it would be epoch-making." (*Principe générateur des constitutions politiques,* Pref., 7.)

Among the races his preference goes of course to the Nordics, the *durum genus,* the hardy breed, which has given its character to all Europe, made it superior to Asia, and introduced freedom into the decay of the Roman Empire. In France itself, still according to de Maistre, after the barbarian invasions, the nation was more Frankish than Gallic, but as the Franks were fewer, it became more Gallic every day, with the result that France is a hybrid nation. (*Considérations sur la France,* 441, 445.)

This contention has a familiar ring to modern ears, and we are not surprised when we encounter in de Maistre the belief that "Nations are born and die like individuals . . . they have a common soul especially visible in their language." Nations being individuals, they should not mix, they should endeavor to remain "frankly of one race" (325-27).

The Vicomte de Bonald, in developing a similar system of monarchical-aristocratic government, accepts the idea that conquest gave the French nobility the right to power, and regrets that in subsequent centuries it relinquished its ideal of racial purity as well as of public service and thus laid itself open to attack. (*Esprit de Bonald,* 135, 168; *on Mme de Staël,* 43 n., 48.)

Having refurbished the dogmas of Boulainvilliers, these two epigrammatic writers influenced a man of talent but less difficult of approach, the Comte de Montlosier, who at the behest of Napoleon began to write a systematic History of France suitable to the Imperial accession of 1804. The work did not please the Emperor, but, slightly modified, it was printed after his fall and enjoyed considerable success.

According to Montlosier, the nobility is ancient, German, and frank (free); the bourgeoisie is new and slavish. Its subjection antedated the arrival of the Franks, for it was the work of Rome. Nevertheless, the hatred of victor and vanquished shifted to the descendants of the Franks and the Gallo-Romans and this resulting lack of unity brought about the "great suicide called the Revolution." (I, 108; II, 1-2.)

By that phrase, the Comte de Montlosier means the nation divided, civil war. He offers as a solution, not a return to absolutism but a free government, an aristocratic regime, based on the Germanic ideas of the old Franks.

These three unequal minds—de Maistre, Bonald, and Montlosier—set the tone of the politico-racial controversy that was to rage in France throughout the nineteenth century.[3] In politics, it is the familiar quarrel of liberals and republicans versus monarchists. The race-overtones are nothing new and the rearrangement of Tacitus's Nordic myth was peculiar to France only in its details. Hitler showed how readily it applies to the Third Reich. And one has but to substitute Marxism for liberalism; Aryan (or Nordic) for Frankish; Semite (or Mediterranean) for Gallo-Roman, and the plot remains the same.

In the France of 1815, the pro-Nordic reactionaries found arrayed against them the greatest historians of the period: Guizot, Chateaubriand, the brothers Thierry, Michelet, and Edgar Quinet. The first two were middle-of-the-road partisans; the rest were outright liberals; and all concerned themselves

[3] At the very end of the century, the conservative historian Fustel de Coulanges felt compelled to write a paper entitled "Am I a Romanist or a Germanist?" After his death, despite his balanced views, the *Action Française* used him as a standard-bearer in a political demonstration that turned into a riot.

with race as an explanation or justification of political opinion. The appeal to the past was for them a form of demonstration, and where an obviously selfish interest could not be justified on its own grounds, it was somehow sanctified by relating it to the race that was postulated as inherently admirable. Benjamin Constant, the greatest liberal leader of the first quarter of the century, bears witness to the power of these political devices. In his famous pamphlet on the *Spirit of Conquest and Usurpation in Europe* (1813) he says: "Our fanatical reformers purposely confuse chronology to kindle or keep up hatred, just as others in the past went back to the Franks and Goths to find pretexts in order to oppress in the opposite direction." (121-22; 91 n.)

Guizot and Chateaubriand do not confuse chronology, nor do they side with only one race. They concede the various racial points made by Boulainvilliers, Dubos, and Mably, which means accepting the three political traditions ascribed to Gauls, Romans, and Franks. Guizot's *Essays on French History* (1823) is an attempt to harmonize everything under the banner of legitimacy. But for him as for the others, each of the political principles to be reconciled is a racial heritage. Chateaubriand is equally ready to do justice to the "three races" but he shows a partiality for the southerners: "Let us not exaggerate, as we are only too much inclined to do, this matter of Scandinavian, Slavic and Teutonic origins. . . . Let us remember that the northern peoples are *as peoples* younger than we by several centuries." (*Etudes hist.,* 1833, 8.)

But having studied the barbarians and re-created the scenes of their conquest of Roman Gaul in his *Genius of Christianity* (1802) and *Les Martyrs* (1809), Chateaubriand objects to those who smooth over that troubled time and show it as a period of equality and fraternity. He is probably thinking of the overzealous "Gallic" liberals when he says: "In past history we look for our own image and we are annoyed not to find it. With the spirit of equality now dominant among us, the exclusive presence of a few nobles in our annals irritates us. We ask whether we are not worth a great deal more than those fellows, and whether our fathers were of no account in the destinies of our fatherland." (*Analyse de l'Histoire de France,* 21.)

Such expressions seem less provocative than the later shouting about the Day of the Saxon, but the thought and emotion behind both is the same. The thought is a continual begging of the question by selecting from the past particular traits and tendencies and asserting those to be the root of forces or parties at work in the present. The motive is expediency: race is a convenient living symbol for ideas and principles, and it is useful propaganda for keeping one's followers conscious of their worth. The value of historical essays on racial principles is to persuade the "Nordics" themselves that they have a great past, encourage them to feel superior, and justify their attacks on inconvenient neighbors. The career of an Augustin Thierry, perhaps the greatest French racial historian, shows how impervious to fact or logic is the political idea of race.

Thierry's vocation began at the age of fifteen with the reading of Chateaubriand's *Martyrs.* Thenceforth, throughout a life of unceasing historical labors, Thierry championed the cause of the Gallic Third Estate in its ages-long struggle with the Frankish invaders. It is true that he saw the "fusion" of the two "races" beginning almost at once and being consummated by the tenth century; yet in a half-metaphorical, half-literal way, he saw the fight continuing down to the present. Thierry began by interpreting English history as a race-struggle between Saxon native and Norman invader. Then in the newspaper *Le Courrier Français,* he wrote his courageous *Letters on French History* (1820), the purpose of which was to crystallize liberal opinion against the government of the day by an appeal to national history. And whenever the two conceptions of government, liberal and reactionary, were at grips, Thierry saw the two races locked in unending combat. At the same time Thierry's friend and fellow historian Thiers was refuting Montlosier in the columns of the *Constitutionnel:* history was the handmaiden of practical politics.

But owing to the confusion noted earlier in the uses of the Nordic myth, the banner of liberalism did not always wave over the same racial stock. Edgar Quinet was as much a liberal and a racist as Thierry, but their accounts differ. Quinet thinks that the Romans did not enslave the Gauls only to be ousted by the Franks. He denies any legitimacy of power based on the Roman conquest and condemns the "scholastic mysticism" whereby liberty grows from tyranny and men always do the opposite of what they think they are doing. His pro-Gallic, anti-Roman partisanship is also directed at the contemporary German scholars who "taught us that our Gallic ancestors were incapable of partaking fully of civilization." (*Phil. de l'Hist. de France; Œuvres,* IV, 357 ff.)

With Quinet, the nationalist, anti-German spirit of modern France was grafted upon the racism of internal politics. This explains in part why race-history did not remain in every country a local controversy, but came to serve the passions of imperialism and world wars. When late in life Thierry retracted his insistence on the unchanging character of the race-conflict, it was too late. The mischief had been done and the French racial tree flourished, not in a desert but in a forest of its own kind.

III

The history of Europe is that of the Goths of Europe; that of Ireland is that of the Goths in Ireland.

—JOHN PINKERTON, *History of Scotland,* 1814

THE POINT JUST made needs elaboration: how did this long local controversy among the French take on European proportions? The answer lies partly in the role that France played in Europe from 1789 to 1870; partly in the new taste for reading history which developed during the same period. The nineteenth century is the century of history par excellence. The new forces of nationalism and romanticism both helped to make historical studies paramount and to endow them with a kind of authority which before, as mere literature or entertainment, they had never possessed. Hume's eighteenth-century dictum that if you would know the ancient Greeks and Romans you had only to look at the English and French of your own day was displaced by the belief that each nation and time had its own particular tone and spirit which it was the business of the historian to discover and re-create. Romanticism by its insistence on local color and on the particular as against the generalized view of Man, by its interest in the Middle Ages and its conviction that nothing human was strange or exotic, gave an enormous impetus to historical research.

Not only did Scott, Dumas, and Manzoni capture the popular imagination with historical novels and plays, but the busy pens of a fertile generation made "straight history" a widely salable product. The educated readers of Europe eagerly absorbed accounts of their own past and greatness. But for the French, as we have seen, the nation was split into two warring halves, the Right and the Left. France seemed the appointed battleground of two principles which still divide the world. The revolutions of 1830 and 1848 started in France, and from the racial overtones of the struggle between middle class and kings the rest of Europe took its cue. When the British historians expressed faith in Anglo-Saxon liberty, it was also a faith in their French colleagues' dictum that the English revolution of 1688 represents the triumph of the Saxon over the Roman idea of kingship. About the same time, the anti-Roman hero Germanicus became an idol of modern Germany. Tacitus was re-edited, translated, and even when unread, implicitly believed. Charles Kingsley waxed oratorical over Roman vice and Teutonic virtue. Race-thinking became a commonplace of scholarship as well as journalism.

Other tastes and tendencies spurred the vogue of race historiography. After the French Revolution, it seemed impossible to go on writing dynastic history—the history of battles and kings. Popular history, in both senses of the word "popular," replaced it. Peoples were now invested with the grandeur and sacredness of monarchs. Nations were living entities, and the study of modern nations led back to the study of the tribes or races that composed them. Niebuhr in Germany revolutionized the current notions of early Roman history by introducing the factor of race-mixture and race-conflict; Ranke, Mommsen, and Wolff followed in his train, and Michelet learned at their school. Pinkerton and Prichard in England sought to replace the older political narratives by proposing, one the Goths, the other the Celtic Indo-Europeans as the "makers" of Western civilization.

The more the history of racial groups gained ground the more were they regarded as organisms imbued with eternal life; and from the notion of race-continuity it was a short step to inferring how a modern German or Gaul or Roman might embody the "racial type." Here again, a French historian—Thierry's younger brother Amédée—took the lead and produced an extremely popular *History of the Gauls* (1828),[4] which presents, together with a good deal of involved nonsense, the new kind of historical-physical race-theories. Before launching into panegyric upon Roman institutions as all-important in the development of France, the younger Thierry offers as his contribution the discovery in Southern Gaul of "two races of men," the Gauls and the Kymri, physically different and having distinct capacities, though equally members of the "Gaulic family." The Gauls or Celts, an "eminently intelligent race," are quite distinct from the Germans, though the Kymri, who are a branch of the Gallic family, are "more nearly Germanic in character than the Gauls." (1881 ed., 1-5.)

Let the reader construe this hodgepodge as he may, what

[4] Ten editions appeared in France between 1828 and 1881.

matters is that despite objections to the pro-Gallic thesis, no critic challenged Thierry's complexities or methods. None, on being told that the Gallic race was "eminently intelligent," questioned whether it meant that some, or most, or all of the "race" were so gifted. It is hard to believe that Thierry meant all, and harder to imagine what means he had for finding out if few or many (or any) Gauls were intelligent. His readers were receptive to such ideas regardless of logic or probability.

This "ethnological science" found acceptance in the schools and in the work of many lesser men, and it led, immediately after publication, to a result of great consequence in European thought; for it suggested to an English physician residing in France, W. F. Edwards, a physiological theory of race which is the germ of all later distinctions based on complexion and shape of skull. It will be dealt with in the next chapter.

Meantime, both in France and elsewhere, nationalism was influencing race-theories. By dwelling on common traditions and a common life within the boundaries of the state, nationalism cuts across (and sometimes counteracts) the political division between Right and Left. Italy and Germany achieved unification by making nationalism triumph over liberalism. How did this process affect the race-historians? For an answer we can turn to the work of Michelet.

Just as it was in reading the Frankish portions of *Les Martyrs* that Augustin Thierry found his calling, so it was among the Merovingian relics in Lenoir's Museum that Michelet "experienced the vivid realization of history." The question of race arose first for him in his *Roman History* (1831), in which he praises Niebuhr for having perceived the importance of race (17). Two years later, in the first volume of his *Histoire de France* (1833), a struggle begins in Michelet's mind between the vision of the manifold forces that make up the history of a nation and the convenient scheme that racial interpretation affords. It is one of the penalties of toying with the race-notion that even a strong mind trying to repudiate it will find himself making assumptions and passing judgments on the basis of the theory he disclaims.

After contradictions due partly to the scale of his work and partly to the gradual triumph of the national over the racial idea, Michelet enunciated the famous theory of the "fusion of races" on French soil. Before reaching that point, he sounds very much like a disciple of Augustin Thierry. Not only do we get racist portraits of St. Augustine, Luther, and Descartes, but the development of Europe seems to him a racial product: "The Celtic genius, which is that of individuality, has a profound affinity with the Greek genius. . . . In opposition to the Helleno-Celtic genius of a free personality, the contrary spirit originating in Germany forces it to struggle and justify itself. The Middle Ages show the struggle and modern times the victory" (169, 183). Even in the later Michelet we come upon isolated examples of labeling by race. Thomas à Becket, for example, is a true Saxon defending the liberties of Kent against the Norman Henry II (II, 358, 363). Louis XVI has a thoroughly German nature; Marie Antoinette a wholly French one (XIX, 166 ff.).

Still, Michelet repeatedly disclaims race-bias, and it is fair to conclude that by 1869 he definitely adhered to the notion of fused races. His famous catalogue of the elements that contributed to the identity of France is worth quoting, both for itself and as an example of racial attributions in one who wanted to overcome the very bias he displays:

"The French genius is thoroughly distinct from the Roman and from the Germanic genius: they cannot serve to explain it. . . . All the races of the world have contributed to the endowment of France (I, 185).

"The base which took on all other impressions was the mobile Gaelic race.

"The Iberians gave the hardness and cunning of the mountaineer spirit.

"The Semitic nations gave the South of France its commercial-mindedness.

"The stubborn Kymris . . . , the ancestors of our Bretons, are our builders of Carnac. . . .

"The Belgae came from the north, the Gauls followed. . . . Civil law and order came in the train of the Roman legions . . . the Greek spirit awoke Gaul to herself: . . . Then came the Germans . . . to second the work of the Church towards social organization" (I, 186-89).

It cannot be said that Michelet, whose genius lay in a divinatory understanding and the widest human sympathy, was in any sense the apostle of a narrow race-creed, but it is obvious that, like many of his contemporaries, he took an imprint that was stronger than any one mind: the whole age thought politically by means of race-clichés. Looking back a century later, Camille Jullian could say: "It was a fateful theory that was launched at that time, with the words 'race,' 'Latin race,' 'Germanic race,' 'Slavic race.' . . . From France it spread to Italy and Germany, both ready to receive it." (*Thierry et le mouvement hist. sous la Restauration,* 12.)

In Italy and Germany the Nordic myth was used to help the work of national unification, but in both countries it was held in check by the opposite fiction of the superior southern or Latin race. Abuse and contempt marked the controversy until the two nations achieved political unity, by which time the Nordic idea had formed a broader base than that of the province or class within which it had first taken shape.

In England the corresponding doctrine of "Saxonism" was almost unopposed. Associating Rome with Popery made it easy for patriots to find the roots of modern England exclusively in her Germanic past. Had not French and German scholars told her that English freedom, English power, the English gift of self-government, were a racial heritage from the Nordic tribes that repeatedly conquered Britain up to 1066? In addition, the thrill of discovering the neglected poetry, chronicles, and other remains of the Saxon period carried scholars and publicists to a pitch of patriotic fervor unequaled since the days of the

Armada. Kemble dedicated his work on the Saxons in England to Victoria with the words: "To the Queen's most Excellent Majesty—This history of the principles which have given her empire its pre-eminence among the nations of Europe."

The now famous adjective Anglo-Saxon, which refers to no historic tribe whatever, was invented to make evident the link between "the history of our childhood" and "the explanation of our manhood." Freeman, in a continuous fit of pride, introduced the fashion of Saxonizing every name. To be exact and Saxon both, the battle of Hastings became the battle of Senlac. The pages of history books became dotted with names such as *Eadweard* instead of *Edward;* familiar words sprouted old diphthongs, as well as the signs for the two kinds of *th* in the language now known as Anglo-Saxon. Carlyle helped Germanism as a politico-racial creed with his *Past and Present* and *Frederick the Great,* and by the last quarter of the century it seemed no incongruity for John Richard Green to assert in *The Making of England* that "with the landing of Hengest, English history begins"; or for the distinguished historian of constitutional law, Bishop Stubbs, to particularize the same feeling: "It is to Ancient Germany that we must look for the earliest traces of our forefathers, for the best part of almost all of us is originally German; though we call ourselves Britons, the name has only a geographical significance. The blood that is in our veins comes from German ancestors." (*Lect. on Early English Hist.,* 3.)

In the light of this confident teaching, the common association of national greatness with a given race heritage is not difficult to understand. When H. G. Wells was a young man the mood, as he tells us, was quasi-universal. A few years more and it became the aggressive, jingoistic belief we recognize in popular leaders such as Joseph Chamberlain and Cecil Rhodes. The great empire builder saw and made others see, in the words of Francis Thompson:

> . . . the Teuton and the Saxon grip
> Hands round the warded world, and bid it rock . . .
> He saw the three-branched Teuton hold the sides
> Of the round world, and part it as a dish. . . .[5]

And Rhodes's followers made it clear that his greatness lay in being the first British statesman whose imperialism was not of Empire but of Race. (W. T. Stead, *Rhodes's Last Will and Testament,* 52.) Politics and race-theories seemed natural, not to say necessary, allies, and the Nordic myth has had as many forms as there have been situations to shape it.

Originating in a pamphlet by the disaffected Roman Tacitus, the theory was nurtured in France through the 150 years of the monarchy by the hobbled nobility. Its first form there was the enmity of Franks and Gallo-Romans. After the Revolution, enriched with the discoveries of Celticism and reinforced by the political passions of liberals and nationalists, it achieved European scale. But it was not destined to stop with history-writing. It multiplied its appeals through literature and criticism and added to its resources first physiology, then anthropology, and later evolutionism. Before pursuing the later manifestations of race in politics, the biological side of the theory must be placed in its proper setting.

[5] Ode on Cecil Rhodes.

Chapter III

RACE AND ANTHROPOLOGY

1

Genera, orders, classes exist only in our imaginations. . . . There are only individuals. Nature does not arrange her works in bunches, nor living beings in genera.

–BUFFON, *Histoire Naturelle*

ANTHROPOLOGY OR THE science of man is of fairly recent birth. Its emergence as a separate branch of study belongs somewhere within the latter half of the eighteenth century and coincides with the rise of the biological sciences. Anthropology is ordinarily given a double paternity. Buffon, the French naturalist, and Blumenbach, the German anatomist, are jointly or singly credited with having established the new discipline. In truth, these dates and credits depend on definitions. One could make anthropology go back to Hippocrates or begin in the year 1910 with Franz Boas's *Mind of Primitive Man*. The ancients—Hippocrates, Herodotus, Aristotle, Pliny, Galen, and others—had noted differences in the physical appearance of human groups, and so may be said to have founded ethnology or the science of peoples, which is the forerunner of anthropology. In recent times, the first systematic division of mankind into races is that by Bernier in 1684. Seventeenth-century physical science put a premium on neat systems that might parallel the orderliness of mathematical physics, and it was not long before the organic world was cast into such a mold. In 1738 the Swedish savant Linnaeus gave his *Systema Naturae,* in which the species man stands at the top of the vertebrates and is divided into four races with their physical and moral characteristics succinctly described. The eighteenth century gathered much new material from travelers and colonists all over the globe, and shortly the science of ethnology merged with natural history and incipient biology to form a new compound to which may properly be given the name of anthropology.

As practiced in the first half of the nineteenth century, anthropology thus had behind it a double tradition. It was descriptive in the manner of Buffon and it was addicted to classifying in the manner of Linnaeus and (as we shall see) Blumenbach. Modern French writers who want to prove that race-dogmas are all of German origin blame Blumenbach for having started the business of differentiating skulls as a means of race-classification. But Blumenbach, who was first and foremost an anatomist, had had predecessors. In 1764, Daubenton was measuring in degrees the position of the head on top of the spinal column and correlating the measure of that angle with the amount of will-power in the several races. Camper in 1786 measured the facial angle and thought the perfection of beauty in human beings was to be recorded on a scale of 100 degrees, the maximum which he believed he had found obtaining among the ancient Greeks.

Once the idea had been made familiar, measuring became an increasingly common occupation of anthropologists. Blumenbach, following Daubenton's use of geometrical projection, suggested his *norma verticalis* or "Blumenbach's View" of the skull. That organ was placed between the feet of the observer and, after examination from above, classed as oblong, round, and so forth, for the purpose of determining the race to which it belonged. Gibson and Bell in England declared in 1809 that the posterior balance of the skull—its ability to rest on the posterior edge of the occipital hole and the inferior edge of the orbits—was a distinctive sign of the Negro race. Many workers along these lines were quietly preparing the day of a quantitative anthropology, but for the first quarter of the century description rather than measurement held the field. The usual division of races was into color-groups, which made of the Europeans (or White or Caucasians) a single race. The first important shift of interest from the color-division to what might be called the shape-division came in 1829 at the hands of the British physician W. F. Edwards, who has already been mentioned.

Edwards was a member of the Royal Academy of Medicine of Paris, lived in that city, and wrote in French his epoch-making work: *Des caractères physiologiques des races humaines considérées dans leur rapport avec l'histoire*. It is significant that the work is in the form of a letter to Amédée Thierry, who had published his *History of the Gauls* the year before. What the letter recounts is the piece of field work by which Edwards arrived at his conclusion that two distinct races dwell on French soil. Note that Edwards was a man of science and that according to him these "races" did not merely coexist in France in the fifth century A.D.—that discovery would have been no discovery at all—but that they still coexisted unmixed and recognizable in the nineteenth century.

After giving credit to the brothers Thierry for introducing the factor of race into history, Edwards cites the authorities of the day on anthropology and goes on to assert the existence of "historical races" as distinguished from those already known to natural science. He is thinking here of Blumenbach's fivefold division of mankind by color, and suggesting that within one color-group further racial subdivisions can be discerned. He attempts to prove this contention by analogy with the persistence of physical characteristics shown by the Jews. In France, according to Edwards, the Franks who conquered Gaul, like the

Normans who conquered England, were few in proportion to the native population. They consequently left virtually no traces of their physique.

Edwards's next point is the influential one. He asserts that the form and proportions of the head constitute the principal test of race. Stature and color of hair are also important but secondary. Methodically, he examines various regions of France, locating the Gauls, the Romans, and the Nordics, all these grouped under the two heads suggested by Amédée Thierry—the Gauls and the Kymri. The Gauls have round heads, medium stature, and rounded features. The Kymri are tall, with long heads and salient chins. Here are our modern tall long-skulled and short round-skulled races making their first bow before the public. Subsequent changes of costume in their later appearances will not alter their basic character. Edwards denies, however, that the long-headed type is due to the Nordic invasions; rather, the invaders were absorbed owing to their small numbers and possible resemblance to an already existing group. He extends his observations to England, Italy, Germany, Austria, and Hungary, where the Mongolian Hun is revealed to him by his low brow and thick neck. In Northern Italy he finds a "pure German population," spotting them by their manner of speech, in the same way that Mezzofante, whom he cites, discovered that modern English is descended from original Gallic, that is, by a comparison of pronunciations. How either knew the pronunciation of peoples long extinct remains a mystery of a kind not uncommon in theories of race. Its significance here is that philology is being drawn in as the third partner in the game of building up race-theories.

Edwards concludes his survey of Europe with two perfectly sound observations: he predicts a great future for philological and anthropological speculations of the kind he is inaugurating, and he suggests that this new science will go further into the mental correlates of racial differences by means of an "alliance between historical science and physiology" (129).

What gave Edwards's anatomical distinctions peculiar force was the contemporary vogue of phrenology. This empirical science was made famous by Gall and Spurzheim, both competent anatomists, about the year 1800, and it numbered as adherents many distinguished minds, including Lavater, Balzac, and Blake, before merging into the later anthropology. Phrenology uses several postulates that make it an important forerunner of race-thinking. It assumes that man's faculties are related to certain areas in the brain; that the size of the areas indicates the amount of the faculty, and that the outer skull corresponds sufficiently to the inner brain to afford the observers a means of diagnosing individual character. At the height of its vogue Thomas Love Peacock ridiculed the idea in *Headlong Hall,* making Mr. Cranium say: "Every man's actions are determined by his peculiar views and those views . . . by the organization of his skull. A man in whom the organ of benevolence is not developed cannot be benevolent."

In popular speech we still retain expressions like the "bump of locality" which go back to the heyday of phrenology. Exactly when that science disappeared is hard to decide.[1] It might be truer to say that it was superseded by a more imposing but no more reasonable jargon. Compare, for example, the satirical passage just quoted from Peacock and dated 1815 with the following bit from Arthur Conan Doyle, written in 1902: "You interest me very much, Mr. Holmes. I had hardly expected so dolichocephalic a skull or such well marked supraorbital development. . . . A cast of your skull, sir, until the original is available, would be an ornament to any anthropological museum." (*The Hound of the Baskervilles.*)

True, the passage is from a work of fiction, but the key sentence at least is not meant as satire. It reflects perfectly the

[1] When this book was first published, *The Phrenological Era* was still being issued monthly at Bowerston, Ohio, as the "Organ of the Tope School of Phrenology . . . in behalf of whatever concerns the welfare of mind and body." XXXII, No. 12, Dec., 1936.

thinking that a well-read medical man like Doyle would naturally ascribe to another in a story of contemporary life.

What had happened between Peacock and Doyle was that the phrenological belief in man's separate faculties and in the indicative aspects of the skull had been joined with the obvious idea of the transmission of racial characteristics from parent to offspring. It was therefore possible to do what Edwards had hoped for: to distinguish, within the white color-group, races differentiated by the shape of their skull.

This particular step in classification was taken by Anders Retzius, a Swedish savant, who announced in 1842 that he had found craniological differences between the skulls of the Finns, whom he held to be an indigenous race, and of the Indo-European Swedes, who were supposed invaders from Asia. These differences Retzius expressed in figures and these figures served him to define the now famous classes of *brachycephalic* (broad skulls) and *dolichocephalic* (long skulls). His figures were obtained by dividing the long diameter of the skull into the short diameter. The quotient, multiplied by 100 to eliminate decimals, is called the cephalic index and presumably determines the race to which the skull belongs.

Not until 1852—ten years after his discovery—did Retzius assign fixed limits to his classification. There lay the crux of the problem: Where do the broad skulls divide from the long ones? The answers to that question will be found in Chapter VII, after a necessary glance has been cast upon two other reinforcements of the trend to racial theorizing: materialistic psychology and the theory of Evolution.

II

As the function depends on the organization, disturbed functions will derange the organization . . . and so arises insanity. . . . Religion is another fertile cause of insanity.

—SPURZHEIM, *Observations on the Deranged Manifestations of the Mind,* 1817

THE PRIME ASSUMPTION of the phrenologists, that man possesses independent faculties related to certain areas in the brain, did not originate with those daring scientists. It was borrowed from the eighteenth-century philosophers. The British tradition of empirical philosophy going back to Locke and Hobbes rests upon the belief that all sensations are drawn from experience and all ideas are the result of association among sense-impressions. Enlarging upon this mechanical notion of the human mind, the French and English materialists of the end of the eighteenth century arrived at the idea of an exact correspondence between body and mind. The most impressive research done in this direction was the work of a school of French psychologists known as *Idéologues* or Sensationalists, who flourished—or rather, were kept from flourishing—during the French Revolutionary and Napoleonic periods.

Cabanis, Vicq d'Azyr, and De Stutt de Tracy were the leaders of this movement. Chiefly trained in medicine and the biological sciences, these men and their disciples produced a considerable body of work in psychology, philosophy, and evolutionism, which incurred private and public condemnation as tending toward materialism and atheism.

Forerunners of the Behaviorists, the Idéologues taught that psychology was explicable only in terms of physiology. Cabanis concluded from his brain-studies that the mixing of races was the surest means of changing and improving human nature, and Draparnaud attempted to establish for that purpose an "ideological scale of the different races." In addition, Cabanis systematically extended his physiological psychology with the aid of experiments upon animals, with researches into embryology, and with data drawn from what we should call today abnormal psychology. Throughout his work, the connection between mind and body is a connection of cause and effect. Mind, in the honorific sense of Spirit or Divinity, is excluded. That is why the religious-minded Vicomte de Bonald condemned the ideas of Cabanis as "abject" (*Recherches phil.,* II, 289) and why Napoleon, seeking to make his peace with the Catholics, suppressed the Idéologues and their doctrines.

That these were not entirely crushed is shown by their resurgence in the nineteenth century. Race-theorizing attests survival, for the foundation of all "serious" race-beliefs is the conviction that mind is simply the correlate of physiological structure, that any spiritual or intellectual product is to be explained genetically, that is, by reference to its physical origin. The Idéologues' influence is easily traced. Saint-Simon, the utopian socialist, probably received their teachings through Dr. Burdin, and on them he based his prediction that when physiology becomes a positive science philosophy and history will likewise become sciences. That stage, which he saw just around the corner, he called Physicism. With respect to man, it defines the development of the individual mind as a purely biological function. This is the source of Comte's *Philosophie Positive* which initiated modern sociology, and which remains the faith of all who have tried to create a science of man or to write history as if it were a science.[2] Saint-Simon moreover drew a parallel between the habits of the individual in life and the prevailing attitude of historical races. For instance, the Egyptians' fondness for digging and building corresponds to infancy; the Greeks' love of music and the arts, to puberty and early manhood, and so forth. Such speculations, innocent or unconvincing though they may seem, embody none the less the principle of physiological race-thinking.

Other nineteenth-century figures had direct contact with the writings of Cabanis and his colleagues. The novelist Stendhal was an avid reader of De Stutt de Tracy and based several of his own systems on Idéologue principles. Mignet, the historian, and Sainte-Beuve, the critic, have acknowledged similar obligations. Fourier, Schopenhauer, and Janet in philosophy, Hartmann and Bichat in psychology, take many of the Idéologues' views as

[2] For further details on this tradition, see my book, *Science: the Glorious Entertainment*, 1964.

their starting points. The historians Fauriel, Mérimée, and Augustin Thierry were in touch with De Stutt de Tracy as late as 1821 and Buchez summed up in his characteristically titled *Introduction to the Science of History* (1833) the complex of ideas and beliefs relevant to this study of race. Not only does Buchez betray the influence of Saint-Simon and the Sensationalists, but likewise that of the phrenologists Gall and Spurzheim, whom he cites approvingly. He entitles two chapters "Social Physiology" and "Considerations on Individual Physiology; its Application to Social Physiology." The actual "considerations" are frequently obscure and entirely *a priori,* but his book, though not written to attract, enjoyed a surprising popularity, a second revised edition being called for in 1842, six years before its author became President of the Constituent Assembly of 1848.

Nationalism and the doctrines of the State likewise received impetus from the philosophy of psychological determinism. Buchez was being metaphorical when he said that "a nation is an idea that has made itself a living body" (*qui s'est faite chair*), but many were beginning to take literally the notion that a race (the body) represented a unique idea (the nation or state) both of them coexistent through all eternity.[3] "The difference between races," said Hegel in the *Philosophy of Mind,* "is again a natural difference, that is, one regarding the natural soul"; and Kant as well as Herder, Fichte, and Fr. Schlegel supported similar views.

For most philosophers of racial nationalism it did not matter whether spirit determined matter or matter determined spirit, but for a large group of believers the difference was of course all-important. Jacques Maritain has written some plain words on the subject: "Nationalism also professes the belief that each nation has its mission in history. In this sense it is almost synonymous with racism, and in this sense it is indeed a very dan-

[3] Oswald Spengler's *Decline of the West* (1918) treats of cultures on just the same basis, though he starts with the idea of form rather than the body.

gerous error. . . . To take nations in the sense of the racial families is materialistic and false." (*Opinions sur Maurras,* 1926, 66.) That racism and materialistic philosophies would fall foul of the established religions could have been predicted and how it happened can be told in a few words.

III

But the expression often used by Mr. Herbert Spencer, of the Survival of the Fittest, is more accurate and is sometimes equally convenient.

—CHARLES DARWIN, *Origin of Species*

ON THE AFTERNOON of August 2, 1830, the Genevese botanist Soret went to see Goethe as usual, but in a state of great agitation. The news of the July Revolution in France had just reached Weimar.

"Tell me," cried Goethe as his friend entered, "what do you think of the great event? The volcano has broken out, everything is in flames, and it's no longer something going on behind closed doors!"

"A dreadful affair!" replied Soret. "What else is to be expected in the circumstances and from such a Ministry, but that the reigning family will be driven into exile?"

"We do not seem to understand each other, my dear fellow," returned Goethe. "I am not speaking of those people. It is quite another question I have in mind. I am speaking of the open break that has occurred in the Academy between Cuvier and Geoffroy St. Hilaire over a matter of the highest importance to science. . . . The thing is of the highest significance, and you cannot imagine what I felt on hearing the news of the sitting of July 19." (*Gespräche mit Eckermann.*)

The open break between Baron Cuvier and Geoffroy St. Hilaire was over the question of the Creation, or as it was put in the debates of the Academy, of the "unity of organic life." Was there one human race or were there many? If there were many, as descriptions of primitive peoples seemed to indicate, then the process of differentiation must somehow be explained. Two explanations were possible. Either each race had a separate pair of ancestors, which implied numerous acts of creation at the beginning of life; or from a single original pair (or possibly tribe) the earth had been peopled. If so, climate must account for the present observable differences. The latter school of anthropologists called themselves monogenists and the former polygenists. Not before the full vogue of skull-measurement did the quarrel between these two groups cease, and it ceased only because the old terms were made obsolete by the skull-nomenclature, on the one hand, and the Darwinian idea of species, on the other. Before skull-anthropology, the "races" of mankind were the groups that one still learns about in grammar school geographies. Color of skin, appearance of hair and features, were the distinguishing marks, whether one followed the fivefold classification of Blumenbach into Caucasian, Ethiopian, Mongolian, American, and Malayan, or whether one preferred the more refined and hence larger classifications of Desmoulins and d'Omalius d'Halloy.

Goethe was particularly interested in questions of morphology and evolution and his comment to Soret on receiving the news of the debate at the Academy evinced a partisanship shared by many of his scientific and lay contemporaries. A desire to explain the forms of natural life in materialistic terms had, between 1750 and 1800, given rise to various theories of evolution: Bonnet, Maupertuis, Buffon, Erasmus Darwin, and finally Lamarck, suggested schemes of increasing ingenuity and complexity to account for the similarities among living beings. Although the tendency to prove similarity and evolution might suggest that scientists would try to minimize the differences among men, the fact is that evolution and the belief in separate races contradict each other only in part. As so often happens, the confusion of ideas arises chiefly from the definition of terms.

In the classic scheme of Linnaeus, species represent groups that are set apart one from another and that will not produce fertile offspring when crossed. Varieties, on the contrary, show less distinct and less stable differences and do reproduce indefinitely by crossbreeding. Thus the species *Homo sapiens* is divided into four varieties with the following criteria:

Homo Americanus—Tenacious, contented, free; ruled by custom.

Homo Europaeus—Light, lively, inventive; ruled by rites.

Homo Asiaticus—Stern, haughty, stingy; ruled by opinion.

Homo Afer—Cunning, slow, negligent; ruled by caprice.

This is already far removed from the simple biblical account of the human races descended from Ham, Shem, and Japhet, yet it does not conflict with Scripture, for it leaves the human race one and undivided. About the Creation it says and implies nothing. Questioning the account of origins in the Book of Genesis began in earnest with the increase of knowledge concerning primitive peoples which was the result of extensive travel and exploration during the latter half of the eighteenth century. Australia and its natives became known to Europeans about 1770. The navigators La Pérouse, Bougainville, and Cook belong to the same period; and to it also the popularizing of the old idea of the noble savage, so important in the growth of evolutionary sociology and so generally misunderstood in our own day. The result was a widespread curiosity concerning man in nature and his ultimate origins. The varieties of red, yellow, white, and black were themselves found to contain sub-varieties. How could they be accounted for without special acts of creation? Was there a parallel between human and animal forms? Buffon compiled his great *Natural History* (1749 ff.), which added impetus to the study of organic forms and contained a cautious, purposely ambiguous theory of evolution. In England Dr.

Erasmus Darwin and in Germany Goethe were puzzling over the problems of morphology and all gravitating toward the notion that animal forms must have sprung from a few prototypes. But any evolutionary theory had to solve a threefold problem: (1) How to arrange animal species in the order of their evolutionary similarity. (2) How to account for the change that would transform one type into another. (3) How to explain the apparent fixity of now living species.

This is not the place to review the numerous answers offered to these questions.[4] What must be pointed out is that race is doubly involved in any theory of evolution. If species do not really exist, then there are in the world only individuals who temporarily occupy a place in the hierarchy of nature and who may still be evolving toward other forms. But it may also be that the agent in this evolution is the adaptation of certain hereditary forms to environment; therefore certain groups (races) would be especially favored and perpetuated. From this to the assertion that the white race or *Homo Europaeus* is the finest racial product of evolution is but a step. In such a view the world is seen as peopled by a large number of diverse races at various stages of evolution that reflect inner powers of adaptation. Race thereby becomes the material agency determining the various degrees of civilization, thus making Providence unnecessary. Hence the great significance of the debate in Paris which lined up in one camp both religious and scientific orthodoxy against the new evolutionary heretics. Cuvier was the defender of the traditional view of monogeny and Geoffroy St. Hilaire was making a frontal attack against the entrenched position. Cuvier won the day, but a breach had been made.

A remarkable aspect of this discussion is that it split liberalism and conservatism within themselves. Obviously the liberal, or indeed the radical, view to take was that the biblical account was mere poetry and that there were in fact many races. But it

[4] For such a review see my *Darwin, Marx, Wagner,* N.Y., 1941/1958.

happened that simultaneously with the religious issue liberals all over Europe were fighting the battle of Negro slavery. One of the best arguments to show the essential wickedness of slavery had always been that the Negroes were our brothers, an integral part of the human race, with feelings and potentialities or "souls" in every way similar if not equal to those of the whites. The heresy of the polygenists laid them open to the charge of condoning slavery by admitting that there might be on this earth differently constituted breeds of men, some of whom were inferior and thus the natural servants of the others. The abolition of slavery in the British possessions in 1834 and in the United States in 1861-65 killed the quarrel rather than settled the argument. But the question of inequality survived on a larger scale, as can be seen in Gobineau,[5] owing to the scramble of the New Imperialism for colonies among the so-called backward peoples.

By the second half of the nineteenth century, Evolution had become established, even popular, with the writings of Charles Lyell, Robert Chambers, Herbert Spencer, Charles Darwin, Alfred Russel Wallace, and T. H. Huxley. Monogeny and polygeny had been merged into a new doctrine that was not in reality more conclusive on the race-issue. Darwin's book is entitled *The Origin of Species by Means of Natural Selection, or the Survival of Favored Races in the Struggle for Life,* but readers could take the book as showing chiefly that all forms of animate life were related to one another. Others could reflect that the races or varieties were not defined or accounted for, save by a mysterious process that Darwin calls Variation. Therefore the monogenists under new names could say not only that all human beings were brothers but also that they were brothers to all other organic forms. It was equally tenable for their op-

[5] *Essay on the Inequality of Races* (1853-55), discussed in the next chapter. *Race and Reason,* by Carleton Putnam, Washington, 1961, is the latest reassertion of polygeny and its social corollaries. It has been endorsed by scientists and senators.

ponents to assert that races having once taken form, the struggle for existence among them was ever widening the gap by increasing the inequalities. It was good Social Darwinism for the white man to call the amoeba, the ape, and the Tasmanian his brother; it was equally good Darwinism to show that the extinction of the Tasmanian by the white colonists of Australasia was simply a part of the struggle for life leading to the survival of the favored races by natural selection.

Meanwhile, the Catholic Church was bending every effort to uphold the monogenistic doctrine on grounds of both humanitarianism and revelation. The bishop of Montpellier, writing in 1857 to the deans and professors of the University, declared: ". . . without entering into the scientific examination of such or such a question of physiology, but on the sole certainty of our dogmas, we can judge of any hypothesis, most such being only anti-Christian engines rather than serious conquests over the secrets and mysteries of nature. It is a dogma that man was formed and fashioned by the hand of God. It is therefore false, heretical, contrary to the dignity of the Creator and an offense to his masterpiece to say that man constitutes the seventh species of ape. . . . Heretical also to say that humankind is not descended from a single couple and that one can discover as many as *twelve* distinct races." (Quoted in Tyndall, *Fragments of Science,* II, 218.)

The church has continued, through its missions and such intellectual organizations as Aucam,[6] to propound monogenism. The result has undoubtedly been to foster descriptive anthropology while asserting *a priori* the unity of the human race. At the same time, the Church must necessarily respect its own dogmas and cannot consider infidels or heathens its spiritual brethren until they have adopted the Catholic religion, just as the white imperialist or the white scientist is usually unable to consider the Kaffir his brother until the Kaffir has taken on

[6] Association Universitaire Catholique pour l'Aide aux Missions. (See the report of its first Congress at Louvain, April 12-14, 1930.)

European clothing and European habits of work. The most conspicuous instance of a reversal of judgment following the adoption of approved ways occurred after 1867, when the Japanese westernized their nation. Almost overnight the tone of contempt toward them changed to one of surprised admiration. The island people began to be distinguished from the Chinese, and instead of being described as indolent and backward "Orientals," they were accorded a status closer to the Aryan whites.

In our day, opposition to German race-propaganda led the Austrian episcopate to reiterate the Catholic dogma: "Humanity is a single family based on justice and love. We therefore condemn the National Socialist *race-mania* which leads necessarily to hatred and conflict." (Vienna, Dec. 21, 1933.)

The ensuing quarrel in Germany proper between Hitler and the Catholics attests the same antagonism between racial and religious dogmas, which in turn has consolidated the alliance between National Socialism and Nordic paganism.[7] But long before Hitler the fusion of polygenism, imperialism, Nordic heathenism, historical determinism, and racial discrimination had occurred, thanks to cultural propinquity, and had found expression in the works of a Frenchman, the Count Arthur de Gobineau, to whom we must next turn our attention.

[7] Ludendorff is reported to have said at a celebration in his honor: "The Christian faith is not apt to bring about a regeneration of the German people: it is not suited to our race."

Chapter IV

GOBINEAU

I

We do not come from the ape but we are rapidly getting there.

—GOBINEAU

WRITERS WHO HAVE taken a stand against German racism have usually looked for a villain as the head and fount of the evil and they have had little trouble in finding one. The Germans themselves have pointed to Arthur de Gobineau as their master and inspirer. Unfortunately, Gobineau's famous *Essay on the Inequality of Races,* published in the middle of the nineteenth century, is one of those books, like Marx's *Capital* and Montesquieu's *Spirit of the Laws,* that everybody talks about but no one ever reads. It is the common fate of two-volume works of erudition, but it does not seem to prevent their influence from working, from spreading, and from generating powerful myths. Gobineau's *Essay* has unquestionably done these things, yet it is a grave mistake to regard him on that account as a narrow-minded snob or a fanatical theorist. He must answer for much, but he is not the villain sought for by his indignant accusers.

The Count, in fact, is not only personally charming, but he is without doubt a first-rate intellect. Granted that he furnished a host of lesser writers with race-ideas and convenient clichés, he himself was superior to his own doctrine and he applied it with the playfulness of a genius fascinated by ideas. Before the end of his life Gobineau had supplemented, if not actually supplanted, his race-theory of history with the notion of an intellectual aristocracy, and his race-prejudice with a utopian desire that Plato or Jefferson might not have disavowed.

His wavering between Nordic racism and a meritocracy of brains is not hard to account for. The Count de Gobineau, born in 1816, belongs to that second generation of Romanticists who suffered as precocious adolescents from the dull atmosphere of the Restoration Monarchy while they dreamt of a life generous and even heroic. "There are two things in the world," he wrote to his father at 23, "that interest me and for which I am ready to become a martyr: my love and my poetry. But when I uttered a word of this to you formerly you got angry and called me romantic." (July 22, 1839.)

Gifted young men of the middle class threw themselves into the struggle for liberalism, seeking liberty from an extension of the Revolutionary principles. Others, bound by aristocratic family traditions, made the opposite choice, believing that it was liberalism and impending democracy that were stifling the best. Gobineau was among the latter, and his choice is but another manifestation of the rift between the Two Frances. The last of a line of well-to-do bourgeois from Bordeaux, Gobineau received the aristocratic *de* from an indifferent father, but the full significance of the noble particle was made clear to him by an erratic uncle who had been a royalist conspirator. In some ways, the youth's early circumstances remind one of another great Nordicist, also from Bordeaux, the Baron de Montesquieu. Both were aristocrats by temperament, wits by avocation, travelers by choice, and systematic historians by determination. Had Gobineau been vain enough to claim the kinship he might have called his essay *L'Esprit des Races*. The two works, separated by almost exactly a century, fairly represent the change in the general attitude of mankind toward science and history. Montesquieu makes geography and climate the conditioning factors in history. The physical world of matter explains the mind and the institutions of men. Gobineau comes after the "biological revolution." He consequently finds in the physical nature of men themselves the factors of race that explain men's minds and institutions.

Before he arrived at this broad statement and buttressed it with an abundance of historical fact, the Count had gained much practical experience in journalism, politics, and diplomacy. He began his literary career under the July Monarchy in that mood of revolt against petty bourgeois conventions that the heroes of Balzac and Stendhal typify. Gobineau soon formed with a few kindred souls a group who called themselves the Scelti (the chosen) or Cousins of Isis, and who, humorously aware of their own solemnity, argued at length in favor of aristocratic freedom. Like the elder Romanticists, they championed Greek independence, they took up Oriental studies and toiled at epic poems, novels and five-act tragedies. This lively struggle against his milieu was for Gobineau a continuation of the fitful tenor of his early education, first under the guidance of a German Hegelian tutor, then at the college of Lorient in Brittany. The results of this training were on the whole good, French biographers to the contrary notwithstanding. He derived from it a love of travel, a knowledge of German (then as rare in France as it was in England), and an acquaintance with racial and artistic Celticism at that time in full swing. Never quite at one with his eccentric family, Gobineau united in himself before his thirtieth year tendencies which, though logically contradictory, were none the less psychologically of a piece. A hatred of mankind and of Christian ethics was combined with artistic individualism. Both these led to a passion for the Renaissance period, as strong and as keen as Stendhal's, and a corresponding contempt for the pseudo-democracy of his own day. It is not therefore surprising to find Gobineau in his earliest literary criticism battling for the Romanticists and seeing in Hugo, Stendhal, Lamartine, George Sand, Mérimée, and Lamennais the voices of his own desires and despair.

In 1848 Gobineau was momentarily tempted by the possibility of an aristocratic republic. With Louis de Kergolay he founded the *Revue Provinciale* to preach the administrative decentralization of France—the old dream of Boulainvilliers and of the Federalists in the French Revolution. Gobineau's hopes were soon dashed, and as Cabinet Secretary to Alexis de Tocqueville in 1849 he became anti-republican, then Bonapartist, finally an indomitable oppositionist to whatever government was in power. This did not prevent his being an excellent diplomat, entrusted from 1849 to 1877 with various missions that took him to Switzerland, Germany, Persia, Greece, Newfoundland, Brazil, and Sweden.

Before we judge too harshly of Gobineau's variable political allegiance, we must recall that the nineteenth century was not the stream of lava cleft at two or three points that historiography tends to make it. It was a period of multiple confusions, like our own, like every period. It was full of dramatic turns and shocking events in even greater degree than ours, if only because the pace was new. The political evolution of a Gobineau, a Coleridge, a Victor Hugo, or a Mazzini therefore demands more sympathetic attention than the historian, sitting in judgment away from the conflict and the smoke of battle, is willing to give it.

Gobineau, like his other spiritual ancestor, the Count de Boulainvilliers, felt born out of his time; but it would be an error to think that his passion for the past, the future, and the elsewhere was an escape or a retreat from the present. He belongs in that regard with the Romanticists. Perhaps no generation of men since the Renaissance has lived so intensely and perceptively, nor made so much poetry and truth out of a present that was out of joint. Like them a poet at heart, despite his wretched versification, Gobineau's literary output was born of conviction. His critical and political articles, his novels and tales, his travel books and Oriental studies, his letters and his sculpture, his diplomatic work, his friendships and his life, must command the respect of anyone acquainted with them, who is not also blinded by partisanship or bewildered by the versatility of a genuine artist.

It is entirely true that this versatility leads Gobineau to contradict himself on important points in the course of the forty volumes he has left us. But those contradictions, as with greater dialecticians than he, always have their explanation in circumstance. They must be held signs of honesty, rather than weakness, of mind. Gobineau had the realist's eye and he was uttering no more than the truth when he said that in studying a new people he "repudiated any true or false idea he might have had of their superiority." If inconsistency resulted, the fault lies with an unmanageable race-doctrine, not with the man observing history or life.

Now, what is Gobineau's race-theory? It boils down to three ideas: special race-characteristics, blood-mixture, and decadence. As to race Gobineau starts with the threefold division of mankind into white, yellow, and black. To the first he ascribes all the noble qualities of manhood, leadership, energy, superiority. The yellow races have stability and fertility. The black are endowed with sensuality and the artistic impulse. At this point Gobineau's scheme shows a novel feature which is unique in race-theorizing. It is only when two races mix, he says, that civilization occurs. Art and government are the signs of civilization and no single race can produce these by itself. But civilization leads to more and more mixing of "inferior blood" with that of the ruling caste, so that the "great race" is inevitably bastardized and decadence follows.

What Gobineau is really doing is to offer an answer to the ever-fascinating question of why civilizations rise and fall. Race is for him the answer, and one is forced to admit that Gobineau is so far a good historian that he sees all the European nations as products of the interpenetration of cultures. As a prophet he is again sound in thinking that nothing is going to stop the process of "mixing." It is when *races,* rather than peoples or cultures, are discovered as the elements in the mixture that the historian must take issue with Gobineau. Pessimist and fatalist as he is because of the "inevitability of race," he deserves a certain respect for rejecting the hope of a "pure race" preserving its "blood" intact. For him—and this is the result of Aryan philology in the manner of Prichard or Max Müller—the primitive *Aryas,* who were the progenitors of the great white race, have left very few pure specimens in our midst. What happened to the great majority was contamination by yellow and Negro blood. The Semites are Negroid and the Semites have infected the whole Mediterranean basin with their "nigridity." That is why the so-called Latin nations—France, Italy, Spain, Portugal —are a decadent, slavish, and worthless stock: they are thoroughly semitized, melanized (μέλας-αν, black). Gobineau paints us the portrait of these unfortunates with the colors of his own disgust for democracy, servility, corruption, and mediocrity.

Obviously, Gobineau, reversing the usual process, starts with a desire for the truth about a great historical question, and ends by finding a confirmation of his hypothesis in the contemporary scene. At his narrowest, Gobineau is actuated by defensible motives—a genuine passion for art, for selectivity, for energy and devotion to causes transcending self or national interest. The vehemence of his racial denunciations is never ignorant fanaticism, and one comes to feel about him what Swift said of himself—that he hated the human race as a whole, but "heartily loved John, Peter, Thomas, and the rest."

The proof of this comparison is that when Gobineau was sent as minister to Persia in 1856, after the publication of the *Essay,* he acclimatized himself readily and conceived a love for the "semitized" and "melanized" Persians inconsistent with his written profession of faith. His work on the history and religion of the Persians breathes sympathy and understanding in a measure that few writers wholly innocent of racial bias could achieve. His next diplomatic post took him to Greece, for whose people and art he had conceived an aversion ever since becoming aware of their semitization in Macedonian and Hellenistic times. But, once on the spot, Gobineau observes, absorbs, and grows enthusiastic.

In Newfoundland and Sweden, despite some frankly acknowledged disappointments of his racial forecasts, he found himself completely in tune with his surroundings. Only in Brazil did he show intractability. He hated the "nigridized race," even though he became a close friend and confidant of the Emperor Pedro, hardly a pure Aryan. But one suspects that Gobineau's distaste for Brazil was due to the climate, which made him suffer, and to the political rebuke of his appointment there, which made his proud and clear conscience suffer even more.

Gobineau's ideas on France itself have made a number of his biographers justly call him a continuator of Boulainvilliers and Montesquieu. He is a Nordicist like them, wielding the added power that, since their day, belonged to the new adjective Aryan. Racially, says Gobineau, France has only a few Aryan Nordics left; the rest are a Gallo-Roman mob whose chief instinct is envy and revolution,[1] and whose highest taste in politics or in art is the circus. Using the word "race" in an honorific sense, Gobineau declares that these Latins are anything but a race. What has happened is of course the hopeless semitization of the breed, with the result that mediocrity is everywhere in power. Their political mismanagement, their moral corruption, was at no time more evident to the Count than during the war of 1870. On the conduct of that war he wrote a harsh but convincing pamphlet which he himself considered his best work, the fruit of twenty-one years' observation and reflection. The severity of its strictures, which will be detailed elsewhere, has prevented many French racists, otherwise in agreement with Gobineau, from

[1] The Count unfortunately had to celebrate his own birthday on the 14th of July.

avowing his influence; it was precisely this brand of unintelligent patriotism which Gobineau most abhorred. He had traveled too far and knew Germany too well to believe, much less to be willing to repeat, the absurdities about the Germans current during the Franco-Prussian War. He thought patriotism a tyrannical invention of the Semitic race. That conclusion, if true, would greatly embarrass those French nationalists who combine rabid patriotism with anti-Semitism. Shortly before his death Gobineau further qualified his opinion. "One must love one's country soberly, to be able to forgive it much. One must love everything in the world in the same way for the same reason, that everything needs great indulgence." (*Catal. Expos. Strasbourg,* 4.) This is not the utterance of an anti-patriot, but of a stoical moralist.

Whether motivated by pessimism or by stoicism, Gobineau was among the first to term the Latin races decadent and to sound a warning against the yellow peril. Already in the *Essay,* the hordes of silent yellow men are pictured as bound to engulf the decreasing race of whites precariously perched on the peninsular tip of the Asiatic continent we call Europe. The Count was perhaps not so much inconsistent about the East as fascinated and frightened by it. As an early orientalist and philologian, he had translated cuneiform inscriptions, but he also wrote articles against the Asiatic menace. He was attracted by magic and talismans, by fatalism and the ascetic life, so much so that during his own lifetime theosophic circles gave his works ready circulation and quiet renown. But he had moments of revulsion. In Scandinavia, swayed by the associations of the language and the surroundings, his orientalism fell away from him and he returned with zest to the Norse mythology admired in the *Essay*. His new acquaintance with Richard Wagner made this rediscovery doubly fresh and attractive. He sculptured a Walküre; yet there was a Buddha nearby swathed in damp cloths.

Behind this mixed love and fear on the philosophical plane,

Gobineau was moved by practical considerations. In 1867 he writes to his friend Adalbert von Keller: "The Orient is our great enemy: the danger began with the death of Alexander." He had seen in Persia the process of religious and racial mixture bringing about urban democracy, and he thought he saw a close parallel between the progress of Proudhon's philosophical anarchism in Europe and the spread of the economic-evangelical movement known as Bab-ism in the Middle East. The East, history suggested to him, always kills the civilizations that conquer it—hence the grave danger of European imperialism in Asia. As the struggle of the powers shifted more and more to the East, awareness of the yellow peril grew in Gobineau's mind, and in an article dated 1880-81 that did not reach the public until after his death,[2] he reviewed the gradual encroachment of "Semitic blood" in Europe from Greece to Scandinavia, analyzed with much insight the Anglo-Russian conflict in Asia, and predicted a world upheaval as the result of imperialism. Imperialism spelled danger to him because it augmented race-mixture, and race-mixture "having gone so far in the modern world can only accelerate the evil to the final extremity." The panicky doctrine of the early 1900's clarioned forth by the newspapers and the German Emperor is here in more than embryonic form, as is also the chief point of modern prophecies like Henri Massis' *Defense de l'Occident*.

To reconcile the Count's writings with his tolerant behavior needs really no legerdemain. Gobineau was first and foremost a cosmopolitan spirit curious about the world. He belonged to that small but permanent class of Frenchmen who travel and who, doing it with their eyes and minds open, never make the mistake of supposing that the Alps, the Channel, and the Pyrenees are the outer edges of civilization. This class has somehow to overcome the whole weight of French habit and opinion,

[2] Ironically enough, in the "semitized" pages of the *Revue du Monde Latin*, 1885, 397 ff.

which accounts for their unpopularity at home. Such men learn foreign languages, appreciate foreign cultures, and do not wither and die when outside the limits of their native Paris or parish. Historically, they often occur in bunches: the explorers of Renaissance times, the eighteenth-century philosophers, the Romanticists, and in modern times a goodly number of young diplomats and colonialists, who continue an important French tradition that has been obscured by clichés.[3]

It has been said that Gobineau was anti-nationalistic and anti-patriotic (despite an effective devotion to the interests of his country) because he owed allegiance only to his race—the Nordic-Aryan breed. The remark is superficially true but misleading. Gobineau found very few true Nordics wherever he went. His son-in-law, the Baron von Guldencrone, was one of those few, and that fact made Gobineau, according to the bride, the happiest man at the wedding. But Germany had scarcely more Aryans than Northern France. Sweden was heavily stocked with a short, round-headed population very similar to the mongrel French. The Count himself was brown-haired, and there remains an insoluble ambiguity topped by a paradox—as so often in questions of race—about the color of his eyes. One of his earliest disciples among the younger generation, the historian Albert Sorel, refers categorically to the Count's "handsome, mocking blue eyes." (*Notes et Portraits,* 232, and *Le Temps,* March 22, 1904.) Another description, furnished by the friend and companion of Gobineau's last years, Madame de la Tour, tells of his light chestnut hair and golden-brown eyes, which she faithfully reproduced in the portrait she painted of him. The paradox comes in when we find Gobineau making blond hair and blue eyes the indispensable mark of the Aryan race:

And all the Merovingian tribe displaying its ancient vigor,
A noble crowd with blond tresses flowing on broad shoulders

[3] See, for example, the article by Abbé Ernest Dimnet, *Literary Digest,* Dec. 23, 1933, 15.

White as the snow at the poles, and dazzling with its blue eyes
. . . Said to me: "Dost know that heaven belongs to the strong-armed?" (*Paradis de Beowulf*)

Despite the difference between this description and his own features, Gobineau truly believed that he was just such a Nordic-Aryan, descended through Norman stock from Ottar Jarl, a Viking hero whose native soil was one of the Skaeren, an islet in the North Sea. Standing on this pine-fringed rock, Gobineau felt a sudden mystic conviction that here *his* race had originated; but this poetic vision or naïve nonsense, as one chooses, need not obscure a lasting element in Gobineau's thought, the belief in nobility of mind, as important to him as nobility of birth. He held aristocracy to be an individual and not a racial matter. He says so, ambiguously perhaps, in *The Pleiads:* "Whoever finds the qualities you speak of hung round his neck from birth, that one without the least doubt has received in his blood through whatever lineage, superior virtues, the sacred merit that one can see shining in him. . . . He is a 'son of kings.' " But in a later, less fanciful work, in which he discusses democracy, he asserts categorically the existence of "a small number of chosen spirits (*esprits d'élite*) who, to the honor of mankind, live in all periods and places, in all milieux, and who by reason of their very excellence defy all classifications; they belong in truth to no class or order but that of select natures (*natures d'élite*), no matter how humble their condition; they cannot, therefore, qualify as representatives of the working classes any more than as representatives of the upper orders." (*Nachgelassene Schriften,* II, 127.)

That conviction, similar to Balzac's, doubtless explains the paradox of hair-and-eye color: his own and that of several of his fictional heroes and heroines who are brunettes with ancestries as tenuously Nordic as the Count's.[4]

[4] Gobineau, belonging to a family of merchants from Southern France, hence "semitized" at one time or another, apparently had a genuine English ancestor in the fifteenth century who helped bridge the missing

II

I knew him. . . . One was aware that he had written some books, but no one had read them. . . . And so he was a genius? How curious!

—ANATOLE FRANCE on Gobineau

TO UNDERSTAND A man's mind in its strength and weakness is one thing; to measure the effects and distortions of his thought is another, far more difficult task. Gobineau himself is a sympathetic character, but there is no doubt that he is responsible for a particular set of influential race-beliefs. Aryan, Germanic, inferior and superior races, race-mixture, degenerescence, semitization, and nigridization are ideas or at least words that he dinned into the minds of his contemporaries and descendants. The habit of quotation-picking among scholars and the echolalia of publicists have done the rest. To make Gobineau solely responsible, as certain detractors have done, or entirely uninfluential, as some French critics still persist in doing, is to go against the facts.

During his own lifetime, the *Essay* was read by at least a score of notables: Renan, Taine, Nietzsche, Wagner, Quatrefages, Schopenhauer, Philip von Eulenburg, Vanderkinder, Hans von Wolzogen, Jacques de Boisjolin, Viollet-le-Duc, Mérimée,

---

link in the genealogical fiction elaborated in the *History of Ottar Jarl*. The whole matter is of slight importance except for the ever-interesting question of the "quality of belief" that a fine intellect accords to myths of its own manufacture. Newton's theology, Auguste Comte's late mysticism, Nietzsche's descent from the Polish nobility, Goethe's self-fictionizing, and similar manifestations of the creative power have not been studied with sufficient understanding by critics for whom, in general, whatever cannot be verified in court records is either vanity or lunacy. A pragmatic approach suggests that a belief of this sort is accessory to other functions in the man's mind. At any rate, Gobineau is not the first nor the last man to take pleasure in a galloping genealogy. A visit to the Theodore Roosevelt Museum in New York City is instructive in this regard, and we shall see in the following pages how often artists and thinkers find it necessary to choose this or that race as their own.

Broca, Paul de Rémusat, Robert Bulwer-Lytton, Albert Sorel, Roget de Belloguet, Comte de Leusse, Baron Prokesch-Osten, Jules Mohl (President of the Asiatic Society), and the American anthropologist Charles D. Meigs, who boasted of having read the book ten times, and who regarded it as a kind of gospel to be preached. In effect, these men did more than read this or later works by Gobineau. They were so struck by the idea of race as the key to history, or so aptly confirmed in their thoughts on cognate subjects, that they adopted the system and made it within a half century the common property of men who had read at first hand neither Gobineau, nor Taine, nor Renan, nor anyone else. It is a mistake to confuse publisher's sales and salon popularity with influence. Many a work that is on everybody's tongue for one or two seasons plummets into oblivion and dies with its own ripples; whereas a work like the *Essay,* if read by a dozen persons will—provided they are the right dozen—live and act long before its author's name becomes known. Moreover, though the *Essay* is in its way a technical book, the same ideas are so easily discoverable in Gobineau's fiction and travel notes that it is impossible not to see in these various sources the cause of much scholarly race-theorizing in the manner of Renan or Taine, and of nearly all the popular dogmatizing of the casual racists.

The dates of the *Essay* and of Renan's manuscript on *Semitic Languages* seem to show that Gobineau merely reinforced the distinction Renan made between the "objective" Aryan and the "subjective" Semite. But that a feudal Germanic constitution was the primitive form of the old Iranian government seems too special a notion for Renan to have come upon coincidentally after Gobineau had voiced it in his *Three Years in Asia.* We know that Renan carefully annotated Gobineau's *Essay* for his own use, though he never publicly acknowledged his many debts to the Count. Neither did Taine, who in public only smiled at the diplomat's "paradoxes," yet brought out a very complete theory of race applied to literature in 1863; nor did Nietzsche, whose sister read the *Essay* aloud to him and testified after her brother's death that he had been profoundly struck by Gobineau's views.

As early as 1856, Pott had published in a work of his own a synopsis of the French writer's thesis, and this may have been the start of Gobineau's fortunes in Germany. At any rate, some twenty years later, Wagner, as was his wont when any fresh system swam into his ken, sat down to the composition of a Gobinian Essay joining anti-Semitism, the love of renunciation and the renunciation of love, blatant Germanism and a Nietzschean view of Greek tragedy. He met Gobineau and, finding pleasure in his witty conversation and musical tastes, feted him at Wahnfried. One wonders whether in these delightful talks of which we hear, the diplomatic Count mentioned his conviction that music is the native gift of the Negro race to white civilization. Did Wagner find the idea compatible with his recurrent faith in a German (Nordic) musical monopoly? Certainly he must have preferred being told, as he was, that the Ring embodied the quintessence of Gobineau's principles of German race-superiority. There was throughout an unconscious play on words, for by German Gobineau never meant Deutsch, and Wagner seldom meant anything else. Nothing, however, arose to strain the friendship. The pages of the *Bayreuther Blätter* were opened to the French writer, Hans von Wolzogen became his devoted disciple and press agent, and Wagner sealed the bond of race-fraternity by inscribing his complete prose works to the Count with the following untranslatable doggerel:

> Das wäre ein Bund,
> Normann und Sachse,
> Was da noch gesund,
> Dass das blühe und wachse!

Through his appreciative Wagnerism and his personal relations with the Master, Gobineau was enabled to reach directly or indirectly the younger generation of writers who established his fame in Germany. Schemann, H. S. Chamberlain, and

Eulenburg were his earliest apostles. It was from the pen of the last-named that Gobineau received the only enthusiastic summary of a life of thought and toil upon leaving it. But that eulogy was only the beginning.

Even if Nietzsche had not privately admitted his sense of loss at never having met Gobineau, one could have guessed from internal evidence that the Count's ideas had struck fertile ground. Then, too, Nietzsche knew his Schopenhauer, and Schopenhauer had also read the *Essay,* and read it well, to judge from the citation in the *Parerga.* The affinity between Gobineau and Nietzsche is not hard to understand. A common admiration for Stendhal meant in reality a common love of the *Renaissancemensch*—bold, active, artistic, and morally beyond good and evil. Nietzsche was not yet born when Gobineau began to discard the Christian ethic and to admire barbarian life, but with this cult of the ego a contradictory orientalism shared Gobineau's soul. The phenomenon is so common among nineteenth-century poets that it may be unfair to atttribute it in Nietzsche to a reading of Gobineau. Goethe had seemed equally at home on the Brocken and with Confucius. Wagner, after the Ring, thought of writing a music drama about Sakya Muni, the Aryan noble turned tribune of the people, and that design became the mystic *Parsifal.* So Gobineau during his Brazilian period was for renouncing all earthly ambition and adopting brahmanic asceticism; and we find the heroes of his new works, *Amadis* and *Beowulf,* turning out to be chaste protagonists who refuse carnal love, precisely like Parsifal. Nietzsche, in turn, could set up Zarathustra and Dionysus as his idols and yet preach the life of the blond beast destined for Valhalla.

The similarity in contradiction goes even further. Gobineau's championship now of race and now of the superior individual is paralleled in Nietzsche by the two different types of supermen he longs for. Up to 1883, Nietzsche's ideal may be defined as the Romanticist genius; thereafter, starting with the fourth book of *Zarathustra,* his ideal is the conqueror breed, that is to say, a racial type in place of an individual. Both men oscillated between their two predilections for the barbarian, with his pagan vigor, and for the highest type of cultured man—Gobineau's "son of kings," Nietzsche's "good European." Stendhal had swung within the same arc of preference, and in cruder form the modern Nazi ideal wobbles between similar poles.

Again, bound up with the issue of race as these ideals are, they strike in Nietzsche the same difficulty that makes Gobineau perpetually contradict himself. In the *Essay* he asserts the race-mixture theory: melanization is the cause of degeneresence. In *The Pleiads,* in *Manfredine,* in *Ottar Jarl,* and elsewhere, the chosen men, the sons of kings, maintain the purity of the "great race" because its essence *cannot* be lost. It is an inalienable heritage that descends with the blood. But if this is so, then race-mixture is impossible: mixing would endow all the resulting mongrels with the imperishable qualities of the great race. In Nietzsche, the blond beast must keep his strain pure, but the good European must not be exclusively Germanic; in fact, to produce him, selected Jewesses must mate with Prussian noblemen. The race-fallacy cannot be teased out. For favored races to exist they must be distinct and their traits permanent. But if hybridism is a danger, those very distinctions must be perishable. "When is a race not a race?" is the puzzle that no philosopher or fanatic of race has yet solved.

If the known readers of Gobineau mentioned on an earlier page were the visible agents of dissemination for the Count's ideas of race, it is also true that they were helped by others, anonymous and unconscious propagandists about whom we can talk only as the "forces" or the "movements" of the century. By 1855, the date of the *Essay,* the first tide of Romanticism had ebbed. The young were seeking new modes of expression, and Gobineau's secondhand Romanticism could not carry him to renown. Imperialism, contrariwise, was reviving. European liberalism, English free trade, and general humanitarianism were followed by a *Realpolitik* which found the inequality of races well suited to its needs. The opening up of China and Japan and the first nibbles at the tempting African continent followed soon after Gobineau's first warning of the Asiatic Peril and the predestined slavery of the non-Aryan whites. "All that is not German is born to serve," says one of his characters in halting meter, and the idea seemed more and more confirmed by the facts, provided one did not scan too closely the Count's definition of German and that one overlooked his gloomy prediction of the outcome.

In France, Gobineau's denunciation of democracy[5] coincided with a defeat of the forces of liberalism and reform at the hands of Louis Napoleon; and although the new Emperor, seeing himself as a reincarnation of Julius Caesar, encouraged Gallo-Roman race-theories rather than Germanic, Gobineau's ideas found favor at Court. Besides, Evolutionism, the new militant religion of scientists and free-thinkers, seemed to fit in beautifully with the notion of superior and inferior races. The word "race" was on everybody's lips, for was not the struggle for survival manifested in the conflict of nations? And within each nation was not the perpetual competitive fight under economic liberalism another aspect of the same process of natural selection? It mattered little that both could not be true; that if nations were races fighting for survival among themselves, then the intramural struggle of individuals could not also represent a war of races. Distinguished minds rose above logic to comprehend in one vision economic competition, class struggle, international anarchy, and Darwin's natural selection of favored races. Gobineau may have been aghast at the crudity of the concepts, he for whom nuance and exactitude were an artistic necessity; but he was swept along in the torrent, and when toward the end of the century writers began to sort out the contributions of individual minds, he was more and more often cited with Darwin, Marx, Broca, and Nietzsche as one of the seers and makers of his epoch.

[5] He wished to "do better than de Maistre and Bonald against liberalism." (Letter to Prokesch-Osten, June 20, 1856.)

Quite apart from these considerations, the belief that Gobineau's works fell stillborn from the press is erroneous. He was reviewed by the leading anthropologist Quatrefages in the *Revue des Deux Mondes,* was alluded to in the same periodical by Paul de Rémusat and in scientific circles by Broca. Gobineau engaged in controversy with orientalists over his translations of cuneiform inscriptions, was popular in numerous literary salons including that of the Princesse Mathilde, and made disciples more readily than many a prophet who has never been considered ill-used. Twelve years after the *Essay,* Viollet-le-Duc's dictionary of French architecture appeared, containing a 100-page essay which is pure Gobineau. Jacques de Boisjolin openly became a defender of the Count's anthropological views as early as 1879. Broca refuted Gobineau on certain details, and so did Quatrefages, but both treated his ideas with respect. When Gobineau came back from Brazil he was "adopted" by the young Albert Sorel, a fellow diplomat and later a famous historian, who remained a warm admirer, though he never rightly understood what the Count meant; or rather, never knew when the Count seriously meant what he said.

Across the Channel, Robert Bulwer-Lytton, who was as disgruntled about home affairs as Gobineau was about France, propounded the notion that English decadence was due to race-degeneration resulting from the admixture of Irish (Celtic) and German (Slavic) blood. This illuminating discovery may have spurred on the English nationalist writers already awakened by Carlyle, Freeman, and Kingsley to the superiority of the Anglo-Saxon race and the beauties of *Beowulf*. Simultaneously, in the United States, some Southern gentlemen printed a garbled version of the *Essay* as a pamphlet in support of slavery. This distortion may not have flattered the author, but it was at least a token that his was not a voice crying in the desert. Although the Count never saw any of his books become a best seller, he found publishers for most of them without much difficulty and was awarded the Bordin Prize by the French Academy for his *Renaissance.*

To be sure, living on after 1870 must have been a trial for a man who saw his compatriots receding further and further away from the political path he advocated. He himself was shelved as a diplomat in 1877 and thereby forced to sell his château at Trie.[6] His articles on French ethnography were becoming difficult to place because his racial conclusions sounded more and more unpatriotic. His assertion that patriotism was a piece of Latin provincialism was felt as a crime against the sanctity of a wounded national pride. In spite of his alienation, he served his country well during the Franco-Prussian War. Not only did he organize local hospitals and refugee shelters in the face of invasion, but through his knowledge of the German language and officialdom he obtained a reduction of nine million francs on the war indemnity assessed upon his Department. Modern critics like Maurice Lange, who accuse him of having been anti-French because he retained his German friendships—principally Wagner's—simply disregard his genuine though peaceful war service.

He lived on until 1882 but the last five years were neither gay nor glorious. He wrote some of his maturest political tracts during that period, without hope of a hearing. Yet hardly a decade after his death the following he had created in Germany resounded in France through the *Gobineau-Vereinigung* and encouraged the growing band of faithfuls in his native country. Paul Bourget's works in the nineties, impregnated with the ideas of Stendhal and Taine, are no less full of Gobinism: the man who wrote the *Sensations d'Italie* in 1891, *Cosmopolis* in 1893, and the *Idylle Tragique* in 1894, joining the Gobineau Union in that same year, cannot be called a new convert or a lukewarm follower.

About this time also Gobineau found a sympathetic biographer in Armand Hayem and an influential critic in André Hal-

[6] Gobineau, who had warned his wife *not* to select a house such as Rousseau wanted for his old age, came to inhabit the very rooms where Rousseau wrote his later works.

lays of the *Journal des Débats*. Cheramy, the lawyer for Eiffel in the trial of Lesseps after the Panama Scandal, was known to be a fervent Gobinist, and Romain Rolland not much later was recording the Gobineau-peril by means of a character in *Jean-Christophe*. Royalist, or at least anti-revolutionary, opinion was being told by Paul de Leusse that Gobineau held the key to universal history, hence to French history, past, present, and future: race-degenerescence means democracy, which means national decadence. These Gobinian ideas were percolating through milieux where young men discussed *la question sociale* and were about to answer it by means either of the *Action Française* or of the *action socialiste*.

Meantime, with the rise of the sociological school of Tarde, Le Bon, Durkheim, Lévy-Bruhl, Vacher de Lapouge, Ammon, Gumplowicz, Muffang, and Closson, all of whom were writing or being published in French before 1900, Gobineau was entering the company of the new "social scientists." He was being pulled and mauled to fit many divergent doctrines, but he was being held in increasing reverence and, above all, he was not forgotten.

It is clear that Gobineau's initial effect in France, though not at first conspicuous, was as great as his success in Germany. His disciples before 1900 may be divided into two or three groups whose composition and opinions did not change for forty years. There were, first, those who adopted the race-theories contained in the *Essay* almost as they stood, that is, who affirmed the superiority of the Nordic-Aryan over all other races. Second: those who recast the doctrine by adopting the basic idea of race-character and race-superiority, but put some other race than the Germanic at the top of the hierarchy. And third: the numerous eclectics who mixed the elements of Gobinism and other racial and national doctrine into a hodgepodge from which no conclusion emerges save that the author is satisfying his vindictiveness behind a smoke screen of incoherent erudition.

In the first group belong Renan, Taine, Viollet-le-Duc, Rémy de Gourmont, Boisjolin, Baron Carra de Vaux, Leusse, and others dealt with in their place. In the second group, the nationalists from Bourget and Faguet to Maurras, Barrès, and Suarès. Their French patriotism obviously does not permit them to take the Count openly as their standard-bearer. They often call him hard names for his Germanism and his clear-eyed criticism of French policy and manners. They then change the names of the races in the Count's historical drama, talk of the imminent danger of racial mixture (métissage), the inalienable traits of the great race (Latin or Lorrainer or French), its function as the civilizer of mankind, and its duty of self-preservation from the poison of cosmopolitanism. Semitization is their chief bugbear, as it was the Count's, but Protestantism and free-thinking come in for their share of abuse as the products of undesirable "races."

The third group, the makers of potpourris, from its nature defies description. Camille Spiess is the extremest example of this type and a single characteristic passage from one of his works will give an idea of the stretch that Gobinism can stand at the hands of a man with a will to discipleship: "To the anthropology of race, I have wished to add biopsychology, which is the science of the sexes, of life, and of genius: the Aryan, Uranian, Dyonisian and Super-Christian mythology."

III

You consider yourself a man of the Past. I am firmly convinced that you are the man of the Future.

—PRINCESS CAROLYN VON SAYN-WITTGENSTEIN to Gobineau

SHORTLY AFTER THE declaration of war in 1914, the philosopher Bergson boasted to the Academy of Moral and Political Sciences that the French did not read Gobineau and took no stock in his ideas, thus differing from the Germans whose pride of race was the cause of the present aggression. Yet less than ten years before, Robert Dreyfus, a respected critic, who in view of the current anti-Semitism could easily have been unsympathetic, reviewed the life and prophecies of Gobineau and concluded that the Count's ideas "though highly original in 1853 run the risk of appearing commonplace and irritatingly banal today, so completely is our political atmosphere saturated with them." Not long after, a Catholic professor in the South of France admitted in similar terms the influence of Gobineau on French social life and politics. Sorel, less sympathetic than these two, was commenting on the obvious when he spoke of "our epoch of esoteric Aryanism and Yankee imperialism." Bergson's hasty dictum is therefore typical of the blindness that comes from either self-persuasion or a guilty conscience. Nothing is more common among a certain kind of race-thinkers than to repudiate the belief in race and to follow up the disclaimer with racist judgments and assertions. Like many scientifically minded moderns, they resent being suspected of superstition and knock on wood lest they fall into error.

In the spring following Bergson's presidential address, a cultured critic of conservative leanings wrote a book attempting to disentangle the good from the bad in German culture and to exonerate Nietzsche, Gobineau, and others from the "war-guilt" which patriotic scholars had tried to fasten upon them. Toward the end of the War, also wishing to clear Gobineau, Spiess wrote the work already referred to, but actually the anti-Gobineau party during the War was small and ineffectual when compared with the anti-Kant party, the anti-Fichte, anti-Hegel or anti-Wagner. After the War the Count's detractors virtually disappeared, which does not mean that all Frenchmen believe in Gobineau, but that there is no organized opposition to the work of the organized faithful.

Gobineau has in truth attained the rank of a recognized classic. "He has been read with delight these twenty years past," wrote a critic in 1926. His pinnacle was not conquered without difficulty, for there was not only the taint of Germanism to overcome but also that of Romanticism. Besides, the vested interest of those who did not want their source of inspiration revealed, or their own heroes—Taine, Renan, and Comte—overshadowed was an obstacle to Gobineau's fame. Its solid position may be seen, however, in the unceasing publication of Gobineau material since 1920. A full-length biography by Faure-Biguet was awarded one of the Academy prizes in 1931, but it was as early as 1923 that the magazine *Europe* devoted a whole number to the canonization of the Count, engaging distinguished writers and specialists to contribute. Eleven years later the *Nouvelle Revue Française* accorded him similar recognition (Feb., 1934). Every year one or another of Gobineau's early critical works has appeared, his novels and travel books have been reprinted, his correspondence has been collected and edited, until it seems superfluous for the writer of an introduction to say that Gobineau was "among the most profound thinkers and greatest writers of the last century." His disciples and admirers are to be found in every camp. The Stendhal Club treats him with respect. The *Action Française* continues to borrow surreptitiously and to attribute to Edouard Drumont or to some other journalist the "quickening of the racial sense among the French." The reason why this and other extreme nationalist groups do not admit Gobineau to their charmed circle of thinkers is that, although they take large doses of his political doctrine and maintain that purity of race is the safeguard of the nation, they are forced to preach the immovability of Race itself; the prime mover of history must itself be motionless. Gobineau, on the contrary, shows that everything in history is mobility and change. Gobineau sees no help for the ultimate degeneration of Europe, and after 1848 he has no program to offer; whereas the nationalists, particularly the *Action Française,* have a political remedy to sell. While he gloomily predicts world-fraternity through race-mixture and international leveling through socialism and democracy, the nationalists offer a nostrum guaranteed to cure these evils. They hope and he despairs. At the same time, the racial-evolutionary point of view contained in the *Essay,* which made Gobineau hint that his ideas had been taken without acknowledgment by Darwin and Buckle, conflicts with the Catholic dogmas of a Maritain, making him reject race as materialism, while he espouses nationalism as spiritual.

In the realm of art, no such objections stand in Gobineau's way, and his racial aesthetics is best continued by the distinguished art-historian Elie Faure, and in a less exact manner by such critics as the late Paul Souday, Adrien Mithouard, Henry Bordeaux, René Bazin, Jacques de Lacretelle, and others. It is no longer quaint or criminal in France to be a Gobinist, or a part-Gobinist, and the statement by Anatole France quoted at the head of the preceding section would now appear a mark of ignorance. It is true that since the second edition in 1884 no reprinting of the *Essay* has come from the press, very likely because its erudition is both out of date and fatiguing and that the central idea, so congenial to the French tradition of racism, can be painlessly had in the brilliant fiction, the engaging letters, and the lively travel books. The fiftieth anniversary of their author's death was fittingly celebrated in 1932 by an exhibition of Gobiniana at the University of Strasbourg, which had purchased the collection from the old *Gobineau-Vereinigung* in 1903.

To sum up, Gobineau waited only twenty years for posthumous fame at home. To a historian and philosopher, particularly a dead one, these twenty years cannot have seemed very long. Whatever may now be surmised, it is not because of his race-ideas that renown was slow in coming. De Maistre and Augustin Thierry were more narrow-minded racists than he; Taine and Renan were equally fanciful and far more rigid in their interpretations, and hence less assimilable. No, the Count

Arthur de Gobineau had to wait twenty years for recognition in France because he was a Romanticist, a cosmopolite, and an original mind more than touched with genius.

In modern England his influence cannot be traced directly but his ideas are well-rooted. Whether owing to a parallel development of evolutionism and anthropology, or because of the infiltration of Gobinism through the channel of German publicists like Penka, from 1870 to 1914 English public opinion was saturated with the notion of a superior Anglo-Saxon race, of which England produced the fine flower. The decadence of France, Italy, and Spain was contrasted with the political and economic success of the Teutonic sister-nations, England and Germany, and this self-righteous pride was heightened by racial contempt for the Irish. Whether we open the pages of John Richard Green, Sayce, or Lord Acton, or listen to the less polished utterances of Cecil Rhodes and Joseph Chamberlain, we hear fragments of the same hymn to Aryan Germanism. In Robertson's *The Germans,* Grant Allen's *Anglo-Saxon Britain,* or Isaac Taylor's work on the *Aryans,* there are modifications of thoroughgoing belief, but the ground plan of race-determinism is unaltered.

The propaganda of Mosley and his Blackshirts in the thirties may be discounted as a trivial sign of racist feeling, but its political unimportance does not measure the extent of race-assumptions current in England. The correspondence columns of the *Times,* the speeches and books of Sir Arthur Keith,[7] the critical and biographical writings of Havelock Ellis, show the temper of articulate public opinion, just as Sir John Simon's previously reported assertion that he is an Aryan reveals the mind of the newspaper-reading masses.

The different responses to Gobineau's ideas in France, Germany, and England might be summarized by saying that in England these ideas have been adopted or paralleled without

[7] Analyzed and quoted from in Chapt. X.

reference to him; in France credit was somewhat delayed and partly withheld, and in Germany recognition, both early and full, prevailed from the first. Gobineau was held in high esteem there even before 1894 when the *Gobineau-Vereinigung* was founded with Ludwig Schemann, another Wagnerite, at its head. A biography of the Count and the publication of his posthumous literary remains occupied Schemann with slight interruption from that time through and beyond the First World War. Many of Gobineau's works in every kind first appeared in German dress and the best of them are included in numerous lists of low-priced classics. Scarcely one German racist fails to acknowledge the inspiration of the master, and he is equally revered by the scientific, the political, and the academic writers. The guides to the literature of the Third Reich place him among the forerunners of the new dispensation, and sometimes called him *the* discoverer of the spiritual import of race. He had his place in the most scholarly works on anthropology, and was the hero of special studies on "race-hygiene" and the sterilization of the "unfit." Art and music critics paid him homage for his good influence on the arts, on Wagner in particular, while literary historians awarded him a high rank in the world of nineteenth-century letters. Philosophers built systems on his systems, some going even so far as to belittle Nietzsche in his favor: "Towering high over Nietzsche," wrote Dr. Karl Kynast, "stands Gobineau. If the former was a poet-philosopher, a productive mongrel in whom were combined and confused the poet's and the thinker's gifts and who was great only when he destroyed, the latter was a penetrating philosopher of history and a great poet as well." (*Nordisches und Unnordisches,* 1927, 113.) Kynast complained of the confusion between the Gobinian idea and the Nietzschean pseudo-ideal and called for a distinction between "Nietzsche the comet and Gobineau the fixed star."

To familiarize the German public still more thoroughly with the figure and ideas of Gobineau, a new *Vereinigung* was planned and started under the initiative of Dr. Julius Schwabe about the same time that a complete edition of the French writer's works in German began to appear in Leipzig (1924). In general, the German appreciation of Gobineau was sincere, for he never asserted that Germany as a nation had any monopoly of Nordic blood. He rather favored the English as depositors of Aryan supremacy, and it is simply untrue to say (as some French critics have done) that Gobineau was hailed by the Germans because he flattered them. Few German writers make the mistake of thinking that Gobineau meant modern Germany when he said Aryan or Germanic. Besides, other French geniuses—Stendhal, Berlioz, Delacroix, Flaubert, Daumier—found in Germany their first and strongest admirers. This acclaim was genuine and had nothing to do with nationalism or race. The truth is that the French public, supposedly so discriminating in cultural matters, is often a little slow, a trifle blind, and very obstinate about certain types of French genius.

Whether the French like it or not, Gobineau's place is secure, if only by reason of their own leanings toward his type of thought. The words he used have become familiar throughout Western civilization. He did not invent them, he did not make a tight system of the things they stood for, he charged them with no relentless animus, and he did not propagate their use by his own powers alone. But it was something new and pregnant to have combined in however loose a scheme the earlier traditions of racial prejudice and theory. Before the *Essay* most race-theorizing had fallen into two categories—the anthropological racism of Retzius, Quatrefages, and Blumenbach; and the cultural or historical racism of Thierry, Niebuhr, Klemm, Guizot, or Stubbs. The attempted grafting of one upon the other branch of learning by Edwards was too specialized to succeed with the general public. Gobineau had a larger scope and did better. He was scientific and utilized Blumenbach, Prichard, Carus, Retzius, and Morton. He observed in races not only their physical characters in the manner of the old anthropology; but, keeping pace with the new, noted their skull-shapes and stature. He was a political historian and his whole *Essay* was designed to solve the problem of the rise and fall of civilizations. He was a social historian who revivified the thesis of Boulainvilliers, Montesquieu, and Guizot. He was a philologist who appropriated the data of Celtic research, oriental mythology, and Sanskrit literature. Add to these his pitiless reiteration of the term "Aryan-Germanic," and the conviction is inescapable that he is the most comprehensive expounder of a great modern myth. *Omne concipiendum vivit:* whatever must be conceived, exists. This motto, taken from Gobineau, is the essence of race-belief. But for posterity perhaps his most novel contribution is his belief that art results only from the contact of two diverse races. Into what existing body of racial art-theories this new and original idea fitted is the subject next in order.

Chapter V

RACE AND THE FINE ARTS

I

One divines in his pages the eye of a Northerner accustomed to living in an opaque fog.

—BOURGET on Henry James, 1885

AT FIRST SIGHT the arts seem a most barren field for the notion of race to take root in. Culture thrives by cross-fertilization, admiration, borrowings, and even thefts, which are incompatible with the boundaries and fixity of the supposed races. Plausible or not, the fact remains that in the twentieth century it is almost impossible to open a book on painting, music, or literature without at once coming upon remarks like the following:

1. "He [Degas] is neither a classicist, a romanticist, nor a realist—and yet he is all three. Possibly this can be partially explained by the mixture of races which run in his veins, the aristocratic French of the Orleans 'de Gas,' the colorful and generous Neapolitan of his paternal grandmother and the adventurous Creole of his New Orleans mother." (Agnes Mongan, *Catal. Degas Exhibition,* Phila. Mus. of Art, 1936.)

2. "So repeatedly have temperaments of this (i.e., the clas-

sic) character appeared in France that it is difficult not to hold theirs the centrally, essentially French tradition, and not to see in men like Rabelais only the Frank and in men like Berlioz only the atavism to Gallo-Roman times." (Paul Rosenfeld, *Musical Portraits,* 1920, 134.)

3. "He [Charles Morice] was a Provençal and had all the emotional excitability of mind we associate with the South, although as a matter of fact it is thence that so many deep and grave philosophers have emerged." (Havelock Ellis, *From Rousseau to Proust,* 1935, 17.)

Examples could be multiplied *ad infinitum* from the writings of all countries on all artistic subjects and ranging from casual remarks like Kipling's and Oscar Wilde's "the Celt—always the artist . . ." to dissertations like Eichenauer's *Musik und Rasse.* To be sure, this use of race is ushered in with words like "possibly," "partially," "difficult not to," "associated with," as if the critic wished to get double credit for biological insight and for skepticism. But the fact that race is brought in at all as an explanation of art, and this without defining the racial terms used, shows how well-established is the belief in the omnipotence of race.

The injection of race-ideas into the arts follows three distinct lines, illustrated by the three extracts above. The first reflects the most "advanced" ideas of hereditary transmission of mental qualities; the second rests upon the familiar Nordic myth described in our second chapter; the third goes back to the notion that climate determines temperaments. As the last is the most ancient, I shall review it first.

The climate theory was not new in modern times. One could go back to Hippocrates and Aristotle and, taking in Bodin, Vico, and Montesquieu on the way, find in them notions of climate determining history. But in recent centuries, for as long as there was any kind of cosmopolitan ideal in Europe—which is to say as long as the division of European society into classes was stronger than its partition into nations—the ascribing of national characters remained a mere pastime. Such it was in the eighteenth century to a Montesquieu or a Chesterfield. The wars of the French Revolution, by setting in motion huge masses of men of all ranks, intensified the feeling of national differences. In the arts, these differences were reflected by the Romanticists, who instinctively shared Herder's conception of cultural nationalism, a nationalism not to be confused with our aggressive kind. Herder's theory was that the several European nations embodied each the soul of a race, the genius of a people peculiarly fitted to produce a given culture, unique and precious, as its contribution to the general fund of European civilization.

It was inevitable that the Romanticists should give to race-theories a new impetus. For in its origin the desire to distinguish cultures is only the desire to particularize, to replace abstractions by a concrete sense of the endless variety of life and nature, to introduce local color, even to show sympathy with what is alien to one's customs and prejudices. From this Romantic philosophy of art it is easy to pass to detailed climate-and-race theory. Accordingly it was not inconsistent for cosmopolitan minds like Madame de Staël and Stendhal to elaborate such notions and to give certain formulas a currency that has not been impaired by the length of time they have been in circulation. These may be briefly designated as the North-and-South principle of criticism. It is not to be confused with the Nordic myth, because it does not necessarily imply a superiority of race, but merely a difference of temperament caused in man by the climate in which he lives. But let Madame de Staël[1]

[1] As the daughter of the Swiss financier and statesman Necker, the future Madame de Staël had been reared among the most cultured Parisian circle of the old regime. Her marriage at twenty with the German diplomat, the Baron de Staël-Holstein, and her unacceptable political views during the later Revolution, Consulate, and Empire increased her opportunities for travel outside France. She therefore was by taste and circumstance at the opposite pole from narrow nationalism. Indeed the main purpose of her two great books—*Literature Considered in Its*

explain how in the Europe of her day there were "two distinct literatures, that which comes from the South and that which descends from the North: that of which Homer is the source, and that of which Ossian is the origin." (*Literature Considered in Its Relation to Society,* I, 210). Eighteenth-century enthusiasm for Ossian apparently did not distinguish Celtic from Germanic, hence Madame de Staël's confidence in the fact that the imagination of the North is melancholy and world-weary, yet fond of natural sights and sounds. The Southern poets, on the contrary, delight in all the joys of life; their love of nature is of a different sort, more moderate in its objects and intensity. Even for Madame de Staël climate is only one factor making for difference. She senses a second cause, something native and permanent in the character: "One must seek in a people as in a man his characteristic trait; all others are the effect of a thousand diverse chances; that one trait alone constitutes his being" (214).

The climate theory of art is racist insofar as it treats a group as if it were a single individual, and as it shows a passion for finding one trait, one formula, to cover diversity. Like race, this trait *alone constitutes the being* of the group or the man. In the arts this amounts to the negation of criticism and of aesthetic experience. It leads directly to the disregard for what does not jibe with preconceived theory. It leads to word-juggling—Northern, Mediterranean, Classic, Latin, the Greek mind, French clarity, Celtic melancholy—terms which are cloaks to conceal complexity, arguments to the crowd for praising or damning without the trouble of going into details.

It would be unfair to Madame de Staël to accuse her of more than a rudimentary form of the mania. What interests her is thought and literature, not classification. The inversion of

---

Relation to Society, 1800, and *De l'Allemagne,* 1810—was not to foster race-theories but to introduce the new Germany of Kant, Goethe, and Schiller to the French. This remains her great achievement despite cavil from nationalist critics on both sides of the Rhine.

these concerns comes later; but it builds on her foundations. We may well wonder why she laid them on just such grounds. Until one reads her books one can hardly imagine the cultural chasm she was trying to span. The formalism and emptiness of French literature, especially of French poetry, in the last quarter of the eighteenth century offered no standard of comparison by which the new German literature might be understood. It required a great emotional and intellectual effort to learn a new artistic idiom, and Madame de Staël had to account for its strangeness, the wildness of its effects, the passion and profundity of German Romanticism. How could these novelties be explained? First, by climate and geography—a perpetually dark sky, a long cold winter, impenetrable forests, scattered habitations. (*De l'All.,* 13.) Second, by the nature of the Germanic race: loyal, good, and simple, but dreamy, melancholy, full of sentiment, music, abstract thought[2]—and beer, added unsympathetic observers. The German tradition included in equal measure the furious valor of the Norse sagas, the Christian medieval epic, and the pagan mysteries. In contrast to these the "Latins" were felt to be more practical and worldly, little given to abstract ideas, and the only masters of the art of domination. The racial character common to the Germanic tribes, despite the geographical differences between North and South Germany, explained the ballads of Burger, the *Faust* of Goethe, the philosophy of Kant, and the painting and architecture of the German Renaissance.

This picture has remained lodged in the minds of many French critics, with only one serious alteration concerning the frank, honest, and dreamy character of the German "race." Brutal, cunning, and stupid have been substituted in the heat of three wars and as many succeeding periods of resentment. The rest of the portrait stays fixed in the face of the most obvious facts. It would have been idle, for instance, to tell the late Ernest Babelon, a Member of the Institute, that Germany is not

[2] Note the reversal of all these race-characteristics in the hundred years from 1810 to 1910.

covered with forests, that in winter there is as little sunshine in Paris as in Berlin, that Germany has scenery as smiling as that of France—in short, that it is absurd to call Germany the North and France the South as if the boundary between them were horizontal and not vertical. M. Babelon would not believe it,[3] for it would go counter to the clichés. Yet it is unjust to blame Madame de Staël for their creation. Her understanding is not to be compared with his provincialism.

At the risk of repetition, one must not dismiss the North-and-South critical dogma without speaking of Stendhal. For one thing, Stendhal has been repeatedly called in France the father of "Mediterraneanism," which is a clumsy name for an appreciation of the South. Stendhal did for Italy what Madame de Staël had done for Germany. He forced the attention of the French on the new literature and lively mores of a people who had been neglected or else seen as foils to the ideally draped figures of Roman history. Stendhal's innumerable sallies on race, climate, and art are suggestive without being literal, form no system, and are scattered in works of the most diverse character: novels like the *Charterhouse of Parma,* travel notes like *Rome, Naples, and Florence,* critical works like the *History of Painting in Italy,* biography like the *Life of Rossini,* and disguised autobiography like the *Life of Henri Brulard.*

Finding the narrow affectations of French society intolerable, Stendhal became a traveler from early years, a *déraciné* or uprooted man, as the home-loving critics like to call him. In the wake of Napoleon's armies, he crisscrossed the Continent, from Paris to Milan to burning Moscow in 1812, added England and Spain on his own account, and finally fixed on Italy as the land of his heart's desire. He discovered in the "native passion" of the Italians the freedom and energy he demanded of life. He soon began to call himself a Milanese and thought of giving up

[3] See his two-volume work of erudition and hatred: *Le Rhin dans l'histoire,* Paris, 1916. It bears the device: *Germani, genus mendacio natum* (The Germans are a race of born liars).

his French citizenship. While Madame de Staël was publishing her first work on German literature, Stendhal was delving into the possible Italian origin of his family.

His motive is of course that "Italy is the fatherland of the arts." On January 12, 1833, he informs a young lady that he is "altogether Italian," meaning that because the arts are his spiritual homeland he must be a native of the physical land—a typical mode of race-thinking in the arts. When you cannot infer a man's temperament from his supposed race, you infer his race from his temperament. So Napoleon felt on one occasion that all great men of letters were French, and so Ludwig Woltmann and his followers find Germans wherever genius of a kind they admire makes its appearance.

But like most Romanticists Stendhal is too much a realist to make a system of his views on the relation between climate, temperament, and works of art. The hypothesis that Taine was to make famous a quarter of a century later as the theory of the influence of *milieu* is explicit in Stendhal, but never rigid: "This kind of effervescence called the Fine Arts is the necessary product of a given fermentation. To account for the foam one must show the nature of the ferment." (*Vie de Rossini,* Prunières ed., I, iii.) In the same book a chapter on "The Nordic in Relation to Music" gives the usual interpretation of cold climate, rude vocal organs, and imaginative qualities. What Stendhal calls temperament is what we mean by race or type, as we can judge from the following unfortunate extract: the German is "well-fed, very blond, very rosy, drinks beer, and eats *Butterbrodt* all day"; whereas the Italian is "slender, almost thin, very dark, with blazing eyes and a sallow complexion; he lives on coffee and a very few abstemious meals."

Stendhal has only forgotten the thin Germans and stout Italians of his acquaintance, which is bad enough; but how much worse that in writing the passage his pen did not balk at the thought of his beloved Mozart, whose music he would certainly not associate with beer and *Butterbrodt*. The recklessness of the would-be physiologist is only too evident. If he assumes that embonpoint and art cannot dwell in the same human frame, he is disregarding a sufficiently obvious fact and forfeiting our respect for his imaginary science. It is the Idéologue philosophy confronting us again, with its faith in the correlation of body and mind. Stendhal, as a good disciple of De Stutt de Tracy, wanted to establish in the realm of art a "biological psychology." (*Hist. Painting in Italy,* c. 41.) But what faith are we to place in the critic, let alone the psychologist or geographer, who can say that "the thing that keeps the English from developing any arts is the lack of sunshine"? Stendhal maintains plausibly enough that in art "climate and temperament condition the strength of the drive: education and manners shape the direction in which the drive is applied." But this is an empty formula, for the temperament defined above and the climate instanced below are pure fictions. The English landscape school contemporary with Stendhal is enough to shatter the nonsense about lack of sunshine.

This does not mean that a man is not free to prefer the products of one culture to those of another. But Europe has been a battleground of thought and opinion for so long that it is a question whether it can boast "pure cultures" any more than "pure races." When Stendhal says, "I feel a natural inclination for the Spanish nation," or when he criticizes the French for their "Gallic" delight in fashion, he is not telling us what he is really thinking of. Just what was it that attracted him in Spain—places, people, palaces, paintings? And the French fashion of his day to worship Rossini—doesn't Stendhal approve of that "Gallic" trait?

So obvious are these objections that he himself inveighs against those who mix patriotism with art and "dislike a quartet because it is German." Divested of their unfortunate racial terminology Stendhal's preferences, like de Staël's, are positive and genuinely artistic. Taken as the words of a genius upon his favorite masterpieces, as the working philosophy of a creative artist designed to combat reactionary creeds, Stendhal's Mediterraneanism can be tolerated and even regarded with affection. But in the hands of later comers the scattered hints become rules, the fine *aperçu* becomes an axiom, and the preference becomes a condemnation of everything outside its compass. Literal-mindedness could not go further perhaps than the interpretation placed by certain German writers on what de Staël and Stendhal had both recognized as the "lure of the South." Madame de Staël was thinking of Winckelmann and Goethe; Stendhal was thinking of himself: all drawn "south" by artistic passion, a love for the famous sunshine and the hard outlines of reality. But in our scientific twentieth century a writer bred on these metaphors does not hesitate to identify Ludwig Woltmann's death by drowning in the Mediterranean with the "siren call of the South."[4]

II

If Buffon has done a magnificent thing in trying to represent in one work the whole of zoology, is there not a similar task to be performed for society? Does not society make of man, according to the milieu where his activity takes place, as many different men as there are varieties in zoology?

—BALZAC, Preface to *Comédie Humaine*

WHEN THE SWISS critic and traveler Charles-Victor de Bonstetten, in youth the friend of Voltaire, Rousseau, and Bonnet, published his study *L'Homme du Midi et l'Homme du Nord* in 1824,[5] the public was already familiar with the North-and-South theories of art. The clichés were established, and a grave critic like Sainte-Beuve could rely on their general acceptance.

[4] Lapouge, *Race et Milieu Social,* 1909, 331.

[5] The book was still deemed useful by Havelock Ellis at the turn of the century when he wrote his *Studies in the Psychology of Sex, passim.*

In the following thirty years no important change occurred in the racial criticism of art.

It was in the decade from 1854 to 1864 that a new type of doctrine made its appearance and from various points at once. First Gobineau published his *Essay* (1853-55) ascribing the birth of art to the conflict of races: we examined it in the previous chapter. Also in 1853, a now obscure critic, Eugène Loudun, published a series of articles in *Le Pays* under the title of *The Three Races,* classifying contemporary French writers according to their race. We are left in no doubt that Loudun is speaking "not of peoples but of three races of men." Climate and citizenship have no importance for him, only the racial characters matter: the Germans have imagination: the English have positive [practical] minds: and the French are a happy melange of the other two. The three impelling motives of the three races are, respectively: absolute reason, self-interest, and common sense. Now, the amazing thing is that chance can cause any or all of these race-types to be born in the same country. For instance, in France, Victor Hugo, Louis Blanc, Balzac, and Louis-Philippe are English. Lamartine, Edgar Quinet, and Lagrange (the mathematician) are Germans. Thiers, Falloux, Berryer, Ledru-Rollin, Cavaignac, and La Rochejaquelein are French. Going back into the past, Fénelon, Rousseau, Sénancour are Germans. Chateaubriand, because he was a dreamy Celtic Breton, is likewise a German. Socialists and other fanciful writers are always German.

As for the English men of letters, Scott like Shakespeare is held to be only in part a man of imagination. There are no English painters or musicians because of the practical instinct which made the Industrial Revolution possible. Goethe typifies the German race and he is the "father of all melancholy lovers of nature." German thought is in fact but a vague idealistic philosophy, and the German universities can boast no specialty or science. Politically, Germany must be a republic to accommodate the race's lack of order. More than that, the Germans must be socialists and communists; but they are harmless, because they are honest and respectful of tradition. Besides they do not know how to fight. They lazily wait for trouble and their land is always the theater of war.[6]

Published in a strongly imperialist paper, two years after the *coup d'état* of 1851, these articles are a kind of manifesto in support of Napoleon III and the new nationalism. They end with an explicit warning against "the foreigner" and a rallying cry to the tune of "France of the French."

To the historian of culture, Loudun is a sign of the times. The particular statements, like the insignificance of the writer who made them, do not matter. The form of the thought is what matters. In the next hundred years, that is, down to our day, that form was to be filled with thousands of contradictory assertions by writers ranging from the journeyman to the inspired. And usually the impetus was hostile or boastful along national lines. In a word, cultural racism had become political-minded and aggressive. Not climate but innate racial traits were now the factors looked for in art. Gobineau's theory, as we saw, was competent on the aesthetic side, but it dug its channel in the same direction of insistence on racial traits. By the mid-1850's these new ideas were to be given simplicity and strength through a new concise formula, Taine's famous three-in-one. Taine starts with the notion of complete determinism in human affairs. "Whether facts be physical or moral matters little; they always have their causes. There are causes for ambition, courage, veracity, as for digestion, muscular movement, animal heat. Vice and virtue are products like sugar and vitriol." (*Hist. of English Lit.,* Pref.)

Like the Idéologues, like Stendhal, Taine wants to establish a "zoology of the human mind with psychology as a physiological

[6] This piece of profound racial psychology was composed sixteen years before the Franco-Prussian War and sixty before the war of 1914.

and anatomical principle."[7] And his study of English literature leads him to think that the *race,* the *time,* and the *environment* shape all intellectual activity and serve to explain it. The time and the environment can be described as historians have always done, but determining the race requires special knowledge. The critic must find the "dominant trait" (*pensée maitresse*) of the work of art, the man, or the nation. The racial element is immutable and irresistible within the changeful time and environment, wherefore Taine blames Hegel as a historian for failing to note this "physiological background—race, skull, color." (*Notes of 1851 on Hegel,* Obj., EIGHT.)

Taine applied his theories to English literature and to La Fontaine's fables, where he finds Gallic laughter as well as Greek and Flemish racial traits (ed. 1875, 14-16); and again to the Italians, and finally to *The Origins of Contemporary France,* a critique of the French Revolution (e.g., *Anc. Rég.,* 15th ed., 159-60; 258-59; *Rég. Mod.,* c. I). Since Taine the doctrine of race, time, and milieu has become an accepted commonplace of French critical writing. It is no more surprising to find it cropping up in a popular novel by Paul Adam than in a political speech by [President] Poincaré (Nogent-le-Rotrou, Mar. 14, 1897).

Side by side with this popular tradition which stems from Gobineau and Taine, there exists a more recherché application which is best exemplified in the great Dictionary of French Architecture by Viollet-le-Duc (1866), the chief restorer of Gothic monuments in nineteenth-century France and the leading architect under Napoleon III. That scholarly work, which still stands as a great piece of erudition, contains a long essay showing the influence of Gobineau, in which the writer sees race as the explanation of certain aspects of Gothic sculpture, and he extends the principle to other times and peoples. According to

[7] See André Chevrillon, *La jeunesse de Taine, Revue de Paris,* July and Aug., 1902.

him, the faces represented on the portals of Vézelay and Autun reveal the presence on French soil of two races, distinct in origin and appearance, differently gifted, and devoted to incompatible aesthetics. At Chartres, the famous King of Judah is "truly French or Gallic, or Celt if one prefers—nothing of the German, Roman or Frank" (VIII, 117). The pseudo-Clovis at Notre-Dame de Corbeil, on the other hand, is a Northern type (118-19). "It is clear," he adds, "why type 8 [Clovis] should rule over type 7 [King of Judah] by his daring and the consciousness of his dignity; but it is also clear that the latter, in whose physiognomy there pierces a certain skepticism, will end by becoming master again" (119).

Despite this liberal historiography in the manner of Thierry and this ascription of dominant racial traits in the manner of Taine, Viollet-le-Duc asserts the essentially Gobinian idea that "any flowering of art—and this is pre-eminently true of sculpture—occurs in history only by the contact of two different races" (98). The remainder of Viollet-le-Duc's race-characterizations would be tedious to recount; he borrows from Gobineau without adding anything new. Yet the entire chapter must have exerted a separate influence, for we find vague echoes of it here and there among writers particularly concerned with art—for example, in Proust (*Swann's Way,* Mod. Libr. ed., 194-95, 213) and in a scientist like Le Dantec. (*Infl. Ancestr.,* 1905, *passim.*)

The late Elie Faure, a respected historian of art, represents not a vague echo but a complete adoption of Gobineau and Viollet-le-Duc. His book, *The Three Drops of Blood* (Paris, 1929), arrests the eye first by its dedication: "To the tragic genius of the hybrids—Michel Montaigne, Jean Racine, H. de Balzac, Eugène Delacroix, rhythm-breakers and rhythm-creators." The three drops of blood are, as in Gobineau, white, yellow, and black; but Faure adds a new notion to the artistic requirement of race-mixture. He hopes that someday "haematological science" will be able to determine "the dosage of bloods constituting, ethnically speaking, a human being selected at random" (223), and by inference that we shall recognize—or supply—our artists thanks to this science.

Not content with blood-tests, Faure orchestrates the leading race-theories of the nineteenth century. He regrets that the "craniometric nature" of the ancient Greeks has not been "agreed upon" (226). He invokes Darwinian evolution and the Mendelian laws as suggestive of aesthetic principles. He classifies Dumas *père,* Renan, Racine, Hugo, Lamarck, Delacroix, Proust, Montaigne, and others by the race of their parents and asserts the correlation between "ethnic stigmata" and mentality. Finally, he reproduces the well-worn categories of the historians, adding flourishes of his own in explanation of such phenomena as Gothic architecture: "The Franks did not fail to impregnate with a Germanic spirit—apparent in the musical combinations of the groining of the nave—this miraculous efflorescence of the melanized Celtic genius" (39). In the light of such a passage as this, Faure's tribute to Gobineau sounds like unwitting condescension, and any critique of the Germans' racist madness like envy of superior numbers.

III

What would a Frenchman have to do in order not to think like everybody?

—STENDHAL

THE QUESTION OF NUMBERS raises a point of some importance in the history of nineteenth-century culture. Race-theories were abundant but were racists many? Before passing on to a critique of race-critiques, this query requires an answer which, for brevity's sake, must be allusive rather than fully descriptive.

In Germany, from the time of Heine to that of Wagner, the criticism of art chiefly followed the loose North-and-South pattern. Heine divided all minds into Hebrews and Hellenes. Nietzsche wanted cultured men to be good Mediterraneans: Burckhardt followed Stendhal. Wagner himself hated Jewish art—was it jealousy of Meyerbeer?—and was a Gobinist.

In England, Anglo-Saxon literary pride took many hints from Thierry. People counted the words in Shakespeare and pointed out how many more Saxon than Latin ones he had used. At the same time, Matthew Arnold was dealing with Hellenic-Hebraic parallels and turning his sympathetic eye upon Celtic literature, finding the usual race-virtues as he went. Ruskin, committed to a social theory of art, pointed out that great art, being the product of collective rather than individual effort, must depend on common virtues, among which is that of a "pure race."[8] Still, in England, the Bible-bred nonconformist conscience combined with revivified Catholic doctrine to keep racial divisions out of ordinary intellectual judgments. As H. W. Nevinson put it, " 'Thy people, Israel,' were ourselves, the English race." (*In the Dark Backward,* 1934, 74.)

The "scientific" approach to race-aesthetics made itself felt more strongly after the work of Darwin, Galton, and others on heredity. It culminated, perhaps, in Havelock Ellis's *Study of British Genius* (1904), based on statistical data concerning hair-and-eye color as observed by him in the pictures of British geniuses in the National Portrait Gallery. In this, only the method is new. Ellis's assumption is the old one of Bonstetten plus the faith in transmission: Sir Isaac Newton is "the supreme representative of Anglo-Danish genius" (42).

In France, from which we purposely draw the chief examples of race-criticism, the question of its prevalence as a mode of thought is plain. A bare list of well-known names, supplemented by others in the Bibliographical Notes and extracts in the Appendix, is sufficient proof: Balzac, Mérimée, Lamartine, Victor Hugo, among the creators, attest race-judgments of art. The

[8] See, for example, *The Crown of Wild Olive,* "War."

same holds true of many historians of literature: Edgar Quinet, J. J. Ampère, Villemain, Philippe le Bas (the tutor of the future Napoleon III), Francisque Michel, Renan, Léon Bazalgette (translator and promoter of Walt Whitman), Lanson, and Faguet; the music critics, Fétis, Tiersot, and Boschot; the philosophers, Emile Montégut, Philarète Chasles, Théodule Ribot, and Alfred Fouillée; the literary politicians, Challemel-Lacour, Prévost-Paradol, Napoleon III, Gambetta, Clemenceau—these and scores of others evince in their casual or considered remarks the ever-spreading belief in race-determined art.

In the face of such near-unanimity, one almost hesitates to doubt. Why is the general belief not true? The best answer is that the particulars contradict one another. Rabelais is called a Frank by Paul Rosenfeld, but to Bazalgette he is an old Gallic spirit, while J. J. Ampère accounts for him and his time by "a return to pure Latinity." For Rosenfeld again, Berlioz was the Gallo-Roman, but the Germans discant on his *germanische Seele,* and his French biographers battle over his "racial origins": Tiersot, Gauthier-Villars, and P. L. Robert find him a classic Latin type; Boschot delves into genealogy seeking a Germanic origin for the root *Berl* which is the first part of his name. Where, in all this, are "science" and reasonableness?

Race, moreover, makes the critic shirk his proper task. He should tell us what he finds, refer us to Rabelais's wit, style, vocabulary, and opinions; to Berlioz's imagination, orchestral skill, and melodic genius, describing these in human and, if need be, technical terms of art, instead of talking about either's Latin soul or German race.

Again, the idea of racial genius is arbitrary. Masson-Forestier and Gaston Gaillard happen to agree that the Germanic origin of Racine's mother explains "his ardent nature, his vigorous sexual appetite, his violent and aggressive temper, his dangerous sensuality" (*Bull. Soc. Anthrop.,* Oct. 16, 1913, 589), but the relation of these to great poetry is hardly clear. Havelock Ellis seems to believe with August Möbius that "a poet's heredity is from his mother" (*Study Br. Genius,* 84 n.), but this is mere assertion. In spite of Taine, genius is *not* a substance like tin or lead. No wide agreement exists in the critical world about the characteristics of genius and its products. The elements of genius are intangible and their transmission is doubtful. If Racine's mother gave him all his qualities why did *she* not write *Phèdre* and *Andromaque?* If Elie Faure thinks Montaigne and Delacroix were great because they were hybrids, why does he stop his racial investigation at their father and mother, instead of going back the ancestral ladder to the very first appearance of the drops of blood which infallibly contain philosophical skepticism and the ability to paint? If he did he might find that every great artist was no more and no less "mixed" than the common man.

The climate theory seems on the surface more logical than the physico-psychical explanation, but it is equally fallacious. As Ellis himself concedes (see above, p. 79), the South has produced both "emotionally excitable" men and "deep and grave philosophers." There have been puritanical Protestants in the sensual South and tyrants in the liberty-loving North, dreamers and realists in both regions. Besides, where does one take hold of geography? Central France is undoubtedly south of Northern France, but it is to the north of Provence, which is again north of North Africa. Climate is not latitude, nor is it an unchangeable factor. Montesquieu thought that one had to skin a Russian alive to make him feel anything; he might now complain that Dostoevsky and Chekhov are oversensitive, skinned alive by other things than climate. Paradoxically, it is the flaws in the climate theory that often throw the critic back on explanation by race, for the action of the climate is slow and the supposed force of race is eternal. If a Southern Frenchman (unruly, sensual, and realistic) emigrates to Scotland, we shall not expect him to become instantaneously a Nordic (home-loving, dreamy, and poetic). Holding in reserve either race or climate to answer any troublesome objection in the form of particular facts, the racist defends his position by keeping his opponent in stalemate.

One can hardly avoid the further conclusion that in the fine arts as in politics race-criteria have ulterior motives. The simplest and most common is the covering up of ignorance. No one knows what genius is or how transmitted: credit it to the race of the mother, father, granduncle, or national group, and no one will be the wiser. The same applies to qualities in a given work of art. But a second ulterior purpose animates race-thinking, namely, political partisanship.

The interplay of politics and literature has always been great on the Continent, and when racial criteria became available political animus took them up as convenient weapons in the struggle of Right against Left. What other meaning can be found in the remark that Zola (a leftist) writes "brachycephalic literature"? It means simply that Zola was writing sympathetically about the masses, who are slaves because of the racial defect of having round skulls. Lapouge, Drumont, and other anti-Semites assumed that the long-skulled Aryan would invariably manifest his leadership and would therefore always be found in positions of authority in modern society. Hence their protest against Zola for daring to threaten the supremacy of the *dolichos* over the *brachys.*

A reaction against "destructive" influences from abroad also occurred, both in France and in Germany, and inspired artistic movements with definite racial and nationalistic platforms. In poetry, *l'Ecole Romane,* founded by the poets Moréas, Maurras, and La Tailhède sought to make French poetry "essentially French" by sticking close to the classic models of the seventeenth century and by considering Greece and Rome as the only legitimate sources of inspiration. This was but one of the numerous attacks on Romanticism, which was felt to be a foreign product, imported earlier from England and Germany and contrary to the true French spirit.[9] As the rivalry with Germany grew keener after the war of 1870, and the rapprochement with England more secure after 1904, a distinction tended to be made between the English genius "strongly leavened with Celticism"—therefore "related to the French"—and the thoroughly barbarous, incomprehensive, and dangerous German nature. It should be noted that in Germany the exact reverse was taking place and French decadence, regarded as a racial fact, was the bugaboo held up by the Germanists as a national peril whenever German artists accepted French influence. The French poison took its place beside the ever-present fear of Semitism, and indeed was often confused with it on the word of Gobineau, who believed that all the Latin races had been "semitized, that is to say, negrified."

The artistic principles enforced by the Third Reich in 1933 were therefore nothing new: they are old and tried ways of thinking, open to only one objection—that they have nothing to do with art and not enough consistency to deserve the name of principle.

[9] This is a commonplace of French criticism (see Ernest Seillière or Pierre Lasserre, *passim*) which is occasionally repeated abroad (see Margaret Kennedy, *A Century of Revolution,* London, 1922, 52-54).

Chapter VI

ARYAN, SEMITE, AND CELT

I

And he did not succeed in achieving that glory which belongs solely to the Aryan peoples, born and to be born, and to the Sacred Zarathustra.

—ZEND-AVESTA

THE WORD "Aryan" comes from the Sanskrit legends in which the conquerors of the dark-skinned natives of the peninsula of India are called by that name and described as tall, fair-haired, fair-skinned, and in every way superior. The word may mean noble or it may mean pure. It is probably related to *Iran,* the modern name of Persia; but it is very unlikely that there is any connection between it and Eirann (Ireland) or any of the other words which Celticists and other linguists, eager to attach themselves to the noble breed, discovered in the nineteenth century.

The whole controversy about the Aryans, their origin, their physical appearance, and their achievements dates from the birth of the new science of philology in the early nineteenth century. For about seventy-five years before that time, the interest in Celtic literature had led to a great deal of juggling with etymologies, word-relationships, and tongue-relationships. Out of the chaos, the efforts of Jones, Grimm, and Bopp between 1800 and 1830 laid the foundations of philology. They showed that the European languages (except Finnish, Turkish, Magyar, and Basque) were related to a much older tongue, now no longer spoken, and which was either Sanskrit or closely akin to it.

At once the inference was made that the peoples who spoke languages derived from the Aryan mother-tongue were related "by blood" to the group that originally spoke it. Thence it was an easy leap of rhetoric to speak of "the Aryan people" and their "Aryan descendants" scattered throughout Europe.

Since there was the inconvenient group of other languages named above which could not be fitted into any crotch of the great family tree, the question arose, Whence did the Aryan people come? At first it was believed that they had come from Central Asia and spread in two directions, west and south, and had in both places conquered some aborigines upon whom they had imposed their superior civilization. The importance of this hypothetical conquest must not be overlooked. It is at the basis of many arguments in favor of Aryan superiority, an exact parallel to Boulainvilliers's old idea of the Frankish conquest over the Gallo-Romans. It seems to be always taken for granted that the conquerors of any aborigines are ipso facto superior. Reasoning by analogy, nineteenth-century Aryanists looked forward to the time when "the great race" (themselves) would overrun the earth; and as the so-called whites seemed to be doing just that in the form of colonization and imperialism, the notion grew that in the virtues of the Aryans lay the manifest destiny to expand and dominate. It is a curious spectacle to see the intellectuals of the period regarding might as the sign of deserved overlordship and never thinking that it is an ambiguous test, which may destroy their own vain pretensions at any time according to the luck of war.

A wave of enthusiasm for the Eastern religions and philosophies accompanied the achievements of the philologists. No longer termed "fantastic" and "obscure" as they had been by the rationalists of the eighteenth century, the poetry and wisdom of the East was studied and revered by the leading spirits of the age. Voltaire had used oriental myths to preach religious toleration by showing the underlying identity of customs beneath the difference of ritual (see *Zadig,* c. XII); but half a century later, during Goethe's last years and during the formative period of Schopenhauer's thought, we see in them both, as well as in the work of Abel de Rémusat and the young Gobineau, a changed outlook on Eastern thought. Pantheism, the notion of metempsychosis and of the evolution of the individual soul, suited the temper of an age that rediscovered Spinoza and pushed forward a doctrine of biological evolution. For we must remember that Darwin's publication of the *Origin of Species* in 1859 was the outcome of a long period of speculation and argument, and not an original suggestion that caught the public unprepared.

By an interesting coincidence, in that same year 1859 appeared what is perhaps the most representative monument of nineteenth-century Aryan race-belief, a two-volume work entitled *Indo-European Origins, or The Primitive Aryas, an Essay in Linguistic Paleontology,* by the Swiss scholar Adolphe Pictet. Pictet was originally a mystical Celtomaniac who went over to the new faith. The thesis of the work is set forth in the introduction, where we learn that Sanskrit roots give us direct insight into the history of peoples, among whom there is a "race destined by Providence some day to dominate the entire globe." That race is "privileged by the beauty of its blood and the gifts of its intelligence," and these are proved by the "richness, vigor, harmony, and perfection of form of its language." (2nd ed., 1877, 8.)

To account for the diversified physical appearance of the modern peoples who are all descended from this supposed original race, Pictet has recourse to the old climate theory of Bodin and Montesquieu. He conceals it, as usual, under the elastic term "environment." Comparative linguistics, he avers, "has established ethnography on fixed principles by methods that are safe from all criticism" (10).

A moment's reflection shows how plausible and strong the "Aryan" position was—at least before the discovery of fossil man and the craze for skull-measuring ran athwart the closet inductions of the philologists. If the mid-nineteenth-century scholars believed that the European peoples originally had a common tongue—and they based this conviction on their ability to relate all existing European languages to a mother-tongue very like the old forms of Zend and Sanskrit—then necessarily all Europeans must be of the same stock, for under that scheme where could any alien "others" have come from? This piece of "reasoning" was technically speaking a truism, as was also the proposition that "there must have been originally a prehistoric Aryan people, pure and unmixed" (14).

Where, then, is the fallacy? Simply in the usual assumption that language or any other mental characteristic is an inseparable attribute of physical (i.e., race) inheritance. The point is obvious when we see a Senegalese speaking French or a Jamaica Negro talking Oxonian English. But Europeans being all more or less "white" and roughly of the same appearance, philologists like Pictet did not see that they might have come from the four quarters of the globe and still be talking a language not "originally" theirs.

Pictet adds to his ethnological beliefs some theological remarks from which it appears that even though the "Aryans" were polytheists, it was owing to their efforts that Semitic monotheism became "forever" the "world religion." He is bound to have the Aryans on the right side of every question; contrary facts of history must look after themselves. Humanity and "our race" are equally affected by these considerations, he believes, so it behooves him to do the Aryans full justice.

Touching upon more and more contemporary issues, Pictet raises the delicate question of blue eyes and blond hair, which "his German colleagues prize so highly." These features define no special Indo-Germanic group within the Aryan family, says our author, who comically assures us that: "there were no Germans in Central Asia, as A. de Rémusat and Kloproth had believed." (1st ed., 1859, 88.) Whether or no, he thinks the term "barbarian" misapplied when used of these blond Germans: it is fit only for non-Aryans, and the Aryans used it to show their "lively feeling of superiority over other races." (*Ibid.*)

With so complete a picture of Aryan supremacy, it would have been foolish for Pictet to weaken his position by discussing either the biblical account of the separation of races or the origin of man and of language. Nor did he as yet feel the international anarchy of nineteenth-century Europe sufficiently to set up distinctions within the Aryan family. That was left for Pictet's successors, who were unwilling to share a heritage, even one so abundant as the Aryan's, among two dozen European nations; they had to pull the Aryan blanket over their own shrinking band and claim a monopoly of the virtues afforded by that covering.

In the English-speaking world the versatile Max Müller made himself the champion of Aryanism, effectively using his gift for popularization and winning both attention and acclaim. The East India Company subsidized the publishing of the Rig-Vedas under his editorship and the Royal Institution gave him the opportunity, denied by Oxford, to address an ever-widening audience on subjects that may be summed up by the phrase *ex oriente lux*—out of the East comes the Light. That simple metaphor, as is so often the fact in race-theorizing, has exercised a tremendous influence on the minds of both scholars and the general public, until today the Aryan Swastika[1] grips in its tentacles Buddha and Hitler and Kipling. Müller's late re-

[1] The Swastika is mistakenly thought to be an emblem of particularly Eastern or Aryan origin. It is found in the ideography of many different tribes, and children left to themselves with paper and pencil arrive at it readily when decorating squares. (Fylfot, gammadion, *Encycl. Brit.* 14th ed., VII, 260 a.)

traction concerning the identity he had implied between race and language had little or no effect, even on his own subsequent modes of expression; and so the vision of Aryan origins persisted undimmed and flattering to all who made it their own.

Although the English anthropologist Taylor sets 1885 as the date when linguistic Aryanism gave up the ghost before the onslaught of the scientific anthropologists, with their panoply of calipers, quaternary bones, and cubic measures of grapeshot, the change was more superficial than real. It is true that the theories of Pictet, Müller, Lassen, Pott, and other philologists were largely discredited, but their forms of thought, their vocabulary, and many of their "facts" were carried along by the powerful stream of the new anthropological science.[2] The scientist Broca was among other things an Aryanist. As late as the eighties and nineties, Poesche, Penka, Hehn, Lindenschmidt, Friedrich Müller, Vacher de Lapouge, Muffang, Sénart, Tarde, Closson combine their information—like the journalist in *Pickwick*—and prove by philology plus anthropology that the Germans, or the Scandinavians, or the dolichocephalics, or the brachycephalics are pure Aryans. About that time, Wilser of Carlsruhe thought it unpatriotic to make the Germans descend from the Asiatic Aryans and "concluded" that it was the Aryans who were descended from the Germans. (*Rev. Scientifique,* Dec. 19, 1885, 778 ff.) Across the Rhine, the Marquis de Nadaillac, a propagandist laboring under the fear of France's depopulation, also was an Aryanist, though a strongly anti-German one who denied any connection between the "primitive Aryas, whose name means noble, faithful, excellent, devoted, pre-eminent" and any German population. (*Bull. Soc. Archéol. du Vendômois,* 1885, 29; *Le Correspondant,* 1889, 59-70.)

Political hatred kindled the scholarship that produced the vast literature on the subject of race and nation, tongue and

[2] Pictet's book was reissued posthumously in 1877 with a note by the editors claiming its authoritativeness despite the recent advances of "archaeological anthropology."

skull. German hatred of the French, the brachycephalics, and the Semites was openly avowed (see Poesche, *Die Arier,* 44) and was returned with interest by the French Aryanists—Ujfalvy, Chavée, Mortillet, and many others, who maintained that the brachycephalic Gauls represented the pure Aryan strain. An economic twist was given by the widespread belief that the upper classes and nobles were Aryans and the peasants non-Aryans, the social cleavage being only the perpetuation of the original conquest. With dolicho and brachy measurements added in support of historical arguments, it was possible to fashion the "anthroposociology" of a Vacher de Lapouge or Muffang in France and a Driesmans or Ammon in Germany.

To be sure, protests were occasionally heard, even in scientific circles, against this perpetual romancing about the unknowable. R. Hartmann as early as 1876 exclaimed: "The Aryans are an invention born in a scholar's cell and not an 'original people' [*Kein Urvolk*]." (*Die Nigritier,* 1876, 185.) Ten years later Mortillet recognized explicitly how misleading the word "Aryan" might be: "As for the Aryas, I do not know what they are. I do not know them in the least, hence I cannot talk about them." (*Bull. Soc. Anthrop.,* 1886, 311.) But this declaration did not prevent him from talking subsequently of Aryan qualities and Aryan traits. Perhaps the only steadfast rejector of the Aryan fiction was the great pathologist Rudolf Virchow, whose mind always cut through the mist of words to a plain statement of fact: "The typical Aryan such as theory postulates him has not yet been found." (*Correspondenzblatt,* 1889, 121.)

Scholarship could not lay the ghost it had raised. Too many violent emotions fostered the Aryan theory to allow a hearing to second thoughts or common sense. Between 1880 and 1900 the ground of discussion shifted from the attempt to prove the existence of an Aryan aboriginal folk to discovering where it aboriginally came from. Men having started life in a cradle must discover one for their "race" as a whole. National vanities allied to the dolicho-madness resulted in numerous field expeditions and a new quarrel among three groups of contestants. First, those who thought the Aryans came from Asia and conquered Europe. This position flattered the individuals who thought themselves Aryans, for their great-grandfathers must have trounced their neighbors'. The second group took up the converse. The Aryans had come from Europe[3] and with characteristic expansive power had gone out to conquer India, then peopled by a dark race. The parallel with modern European imperialism was neat and serviceable; it justified colonization. The third group differed from the second only in determining where in Europe the chosen group had arisen. Many German scholars, principally Geiger, Poesche, and Penka, confiscated the Aryans and bottomed their cradle in various parts of modern Germany.

Before them, however, d'Omalius d'Halloy (a Belgian scholar), Clémence Royer (the French translator of Darwin), and Henri Martin (an incurable Celticist) had reopened the Aryan question in a manner more favorable to French national pride. These several views, German and French, are so complex that they defy an assessment of merits, concessions, and contradictions. Perhaps a résumé of one section of Penka's very popular work[4] will show how impossible it is to align the Aryanists in orderly ranks, or even to be sure of any one author's position.

Penka thinks that the dark-haired dolichos are a South European race. It is also for him an African race, a Cro-Magnon race, and the Semites are a branch of it. The dark-haired brachys, on the contrary, come from Asia. They fought the former group in France and Belgium. At this juncture the blond

[3] Bulwer-Lytton had propounded this theory as early as 1842 in *Zanoni*.

[4] Sayce in England and Lapouge in France adopted Penka's views: *Report Brit. Assn. Adv. of Sci.*, 1887, 889; and *Rev. d'Anthrop.*, 1889, 181.

dolichos or Aryans, who had left Germany for Scandinavia, return and easily conquer the two other inferior races. They mix with them and form the populations of modern Europe. Among these the Greeks are Semites speaking an Aryan tongue; the Slavs are Mongols that have been semitized, and the Finns are Aryans who have abandoned their native speech.

One could multiply details from this and other authors until the reader would beg for mercy. All use the same words, but with different shades of meaning and different estimates of the praise and blame conferred by the attributes of dark hair and long skull. One could show Penka's Semitic Greeks turning into pure Aryans with Zaborowsky. One could show the cleavage between Aryan and Semitic speech, deep according to Pictet and Renan, being bridged over very convincingly by Delitzsch and Hommel, and being still discussed by Reinach in 1892. More bewildering still, one could show writers not immediately concerned with the controversy becoming adherents of systems they do not wholly accept, and borrowing pieces for use ready made from the most opposite sources. Huxley, van den Gheyn, and Quatrefages, for example, are eclectics to the verge of chaos. Conceive the world of chemists divided on the nomenclature and property of the elements and proceeding to do and publish research based now on one system, now on another, until each worker scarcely knew himself whether Lead meant Gold or Metal meant Acid, and you will have some faint idea of the Aryan battle in the nineteenth century.

II

A person is to be regarded as non-Aryan who is descended from Jewish parents or grandparents. This holds true even if only one parent or grandparent is of non-Aryan descent. This premise especially obtains if one parent or grandparent was of the Jewish faith.

—REICHSGESETZBLATT, I, 175, Apr. 11, 1933

AT THE OUTSET, the political passions behind the Aryan controversy involved chiefly the rival European powers and only incidentally the Jews. How Aryan came in our century to be the antithesis of Jewish can be indicated here in a few words, leaving the details of Nazi doctrine till later. As national enmities in Europe grew sharper and sharper, international groups or ideas became suspect in the eyes of ardent patriots. All threats to the safety of the state were attributed to the "alien in our midst." That alien might be a Jew, a Catholic, a Freemason, or a socialist. In a Catholic country such as France he might be a Protestant. Non-national was automatically taken to mean antinational. The Jews had long been thought of as a distinct blood-group and were now, as a result of Aryan philology, "proved" to be a race "absolutely different from the Aryans."[5] Renan, the most widely read authority on the Semitic languages and literature, had elaborated in the years 1847-55 the theory of the complete disparity between Aryan and Semitic tongues, and had presupposed the existence of the "pure Semite." The weakness for race-portraits popularized this distinction, which Gobineau had independently made the basis of his all-embracing system. Renan, to be sure, had distinguished at least ten separate Semitic types, and philosophers like Fouillée insisted on that important fact when trying to combat the growing anti-Semitism of the great industrial nations. But such ideas were too complicated for publicists with an ax to grind. By 1898 a traveler like the Baron Carra de Vaux, while sympathetically trying to understand the Semite in Islam "with an eye to French foreign policy," reiterates the accepted dogmas. He contrasts the "vast speculations of Aryan thought" with the "oversimple intuition" of the Semitic. Socialism seems to him likely to fit the Semitic

[5] Said Broca: "These words 'Aryan race' are perfectly scientific. . . . Pruner-Bey and Renan have shown the absolute difference of the Indo-European and Syro-Arabic languages." (*Mém. Anthrop., I,* 1862, 234, 242.)

temper, and after an appeal backed by nationalist and imperialistic motives, the Baron concludes: "Aryans as we are, we must take sides with those that resemble us . . . and zealously support in the Orient the efforts to rekindle the flame of our own genius." (*Le Génie Sémite et le Génie Aryen,* 1898, 152-54, 230.)

The association of Semitism and socialism was reinforced by all sorts of factors, and notably the role played in history by Karl Marx and Ferdinand Lassalle. The presence among the Freemasons of many Jews emancipated from religious ties made them suspect: the Jews were always fomenting international revolution. It was just as heinous that Jewish international finance should be "scheming" across the frontiers for the downfall of the state; that increasing masses of Jewish proletarians should be "scheming" from below in anarchist and socialist circles, aided by the "scheming" of Jews in the professions recently opened to them, all of it aimed at the overthrow of Aryan culture. The fallacy of numbers played a part in the growth of the prejudice: if one Jew were arrested among seven anarchists, the public fastened on him as the cause of social unrest, simply because the epithet "Jewish" is in itself a convenient way to remember the personality of at least one undesirable.

And the Jews themselves, like any minority, were also responsible for the fusing of diverse opinions and characters into the pattern of race. From Disraeli, who repeated in his novels that "race is everything," to Isaac Blümchen, who announced in 1914 the coming overthrow of France by the superior Jewish race, most of the defenders of the "Semite" have sought rather to glorify the "hated name" than to deny its validity as a description. Persecution, like adversity, makes strange bedfellows, and in the Aryan-Semite antagonism nineteenth-century pogroms and prejudices only strengthened the irrational bonds that had been forged during the Middle Ages in the name of religion. In both epochs, the link of race rested on superficial appearances fortified by political passion, blind on both sides, and made compelling by the appeal to authority—first theology, then the science of language.

III

> *The Scots (originally Irish, but by now Scotch) were at this time inhabiting Ireland, having driven the Irish (Picts) out of Scotland; while the Picts (originally Scots) were now Irish. . . . It is essential to keep these distinctions in mind.*
>
> *–1066 and All That*

IT HAS BEEN STATED earlier that the science of language which evolved the entities "Aryan" and "Semite" had been originally concerned with the Celts and their tongues. Not the least important feature of Western race-superstition is that it proceeds by the addition rather than the replacement of doctrines. No racist can ever be wholly up-to-date, and all that has ever been said on his subject is just as true as it ever was. Language, cranium, Nordic blondness, artistic bent have been accepted race-criteria equally and simultaneously.

This eternal youth of ideas explains why the Celts are always with us, even though they may have never existed. They were largely invented in the middle of the eighteenth century, when the tide of feeling among literary men began to turn away from the overworked Greeks and Romans. The Celts and their literature then typified everything that was fresh, young, and vigorous. The vogue of MacPherson's *Ossian* and the collecting of popular ballads were signs of a genuine desire for literary ancestors more recent than the classics. Students of language began to discover the beauty, the universality, the surpassing importance of the Celtic tongue. The name *Celtae* (Greek: *Keltoi*) had been loosely used by Caesar and other ancient historians to designate certain tribes fought by the Romans. From a few geographical hints, scanty physical traits, and the likely speech connection between Brittany, Wales, Cornwall, and Ireland, the whole supposititious science was built up. In France, Court de Gébelin constructed a whole historical system on Celtic speech, its affinities and etymologies. In England, MacLean identified the Celtic tongue with the original speech that the animals spoke to Adam in the Garden of Eden. At the turn of the century the Académie Celtique was founded in Paris to collect the "titles to glory of all Frenchmen—Gallic, Celtic, or Frankish." (*Mém. Acad. Celt.,* 1807, 1.) La Tour d'Auvergne-Corret, officially "the first grenadier of France," was an active member of the group and the memoirs of the Academy were dedicated to the Empress Josephine. Stendhal tells us how in this period children were costumed as Gauls and what faddish affectation surrounded everything alleged to be Celtic. (*Racine et Shakspeare,* 1833 ed., 85-86.)

Exactly who the Celts were or whence they came, no one knew, though everyone had his private belief. To combat Celtomania, John Pinkerton published in 1814 his *Inquiry into the History of Scotland:* he was an early Nordicist, convinced that the Scythians or Goths were the great race and that the Gauls were Germans, not Celts—"that dastard race" (II, 89-90). For him the Romans were a Scythian race also; whereas Madame de Staël adopted the more usual belief that the Romans form a separate race from the Nordic Celts or Old Gauls.

The association of the Celtic poetry and temperament with misty landscape can be carried over into the figurative landscape of the Celticists' minds: from the outset their lore was a tangle of contradictory assertions. A hundred years after its beginnings, the archaeologist S. Reinach commemorated it in these words: "Celtomania can be summed up as follows: The Celts are the most ancient people on earth; their tongue, the mother of all other tongues, has kept itself practically pure in low Breton; the Celts were profound philosophers, whose revelations have been transmitted to the bardic schools of Wales;

the *dolmens* are the altars where their priests, the Druids, offered human sacrifices; the 'alignments' [of stones] are their astronomical observatories."

Like every other race-notion current in the nineteenth century, Celticism could be adopted on all levels of intelligence. Matthew Arnold and Renan's interest in Celticism was literary and on the whole fairly intelligible; the *Eistedfodds* or Welsh songfests were likewise a cultural influence of the kind that has produced the Irish Renaissance of the early 1900's with Synge, Yeats, and Lady Gregory as its chief glories. But Celticism had other aspects. To Englishmen trying to cope with the Irish problem, Celticism could be made the "explanation" of misrule. "All the while," said Justin McCarthy about 1869, "five out of six English writers and political speakers were discoursing gravely on the incurable idleness and lawlessness of the Celtic race and the Irish peasant." (*Hist. of Our Own Times,* 1880 ed., IV, 277.) To these and other characteristics of "the two races," George Meredith tried to give fictional form in *Celt and Saxon,* and though the novel was published only after his death, he had earlier sprinkled his works with race-attributes based on this dichotomy.[6] The notion of culture was not yet at hand to permit the desired generalization.

Across the Channel, Celtic blood was frequently felt to be the true bond between England and France. In 1838, at Abergavenny, Lamartine told the assembled Welsh and Bretons that they were brothers. They needed but to look at one another's faces, eyes, and hair—their eyes as blue as the sea, their hair of the same blond color, and their hearts of the same stout quality. The French literary historians and historical littérateurs also became Celticists. Mérimée, the author of *Carmen,* hatched theories of his own about the Gallic Celts who came from Asia Minor to found France and bring it the Greek heritage. Balzac went in for Celtic etymology in *Les Chouans;* Michelet's Celti-

[6] See, particularly, *Diana of the Crossways.*

cism we noted earlier. A whole school of Celtic scholars, lasting into the present, found lifelong tasks and public honors in the devotion to this brand of racial history. Only a few names—no doubt obscure outside learned circles—need be mentioned: Henri Martin, A. Bertrand, d'Arbois de Jubainville, Camille Jullian. But these eminent men were not alone. Numberless dissertations filled with references to Gaels, Gauls, Kymris, and Belgae added to the delights of research by multiplying subtle distinctions. It is not rash to say that no two accounts of the Celts entirely agree.

To remain both Celtic and patriotic in France, it was necessary for scholars to show that the Germans were only a branch of the Celts. The Franks who had invaded Gaul in the fourth and fifth centuries A.D. were proved to be Celts who had left Gaul five hundred years or more earlier under their two leaders Sigovese and Bellovese. Galatia and Galicia in Eastern Europe were names recording the exploits of early Celts or Gauls; indeed the Celtic race was the great conqueror, just as the Celtic soul was the one civilizing element in mankind.

Against these contentions, the Germanists, Aryanists, and Romanists pointed out that everywhere the Celts were a conquered race, that the record shows them a disunited, unstable people; that their charm and other qualities are unproductive: they are too dreamy, melancholy, and impulsive. Even their literature is fragmentary, unformed, only occasionally moving or powerful. Such attacks were of no avail: Celt or Gaul is still in France a term of praise, implying both strength and imagination. De Maupassant called Flaubert a *vieux Gaulois;* no higher praise for Briand's scheme of European peace could be found than that it disclosed the mind of a *vrai Celte;* and few French readers would carp at the idea expressed by Jullian that the Rhine is "an essentially Celtic river." Pronouncements like the following, taken from a serious article on French speech, surprise no one: "I am a conquered foe of Caesar's, a soldier of Alesia, one of the slaves of the Circus, a rebel, . . . an exile.

Like Taliesin [the Celtic hero] I have lived through the past. I have seen and suffered all that our fathers have suffered. I have hated the foreigner's yoke. . . . I have cursed him and his tongue for four centuries." (Aug. Callet in *Poème et Drame,* Nov., 1912, 64.)

IV

Pure Saxon English; or Americans to the Front, by ELIAS MOLEE, Chicago, 1890

Nu Tutonish, an International Language, by ELIAS MOLEE, Tacoma, 1906

FURTHER COMMENTS on Celticism may seem superfluous, for of all the nineteenth-century race-beliefs it looks the most foolish. It is none the less instructive. For one thing, it coexists in the same minds (Broca and Bertrand, for example) with other race-classifications. The most elementary logic would suggest that mankind must fall into a fixed number of races, or else none at all. But racists are able to pin their faith now on a cranial division, now on a color division, now on a linguistic one; to make the three coincide is beyond their intentions or their powers.

Again, Celticism must rely on ancient texts for its generalities. Now it is clear that no one can know what the words "Celt, Iberian, Bryton, Ligurian, Kymri, Gaul, Gael," and so forth mean when applied to peoples. Even less certainty, if possible, obtains about these names considered as descriptions of physical types. It does not seem to have occurred to a single Celticist among those read for this study that the people known in antiquity as Celts may have included individuals of diverse physical appearance—some tall, some short; some fair and some dark. Ancient and modern texts alike form a maze of nonsense to which scholarly method only adds unreality. Every writer makes a choice of what he takes and rejects so that it is impossible to know whether a Celt is a round-headed Gaul or a Gaul a round-headed Celt—and, after a while, to care which is which. Each worker declaims against the "anarchy of terms" and points out the "enormities" of his rivals. But since these enormities become the orthodoxies of the next man, the only reasonable course is to preserve the same skepticism about Celtic origins as about Aryan virtues.

Even where a language is still alive and documents are plentiful, race-theories cannot be safely built upon them. Seventy-five years ago Chavée thought that languages represented the "immutable peculiarities" of the race that produced them. And writers in English, French, or German still expatiate about the racial or national traits that their idiom displays. The French find in the Germans' colloquial use of *Kolossal* and *Fabelhaft* an index to the race's underbred and barbaric mind,[7] while to the Germans the mincing speech of the French proves them to be an *Affenvolk* in their decadence. Such comparisons are incomplete and capricious. The linguistic sounds that are said to mark off the Germanic and the Celtic "races" take no account of actual pronunciation.[8] Nor does the latest modern method of recoding voices utilized by Dr. Willy Peters of Dorpat[9] in order to distinguish the races and spot the Semite seem to offer much guarantee of common sense. It is equally absent at the other end of the politico-racial scale. The Jews discriminate racially among themselves by speech differences[10] and left-wing publicists entertain a similar idea (justly criticized by H. L.

[7] See *Revue de Paris,* Sept., 1933. Of course the French use of *épouvantable* and *formidable* is not mentioned.

[8] To take but one instance: there is a startling similarity between the French and German *ü* and *r* and even between the initial sound of the French words *je viens* as they are heard on the streets of Paris and that of the German word *schwein.* (I am indebted for this example to the keen ears of the musician and linguist Julian DeGray.)

[9] See below, p. 195.

[10] The divisions of "Eastern Jews" among Lithuanians, Galicians, Russians, and Polish exemplify the process of crystallizing geographical, social, and intellectual factors into the absolute of Race, revealed through speech.

Mencken) when they associate speech with class-consciousness (Mencken, *Amer. Lang.,* 4th ed., 368) or when they refute the superficial judgments of nationalists on language by substituting equally superficial class-absolutes. (Margaret Schlauch, *Science and Society,* No. 1.) In short, race-theories shift their ground, alter their jargon, and mix their claims, but they cannot obliterate the initial vice of desiring to explain much by little and to connect in the life of the group or the individual some simple fact with some great significance. How the diameters of the human skull fulfilled this requirement will be told in the chapter to follow.

Chapter VII

SCIENTIFIC ANTHROPOLOGY

I

And when a whirlwind hath blown the dust of the Churchyard into the Church and the man swept out the dust of the Church into the Churchyard, who will undertake to sift those dusts again and to pronounce, This is the Patrician, this is the noble flour, this the yeomanly, this the Plebeian bran?

—JOHN DONNE

THE DISTINCTION between the old "descriptive" and the new "scientific" anthropology is bound to be arbitrary. An observer like Buffon was a better scientist than some plodding latter-day measurer of skulls. But for our purpose a line can be drawn between the bulk of the anthropologists who worked before 1859 and those who came after. The date is not so arbitrary as the line. The year 1859 commemorates in the science of man two capital events: the appearance of Darwin's *Origin of Species* and the founding of the Anthropological Society in Paris under the leadership of Paul Broca.[1] The significance of these

[1] W. F. Edwards had made a start twenty years before but his Ethnological Society had died with the extinction of the slavery issue in 1848. Following the lead of Broca in Paris, societies sprang up in other capitals. Rudolph Wagner founded an anthropological association

two events lies in the virtual extinction of the quarrel between monogenists and polygenists and the proliferation of other issues and methods that led to new conclusions concerning the races of men.

How Darwin's famous book swept out of court the old arguments about the creation of man need not be retold here. Suffice it to say that the rising generation trained in science between 1830 and 1850 no longer felt the necessity of squaring their scientific beliefs with Scripture. In consequence, the period from 1859 to 1914 was given over to materialistic and mechanistic anthropology. In terming this brand of anthropology scientific there is no intention of praising it, but merely of recalling that its exponents chose the term to praise themselves; they chose it because the prevailing definition of science denoted precisely what they were doing—no longer merely observing and describing, but counting, measuring, and experimenting. Buffon had experimented, to be sure, and so had Erasmus Darwin, Charles's grandfather, but they had not made it a system nor deemed it a virtue, as did their grandchildren.

The anthropologists of the later period pursued the quest for certainty in the science of man by means of Number. Anthropology became the science of measuring the parts of the human body, principally the skull, but also the features, the limbs, the genital organs, the stature, the diameter of the heart or of the buttocks. The system required that the measurements be made on large groups of specimens in order to find the common characteristics of the races. The result was a mass of statistics. Where, one may ask, did experiment come into the method? It

---

at Göttingen in 1861 and henceforth coveted the skulls of his most distinguished colleagues at the University, most of whom were amiable enough to die before him. James Hunt established a group in London in 1863. Three years later, Soutzoff followed suit in Moscow, and from 1865 to the revolution of 1868 Velasco sought to endow Spain with a similar body, against the protests of the Catholic regime and newspaper press. The first International Congress of Anthropologists met in 1865 and became a yearly institution in 1867.

was impossible to experiment on human stock: men live too long and will not breed merely in order to satisfy scientific curiosity. Apart from the well-established use of animals (e.g., Broca's work on the fertility of leporides) experiment was limited to the invention of instruments. In this field Paul Broca reigned supreme. Called by Darwin "a cautious and philosophical observer," Broca was also an inventive pioneer. His resourcefulness in devising craniometers, his sphenoidal and other hooks, his consummate gadgetry for discovering the mathematical relations of the various parts of the skull, show talent amounting to genius. One must go to the five volumes of his *Mémoires d' Anthropologie* for plates and descriptions of the instruments he conceived and built for capturing the elusive chimera of race. He was followed, imitated, and finally surpassed by hundreds of researchers all over Europe, whose efforts culminated about 1900 in the 5,000 measurements that A. von Törok took on a single skull.

The greatest diversity persisted, of course, among the conclusions of equally scientific anthropologists during the period in question, but they shared certain postulates in common, together with their common method. The first postulate, in Broca's own words, amounts to a profession of faith: "I am among those who think that the great typical differences which separate human groups are primordial." (*Mém. Anthrop.,* I, 248.) A second assumption, not so universally accepted, was that, since racial differences find their expression in opinions and behavior, the brain has something to do with race and the measured shape of the skull is the best way to get at the contents of the brain. This is nothing more nor less than transmogrified phrenology, and one is not surprised to find Broca paying generous tribute to the pioneer work of Gall and Spurzheim which led to the localizing of brain functions and the focusing of attention on brain studies. (*Ibid.,* I, 199.)

The third assumption is that the measurements of skulls yield positive facts. At first sight this statement sounds like a paradox: how can it be an assumption to state that a measurement yields a fact? Simply because of the nature of the human skull. There are two ways of measuring it—dry, that is, the actual skull of a dead person; and live, that is with the skin and hair upon it. This last procedure involves making an arbitrary allowance for the thickness of the tissues and hair. It is doubtful whether the tissues are of constant thickness on both sides of the skull at a given point and even were it so, whether that arbitrary allowance can be gauged accurately from the external "feel" of the scalp on the bone. The scientist starts therefore with a big "if" in measuring the living skull for comparison with the measurements of other "racial" groups. But what are we to think when we come across the honest admission of a man like Broca that the measurements of the dry skull are no less variable in their accuracy? No two anthropologists, it seems, get exactly the same figures from measuring the same skull, and no one anthropologist gets the same figures from two measurements of the same specimen. The skull, in short, is too bumpy to be precisely measured.[2]

The reassuring thought suggests itself that in a group of skulls those small differences even out, but in fact, before they can do so, too many factors intervene. In the first place the "cephalic index" representing each skull is obtained by dividing the lengthwise diameter of the skull into the crosswise diameter and multiplying the result by 100. The resulting numbers are arranged on a scale starting with the lowest index and approaching 100 as an upper limit. This scale proceeds by decimals (e.g.: 77.10-77.101-77.102) each of which expresses a very small divergence from the preceding skull. Now, the race anthropologist must divide his scale into groups that he calls racial types. The most familiar are the *dolicho* (long-headed) with a small index, and the *brachy* (round-headed) with a larger index. Most an-

[2] For a discussion of the different methods used in France and in Germany and the "unfair" comparisons that resulted, see pages 218 ff. of Vacher de Lapouge, *L'Aryen: son Rôle Social,* 1889-99.

thropometrists recognized subtler groupings, however, in four, six, and even more categories, properly labeled in Greek. Whether a skull is *brachy*- or *dolicho*- or *mesati*- or *ortho*-cephalic is therefore doubly a matter of arbitrary division. Each anthropologist devised his own nomenclature, and the place of each skull in any one class was more and more uncertain at the edges of the series. Skull X, for instance, with a none too exact index of 81.34, might be *brachy* with Broca and *mesati* with Mantegazza. In the racial conclusions these dubieties are lost sight of. Long before the end of the study skull X has become irretrievably brachycephalic, its origin in a city cemetery has endowed it for the anthropologist with "proletarian" qualities, and the anthropologist has discovered a "law" correlating low-class city populations with round skulls.

This example drawn from Broca merits a few words more. He measured 125 skulls found buried opposite the Palais de Justice in Paris. From their position below the surface he assigned them to the twelfth century, and from the aristocratic nature of the district in that century he believed them to belong to the upper classes. He compared with them 259 skulls originating from nineteenth-century paupers' graves. He measured, multiplied, divided, and grouped them, and then showed "the difference between the wealthy classes of the Middle Ages and the modern proletarians." (*Mém. Anthrop.,* II, 3, 5.) That difference is expressed in figures accurate to 0.40, which means four thousandths of a millimeter when one redivides the index number by 100. But what do we really know about the supposed medieval skulls? It is easily probable that among them are the brain-pans of low-class domestic servants; again, among the nineteenth-century paupers' remains were many originating in the Morgue, the bodies of suicides, which not only introduces an abnormality that mars the validity of the series but spoils the "proletarian" and national unity of the group, since a Paris suicide may just as easily be the scion of a Hungarian noble family as an itinerant Swiss tinker.

One is readily impressed by the care, the intelligence, the devotion to science that lie behind Broca's figures. The figures themselves have a comforting air; they seem to speak for themselves. It is unfortunate that being an honest scientist and a competent anatomist and physiologist, as Broca was, is no guarantee of his conclusion that city people tend to have rounder heads than their country cousins. The calipers and the figures refer to little that is tangible. It is not the fault of the statistics, but of the reasoning behind them. When a farmer finds that one orchard consistently yields him more apples than another after he has expended the same care on both sets of similar fruit trees, he is justified in concluding that the land or the exposure of one orchard is better than the other's. His conclusion, though crude, is probably sound because he has compared things identical save in the one respect at issue and *because he has counted apples.* But what has Broca counted? He started with skulls, of which he did not precisely know the origin; then he went to diameters, which he reduced to cephalic indexes—a purely arbitrary notion, though one which we willingly accept, until we discover that the final result is expressed in terms of twelfth-century aristocrats and nineteenth-century proletarians. We started with apples, as it were, and end up with complex social entities.

But there is worse to come: Broca was too intelligent to be taken in by the uncertainty of his method. He points out that the cephalic index is "neither a simple character, nor a natural one." (II, 16 ff.) It depends on the relation of two independent diameters, and can therefore vary owing to the increase of the one or the decrease of the other. Brachy, dolicho, and similar expressions have therefore "a purely conventional meaning." (*Ibid.*) A dolichocephalic does not occur in nature in the same sense as an apple or a horse. Still, by comparing the averages of unreal entities Broca thinks he is "authorized to conclude about the different ethnic elements (i.e., races) when the skull-averages of random series give markedly different figures." (*Ibid.*) Anthropology can therefore say little or nothing about the individual, but it pretends to describe and forecast the nature of the racial group. Broca and many of his colleagues see this clearly, and oppose the racial absolutism of Retzius and Pruner-Bey. Still, it is one thing to acknowledge the limitations of a method and quite another to remember them in stating conclusions. Broca himself continually takes his relative results for absolute ones; he starts with a blind and dumb skull or a fragment of jaw; he translates it into a mathematical entity; and he finally resolves it into a human personality with social attributes and historical antecedents (proletarian, white, lacking initiative, Aryan, non-Aryan, and so on). For he supplements his measuring science by adopting the usual color-division, "Aryan" philology, and plain race-history in the manner of Thierry.

Broca further admits that environment, climate, and occupation may have influenced the cranial characters, though within very narrow limits. He is aware that the post-coronal depression is often the result of tying a band around the child's head; yet he disregards other skull deformations reported by his colleagues as being the result of either the effects of burial or the method of delivery at birth. As far as the skull goes, the question of "racial origins" would accordingly be referable in part to the gravediggers, the midwives, and the nurses of Europe and would have little relation to society, civilization, progress, and the other modern issues linked with race. What is discouraging about Broca is not that he is stupid or fanatical about his methods and conclusions; on the contrary, admissions like the following force us to respect his intellect and make of him the laboratory counterpart of Gobineau:

"The more I have multiplied my cranial researches, the more I have become convinced that the comparison of races can furnish no absolutely decisive criterion [*caractère*]. It is by the sum total of all characters that analogies and distinctions of race can be established." (III, 298.) The second part of the statement often means an attempt to salvage the ambiguous criterion jettisoned in the first. Broca goes on to belie his admission by talking blithely of the "Gallic blood which tended to recover its pre-eminence in the Frankish aristocracy of the St. Barthel Cemetery." If one needs the sum total of characters to compare races, how did he find "Gallic blood" tests in a cemetery and by what does he make sure of his Frankish aristocracy? Babble about "the resistance of the nasal index to crossbreeding" hardly atones for such flagrant inconsistency. We are no further away from the contrasts of Franks and Gauls than we were at the end of the seventeenth century with the crotchety Count de Boulainvilliers, who could utter the same enormities with better excuse, since he did not have the advantage of micrometer calipers. Feeling recurrent doubt, Broca added to his criteria cranial capacity measured with small shot, mercury, or fennel seed; and nasal and orbital indexes, measured with special hooks and rulers.

After working on the nasal index, which he adopted in spite of "the obliquity of the measurements," Broca applied it to modern and ancient nations: "The Franks brought with them a new nasal type. We know that from the earliest times of the conquest, the Frankish aristocracy intermarried frequently with the Gallo-Roman aristocracy; this progressive mélange in which the blood of the conquered race was gradually to supplant the blood of the foreign, was no doubt in the beginning not very uniform. . . . [Now] . . . the Franks were not leptorrhinian [narrow-nosed] like the peoples of Western Europe, but mesorrhinian like the Mongols. They were nevertheless of the Germanic race . . . and . . . the modern Germans are as leptorrhinian as the French. The mesorrhinia of this people [the Franks] belonging to a blond and white race, therefore constitutes a unique exception." (IV, 338-39.)

Broca further admits that the cephalic index has changed its significance since Merovingian times, that the process of ossification is capricious enough to throw off the keenest anatomist, and that "individual variations are always greater within a given race than the distance which separates it not only from neighboring races, but sometimes from all other races." (IV, 356.)

II

There is war, not peace, in the camps of the learned.

—F. J. E. WOODBRIDGE

THESE RESULTS AND CONCESSIONS, though they may no longer satisfy us, do not seem to have daunted the anthropometrists. Not content with ascribing race-differences to modern populations and to peoples that have left no name in history, the scientific anthropology of the nineteenth century confidently reached back to prehistoric times and, trusting in paleontology and archaeology, differentiated primitive races on highly speculative grounds. One of the forces behind this interest was the connection of prehistoric anthropology with Darwinism. For the question of origins brought up in a new shape by the triumph of evolution and the desire to know how the human species had changed were engrossing scientific minds.

Moreover, the confirmation in 1859 of Boucher de Perthes's discovery of human remains dating from the Pleistocene or early Quaternary period necessitated a revision of the geological and archaeological chronology. The existence of antediluvian man, as he was called, led to wonder about his culture, temperament, and physical appearance. Here, too, Broca was in the forefront of speculation, and we find him in 1867 making affirmations on the flimsy evidence of bone fragments, nasal angles, and cranium capacity.

It adds to the comedy of these endeavors to recall that these ancient "races" exist in the form of Arabic numerals and decimal points. The tangible data were stone tools, human and animal bone fragments, and a very few undamaged skulls. And even these were subject to doubt when rival theorists came to grips. Broca showed how two of Retzius's so-called Basque crania were simply unidentified and unidentifiable skulls. Pruner-Bey's plaster replicas of skulls at the Paris Museum of Natural History, which were labeled as "mixed Iberians," turned out to be of Swiss origin and to have had all their labels switched about in the course of setting up the collection. The story of the Truchère skull found near Lyon is a saga in itself. Honest discoverers of genuine remains freely admit that the normal conditions of unearthing a find are liable to the danger of unconscious fraud through the inclusion of spurious bones, as well as to error in gauging the depth of the remains through clumsy shovel work. Yet in the teeth of these handicaps anthropologists who had been nowhere near the spot of discovery, who had not even seen or touched the remains, but who took someone else's measurements and reconstructions, built up theories of prehistoric racial characters, juggled with skull-indexes, called each other names, and filled the general public with prejudices about their national origins or those of "the enemy across the frontier."

The strength of the illusion can be inferred from one of its effects on Broca, whom we must call a great and an honest mind in spite of all his aberrations. He had proved to his own satisfaction that a series of not less than twenty skulls is necessary to make measurements valid. But later, lacking the requisite number, he is tempted to say that ten skulls often suffice. Finally, he is found willing to conclude about a prehistoric race on the basis of two or three skulls in not very good repair. But elsewhere again he warns students that fifteen is the minimum number for a "sufficient series." (*Mém.*, IV, 764.)[3] Such variable minimums served their turn in answering the profound and widely mooted question: whether dolichocephalism represented

[3] By 1879 Broca had acquired a total of 2,000 skulls composing sixty series. Retzius had collected 300 for his original work but based his ultimate results on only five.

a "superior type," that of the Indo-European Celt or Aryan who had conquered the "native" brachycephalics. Broca's answer, not free from the taint of nationalism, was that the Indo-European invaders did not introduce dolichocephalism into Europe, but that the native races whose remains antedate the age of bronze were both dolicho- and brachycephalic. Against the "Nordic contention," he added that the brachys doubtless had larger and better brains than the dolichos. On both sides the belief that skull-shape carries with it cultural qualities was taken for granted. From Broca's involvement one can judge of the soundness of lesser men. Their "thinking" and their quarrels can be seen in dramatic form in the reports of the Congress of Anthropology and Prehistoric Archaeology held at Paris on Aug. 30, 1867, where Thurnam and Barnard Davis, Van Duben, Pruner-Bey, Broca, Topinard, Morton, Nott, Gliddon, and the shades of their predecessors or colleagues, Blumenbach, Cuvier, Prichard, Retzius, Rudolf Wagner, Huxley, Haeckel, and Virchow fought Homeric battles wanting only the laughter of the gods.[4] Three years before the Franco-Prussian War, one can discern in that meeting the ill-concealed animosities of nationalists underlying the vigorous enmity of rival theorists.

This confusion of armies clashing by night could none the less leave on the educated layman who read the newspapers a distinct impression that progress in civilization depends upon race. Broca repeatedly asserted the principle in so many words. He judged the aptitudes of races for progress, and he concluded that the whites as a whole are superior to the blacks as a whole. What this implies about colonization and imperialism was not left unsaid, any more than the suspicion of ulterior motive in other nations' race-theories. "Our colleagues on the other side of the Rhine" was a phrase tossed back and forth by French and German scientists. Anglo-French antagonism was almost

[4] Unless one counts as such the points made in the memoir entitled "*How I learn pre-history while sowing carrots,*" *Mém. Anthrop.*, II, 130 ff.

wholly absent, the belief in Celticism suggesting a prehistoric bond that was not disrupted by the Norman conquest of England.

In this entire scheme of skull-measuring only one question was generally avoided, despite sporadic references to it. It is the capital question of how a race remains a race. In all the scientific anthropology of the nineteenth century the main business of the investigation was to find what races were *like,* rather than what a race was. The distinction is not a quibble. This dolichocephalic skull in Broca's hand is not a race—it is a specimen of human skull. This collection of dolichocephalic skulls is not a race, either: it is a group of similar skulls, presumed to belong to the same race. Possibly the similarity depends on their former owners' having had a pair of common ancestors, for otherwise it is accidental and meaningless. We do not speak of all the round pebbles on the beach as forming a race. In other words, a race must start as a family, a couple with its offspring. But if that is true, then we must turn our attention to a whole new set of facts—the facts of hereditary characteristics, their transmission, their mixture, their permanence or disappearance.

Broca and his colleagues all too summarily dismissed this essential problem. For all they knew, their similar skulls were really two pebbles on the beach. Scientific anthropology might as well class together all human beings born with the ring finger longer than the middle finger and call them a race.[5] One excellent reason why the mid-century anthropologist did not take up the problem of race biologically, but only anatomically, was that the science of genetics was not yet born. An exception to this general condemnation of the anatomists was André Sanson, at one time President of the *Société d'Anthropologie*. His professorship at the Agronomic Institute partly explains his uniqueness: his knowledge of animal species led him to make wider applications of biological conceptions. Broca had said: "Despite the unity of the fundamental type, men present numer-

[5] Casanova laid much stress on this "sign" of artistic sensitivity.

ous profound varieties or modifications based on external, physiological, anatomical, intellectual, and moral characters . . . there still exist pure races . . . and statistical measurement can alone demonstrate whether a race is progressing, stationary or decadent." (I, 7-17.) Sanson replied: "The whole question is to determine experimentally what a species is . . . Broca's method is unquestionably illusory; the shape-of-skull system is chaotic and powerless to distinguish types." (*L'espèce et la race en biol.,* 1, 46.)

The great problem, for Sanson, was that to have validity in scientific work, species must be clear and unchanging, whether or not they have been recognized as such in the past and whether or not they once existed as varieties. He believed that there is no constant variety (*Ibid.,* 310, 317) and that any "race" is the sum of the descendants of an original couple, with or without physical similarity among the offspring—in other words, a collection of families. He concludes that "race is the physical manifestation of the actual species" (317), which is to say that the existence of races in the sense of unchanging varieties is still to be proved.

These ideas have only recently been pursued and then only by a few modern anthropologists. The successors of Retzius, Broca, Beddoe, and Taylor in the first decade of the twentieth century—be they Deniker, Ripley, Montandon, or von Luschan—did not greatly change their methods or point of view. The scientific imagination was slow to grasp the fact that race-definition, on the one hand, and the multitude of living human beings, on the other, must be reciprocally and exactly ordered in biological terms before one can assert: "This man is of that race" and "this race is composed of men who are thus and so."

III

Masses of men will be massacring one another for one degree more or less in their cephalic index.

—ALFRED FOUILLÉE, 1893

IF ONE SURVEYS the sweeping movement of scientific anthropology with the "eye of eternity" and tries to assess its importance, one is compelled to admit that it had remarkable consequences. Scholastic, puerile, and verbose though it was, its effects were practical and extensive. Militarism and criminology were its first beneficiaries. As early as 1868, the efforts of members of the Société d'Anthropologie of Paris contributed to the legal lowering of the stature-exemption for military recruits. It was held unfair to make the several "races" within France, congenitally different in stature, attain the same height, which was consequently lowered to 1 meter 55 centimeters. Already in the sixties the rumor was current that the French race was degenerating. The size of the conscripted men and the falling birth rate were taken as signs of decadence. Since 1854 the number of deaths had exceeded that of births and a copious literature had begun to flood the country without settling either the figures or their social significance. Its authors naturally enlisted the aid of anthropology. The notion that height was a racial character that does not change under social or geographical influence gave rise to an absurd piece of reasoning: human stature is an unchanging character, hence the fact that our soldiers are getting shorter and shorter cannot be due to undernourishment or changing environment through industrialization. It must be that the race is degenerating. The nightmare of the race's disappearing gradually like the Cheshire cat, leaving only an index number behind, must have haunted many a patriotic student of society. How degenerescence, or change, could attack the race—something by definition unchangeable—proved no stumbling block, and "reasons" were as plentifully offered for it as for the puzzle Charles II set his Royal Academicians—why a dead fish weighs more than a live one—without reference to the truth or falsity of the case put.

Under the Third Republic, when the strength of the race was even more an object of solicitude, the science of military anthropology found its most indefatigable practitioner in Dr.

René Collignon. He thought it the noblest task of anthropology,[6] and a patriotic duty as well, to draw up a map of the racial types living together as Frenchmen and to show that the "prehistoric races," far from having been annihilated by conquest, had survived through the centuries. Collignon was an army doctor who carried out his researches as a member of the review commissions for compulsory military service. He prepared a handbook for the use of military colleagues, and he managed to put together his longed-for racial map of France "before railways and the telegraph [*sic*] obliterated the races by mixture." (*L'Anthrop. au Conseil de Révision,* Paris, 1891.)

His races rest on four indexes: height, cephalic index, nasal index, color of hair and eyes. He is careful to show how difficult it is to take these statistics quickly and accurately while doing the main job of passing on recruits. Indeed, he proves the difficulty so well that one is inclined to believe it insuperable and consequently to doubt the value of his figures. By their means he proves that the Celts have round heads and the blond and Mediterranean races long and narrow ones. How does he know that a round-head is a Celt? Simply by finding out from Caesar or Procopius what regions the Celts inhabited in Gallic times and measuring the people in that locality today. Collignon's science walks on crutches—one is a yardstick and the other a five-foot shelf of the classics. But other difficulties surround the military anthropometrist. He measures for the most part youths of twenty, though the period of reaching full growth varies among individuals up to the age of thirty, before which time both extremes of height and shortness have a tendency to be eliminated by death. Besides, the accurate measuring of the chosen indexes is a very delicate business. The posture, the thickness of hair of the subject, his physical health, and the amount of sleep he had before the measurement, all play a part in making uncertain the bare figure from which the "racial" aver-

[6] Ammon was his counterpart in the Grand Duchy of Baden, starting his work in 1886.

age is derived. Collignon's averages produce such contradictions that he is obliged to make hypotheses at every turn. For a given region such as the Department of Côtes du Nord he postulates "four or five stocks intermingled, of which probably two belong to the same race." Even after this he does not appear enlightened by his researches, and if not he, then *cui bono?*

The effect of anthropometry on criminology need not detain us long. From detailed measurements to fingerprinting, the work of Bertillon and others aimed chiefly at the identification of individuals and not of races, so that its validity rests entirely on the fact that a human being cannot effectively alter his physique at will. The criminologists were also interested in distinguishing races, but their method does not differ from that of Broca or Topinard. Nevertheless, the anthropological view of crime "established" one highly debatable point: it ascribed crime not to circumstance and environment so much as to certain conformations of the brain and body. There resulted a widespread belief that all criminals are degenerates and that the offspring of a criminal is fated to be a criminal. It made of criminals a distinct race, recognizable by the long jaw, flattened nose, scanty beard, and certain abnormalities in the size of the head and brain that indicate a reversion to savagery.

This description, paraphrased from Lombroso, the famous Italian anthropologist, was popularized by him in the nineties and it has stuck in the public mind. Facts are powerless against it. In 1900 a typical "psycho-physiological study" by five physicians on the body of a maniacal strangler named Vacher brought out interesting differences of opinion. It was found that the third frontal convolution of Vacher's brain resembled greatly the corresponding part in the brain of the late patriot and prime minister Gambetta. Dr. Laborde insisted that the difference between the depraved assassin and the savior of his country lay in a "simple functional deviation." The others supported the view that an organ and its function are as cause and effect. Over the body of a convict was being fought out the great philosophical quarrel of the century, between strict materialism and the dualism of mind and matter. It was another aspect of the race-question, since the scientific racist must be a strict materialist. For him, given bodily features a, b, c, d, only one type of mind is possible. Critically considered, the argument is bad even as materialist thinking, for it takes no account of the modifications to which the features a, b, c, d have been subjected during the life of the organism. It says: Once a criminal or Aryan always a criminal or Aryan, and refuses other evidence.

The more diffuse results of scientific anthropology upon nineteenth- and twentieth-century culture are not less important than those on militarism and criminology. Taking together the practicing scientists and the qualified publicists, an imposing group of intellectuals were engaged in "investigating" or propagating the great anthropological truths. Ammon, Gumplowicz, Bouglé, Pouchet, Drumont, Colajanni, Clavel, Léon Daudet, J. Finot, Bocayuva, A. Firmin, Souffret, A. Hovelacque, Letourneau, Lefèvre, Muffang, Odin, Velasco, Closson, Nietzsche, Pittard, Seillière, Gehring, Cornejo, H. S. Chamberlain, Aline Gorren, Homer Lea, Havelock Ellis, G. Ferrero, Madison Grant, Lothrop Stoddard, are but a few taken at random from an interminable list. Their names span Europe and the Americas as well as the arts and professions, without including the more recent Third Reich publicists and their German forerunners in purely political anthropology.

Among the latter only one name, Nietzsche's, is of the very first rank, and his is a measure of the importance of the others. The great man is usually without power and influence until a good while after his death—it was particularly true of Nietzsche—whereas the rest, holding down posts in the universities and the civil service, or else established as critics, littérateurs, politicians, physicians, and lawyers, form the miscellaneous leadership of public opinion. This is not to say that the great minds of the period escaped the influence of scientific race-theories. On the contrary, scarcely one can be found who does not show a trace of the superstition, but the great artist, thinker, or statesman ordinarily reflects those superstitions without actually propagating them. We can find some kind of race-belief in Clemenceau, Poincaré, Briand, Claude Bernard, Freud, Le Dantec, Bergson, Brandes, d'Annunzio, Ruskin, Matthew Arnold, and Henry James, but it does not form the core of their thought or the goal of their endeavor. They accept race frequently without question, as they do the Copernican theory and the existence of bacteria. The lesser, more immediately powerful men, on the contrary, think race night and day, see it everywhere, and help out one another's hallucinations by writing books, forming schools, and engaging in a war of words that carries them momently further away from the counsels of good sense and the reality of Man.

Chapter VIII

RACE AND THE NATIONALISTIC WARS: 1870-1900

I

There is in race a latent political genius which is sometimes incarnated in a statesman.

—RÉMY DE GOURMONT

BETWEEN 1870 AND 1914 Europe was simultaneously a prey to all the forces previously described as acting separately toward the intensification of race-beliefs. Nationalism was an acute and universal fever; the unrest arising from industrialization, rapid or slow, was giving rise to a host of revolutionary movements; philosophy and the fine arts faithfully reflected the national and social struggles; science and evolutionary theory were conferring certainty upon the most diverse fanaticisms; imperialism and prestige-diplomacy were clutching at every argument for the furtherance of commercial aims in Africa, America, and the Far East; finally, free public education, the newspaper press, and manhood suffrage were making millions participate in national policies, as either voters or readers; and the nature of the machinery for this participation was such that the simplest ideas, the crudest superstitions, stood a better chance of spreading and surviving than the more complex truths and the subtler speculations.

In such a state of affairs one might reasonably expect a luxuriance of race-beliefs, and the facts bear out the supposition. All systems and ideas of superiority based on race served to express and aggravate current problems. Less and less caution was used by the proponents of race-doctrines in foisting their wares on the public. For one thing, that public was a product of newspaper education; for another, race-words and slogans—Aryan, dolicho, Anglo-Saxon, Celt, tall blond, Nordic, Semite—were absorbed into the common speech of all classes. Then, too, international strife seemed to justify loose thinking and mass-denunciation as patriotic, while the shield of science was raised over the racist to save him from attack by the intelligent layman. At one instant, *Realpolitik* was invoked to cover inaccuracies, and the next, the errors so justified found asylum in the laboratory.

Although no harmony must be looked for in the din of racist voices, it must be introduced willy-nilly in order to describe the period at all. Four general trends may be discerned for that purpose. The one involves France and Germany and deals in Aryanism, Celticism, and Germanism. Another comprises the attempts to connect race with social unrest: it makes of the socialists a race of revolutionaries with Semitic noses and brachycephalic heads. The third divides Europe into two camps—the Anglo-Teutonic in the ascendant, and the Latin in decline; the Slavic group oscillates between the other two. The fourth and last race-grouping sees things in black and white. Europeans must stand shoulder to shoulder against the colored hordes of black, red, and yellow men whom they have aroused from their ancestral torpor in the name of civilization, else European culture—or, rather, Civilization itself—is doomed.

No European figure of importance in any walk of life escaped, during that period, the contamination of one or more of these beliefs. Many took for granted the truth of all four, each in its sphere, regardless of contradictions; and the most vocal were by no means the most inconsistent, since it is easier to hold incompatible views on the same subject when one is not engaged in treating of it. The truth of that generality cannot, in the nature of things, be proved; it can only be tested, here and there, by reference to the politics, the historiography, the arts, and the periodical literature of the time. Even a summary unavoidably reproduces the confusion and the tedious repetitiousness of the data themselves. To summarize, five "moments" will be lifted out of the half century in question: the aftermath of the Franco-Prussian War; the Dreyfus Affair; Germany under William II; the rise of new sociologies; and the First World War. But before these organized "moments," a few illustrations taken at random will help convey the confusion.

While in France the "specious doctrine of race, tongue, and nationality" was leading the Second Empire to ruin (Hovelacque, *Langues, Races, Nationalités,* 1875, 7), Italy was fighting along the path of national unity to an accompaniment of similar issues, involving long skulls, Germanic populations, and inherent capacity or incapacity for government. The same questions of unity and power occurred for Bismarck somewhat later and he decided that "the Gaul was easier to govern than the German," flattering the latter with the possession of unruly blood. (Reichstag, March 18, 1867; March 6, 1874.)

Meantime Mademoiselle Clemence Royer, expounding Darwinism and race in the public press, was considering nations as living organisms competing in the universal struggle for life. The racial inequality of nations thus "placed in the organic series" led to improvement, to a greater display of ingenuity, and to the survival of the fittest. (*Journal des Econ.,* Nov., 1875.) This competition, visible enough in industry and diplomacy, was halted only temporarily by such shocks as the taking of Khartoum and the death of Gordon. A shudder of panic ran through the European press and for a time there was talk of white-brotherhood against Islam. Relaying the news from London,

John Lemoinne called for a "tightening of the ranks among civilized nations in the face of barbarism." (*Journal des Débats,* Feb. 7, 1885.)

Leading to other kinds of alignments, the fear of radicalism also drove publicists and scientists to seek refuge in race. A Stuttgart anthropologist studied the Reichstag election returns from Swabia and found them the "expression of a natural instinct, rooted deeply in the native character of the people. A decided connection obtains between dark eyes and democracy." (Kollmann, *Archiv. für Anthrop.,* 1877, 173.)

The practical value of race-consciousness in settlers among the "inferior races" (to ward off the impending dangers of race-mixture) was made explicit by such popularizers of science as Topinard (*l'Anthropologie,* 1879, 11-12) and by later publicists down to Madison Grant and Lothrop Stoddard. Again, race-feeling was used as an explanation of greater or less success in imperialism by the various nations of Europe in their struggle for a place in the sun. (Laupts to Zaborowski, *Bull. Soc. Anthrop.,* 1898, 392, 397.) The Latins were poor colonizers, the Anglo-Saxons highly successful. Was it irrelevant to ask where Teutons and Slavs fitted into this racial scale?

Race was naturally resorted to in the arguments of subject-nationalities about autonomy and boundary lines. Thus the Albanians in 1883 protested to the great powers against the ceding of Epirus to the Greeks. Their memorandum, supposedly inspired by Italy, said in part: "To understand why the Greeks and Albanians cannot live under the same regime, it is only necessary to examine the entirely different structure of their skulls; the Greeks are brachycephalic, whereas the Albanians are dolichocephalic and lack almost completely the occipital protuberance." (Fouillée, *Psych.,* 1898, iii.)

The nationalist propaganda that had to be exerted for the welding together of the new Germany rested on very similar grounds. A Pan-German League publication dated 1899 refers to the Celtic blood of the Swabians and Bavarians justifying, at the time of the Rheinbund, an alliance with France; while the "proportion of German blood" kept those same peoples from uniting with "the Slav." These proportions of blood having been changed, politics followed suit. (Schultheiss, *Deutscher Vorschlag,* 4.) This explanation of politics by race was so generally accepted that a French *Dictionnaire Général de la Politique* (1884) does not so much prove as expound it, and the *Saturday Review* asserts that "the biological view of foreign policy is plain." (Feb. 1, 1896.) Consequently, the racial antagonism between France and Germany is a quarrel of bodies and not of principles; a local and chronic condition frequently paralleled elsewhere.

Change the proper names and any German pamphlet or article could be signed by a corresponding French writer; while for many other nationals of Europe the racial adjectives themselves could stand unaltered, each side appropriating the name that carried with it the most honor and virtue.

II

The men of my generation are those of whom it has been said that they were hypnotized by the Rhine frontier.

—ALBERT SOREL

THE ERA OF EXASPERATION between the two wars of 1870 and 1914 began in France with psychological depression and it ended in nationalistic fervor. The terms of the Treaty of Frankfort (1871), coming on top of the humiliation of the Second Empire and the unification of the new Germany, was followed by the diplomatic isolation of France at the hands of Bismarck. Among the ruling and educated classes in France these reverses caused a widespread feeling of inferiority. But added to it was a sense of England's renewed colonial supremacy under the leadership of Disraeli and an awareness of the growing power of the United States, which had not only reasserted its unity in 1861-65 but had forced Napoleon III's withdrawal from Mexico. It was not difficult for some Frenchmen to generalize from these facts that certain nations—Germany, England, the United States—were in the ascendant, whereas France, Italy, Spain, and Portugal were unmistakably in decline. But what trait common to each group could serve to explain the facts? Race: the Anglo-Saxon nations were still vigorous, while those of "Latin blood" were decadent.

The lowest depth of this national despair came in the eighties and nineties but conspicuous signs were not wanting in the seventies. Gobineau's illuminating pamphlet on *What Happened to France in 1870* remained unpublished, but the critical views expressed in it were not those of an isolated man or of a traitor to his country. Like his compatriots, Gobineau believed the 1870 disaster unparalleled in history, but he thought that it was due not so much to an exterior enemy as to internal rottenness. He ascribed to nationalism a large part of the ill-success of the war. National vanity he saw as France's "Chinese wall" which had kept the country shut in and favored the "incubation of the germs which the Gallo-Roman plebs carried necessarily in its bosom" (101). The results were centralization, *étatisme,* bourgeois supremacy, corruption and incompetence, and finally disaster. It was an "ethnic fatality" that this should have been so, for "each race finds its food within the circle of its instincts and cannot find it elsewhere. Envy is essentially the malady of the Latin races"—hence their resistless march toward mobocracy. Gobineau inveighs against the increasing materialism and cynicism of the masses. *"On trouve charmant d'être des Français en décadence,"* he exclaims sardonically, and, "to the Parisians, the war of 1870 was a circus—the great passion of the Gallo-Roman mobs."

In his pacifism, too, Gobineau reflects faithfully the mind of the peasants who returned a monarchical Assembly in 1871 in order to have peace at any price. He asserts that after Sedan the

Germans showed no hatred against the French, but on the contrary a desire for peace. He denounces the insane propaganda and lies of the press and the false atrocity stories then current, as they were to be again in 1914.

Gobineau went further in his critique of nationalism and the government than did his contemporaries. But the feelings behind the strictures were the same. Gambetta himself, the republican patriot who carried on the war after Sedan, condemned the levity of the French. More than that, he assumed a race-theory parallel to that of the Count. He praised the Alsatians for energy and tenacity, racial qualities lacking in the French. Gambetta dare not call them Germanic qualities,[1] for the date, May 9, 1872, is too soon after the war. But if "our dear Alsace" was so necessary to French unity "and added invincible energy to French frivolity and nobility," what can it mean but that Gambetta adopts Gobineau's Nordic thesis? Like Gobineau, Gambetta ascribes his own republicanism to race and that race is the "Gallic or plebeian" race. But in Gambetta's eyes his race and his plebeian origin are "noble." He speaks of the "truly Gallic nature" of Hoche, the revolutionary general, which made him bear his trials with fortitude and serenity, and he says that instead of calling each other liars, traitors, and thieves, the Monarchists and Republicans should attribute the defeat of France to the might of Germany and not to internal weakness. In short, "German versus Gaul" serves once again to gloss over more fundamental antagonisms.

Another witness, Gustave Monod, who was later to be one of the great props of the republican regime as well as a distinguished historian and educator, corroborates those conclusions that Gobineau and Gambetta share in common. As a noncombatant hospital aide Monod could maintain his independence of mind, and his strictures on the "deplorable levity of the national character" confirm what we knew of the causes that doomed

[1] But Bismarck, offering flattery from the other side, praises the "Gallic warlike race of Alsace." (June 3, 1871.)

France to severe disillusionment. Though chary of generalities, he sees the German's respect for womanhood as "a national quality and a source of the strength of the German race." (*Allemands et Français,* 13.) Other contrasting characters of the Germanic race are its reforming zeal and scientific spirit, but he sees danger in the Germans' taking the French doctrine of war as an agent of civilization. The same swollen pride that ruined the French will ruin the Germans. Monod shows very clearly the origin of the French superstition about German "barbarism." At first in 1870, according to him, the French were pleased with the fancy of crossing the Rhine to pillage Germany, while they were treating their own peasants' persons and property on the whole worse than did the Germans; but when the French were finally defeated their fury vented itself in the form of lies about German atrocities, German savagery, and the violation of the soil. "The native vocabulary was not adequate to the fury of the patriots" (31). Toward the end of the war the French soldiers began to recognize their inferiority, but they had little influence on the great mass of noncombatants who were to shape the opinion and temper of the next generation.

What is known in France as the "generation of '70" consists of those born roughly between 1860 and 1880 and who came to consciousness in a troubled period of external and internal anxiety. Among them the patriotic racists of the period 1870-1914 were directly affected in their childhood or family environment by some aspect of the war. One witnessed the occupation of his native village by German troops; another vividly remembers the parade of the local soldiery leaving for the front. Many Alsace-Lorrainers were economically or psychologically injured by the German annexation of these provinces. Of France's future writers, Barrès, Bazin, Bordeaux, Juliette Lamber, Georges Dumesnil, Paul Déroulède, Edouard Schuré were among those whose racial antipathies were rooted in the unhealthy soil of war fever and postwar bitterness.

This historical aspect of their vituperative chauvinism consists in seeing the Germans as the perpetual invaders of France. France identifies herself mentally with Rome, so that the "crime" of invasion goes back to the so-called barbarian invasions, and the same process of identification makes the modern Germans nothing more than barbarians thinly veneered with civilization. In the words of René Lote, "German Kultur" is only an "enterprise against Latin civilization . . . Germany is a nation void of inventiveness, imitative, secretly afraid of being still a pupil, perhaps only a barbarian." (*Les relations Franco-allemandes,* 75.) Ernest Babelon, a scholar and a member of the French Institute, traces the whole history of the two nations with reference to this hypothesis of barbarism versus civilization. For him, world history hinges on the struggle of the two principles of Romanism and Germanism. For less systematic publicists and historians, such as Lasserre, Bainville, Faguet, Maurras, Le Goffic, Lavisse, and Gaillard; philosophers such as Bouglé, Boutroux, and Ernest Hello; novelists such as Bazin and Bourget; poets such as Mistral, Strada, and Sully-Prudhomme; politicians such as Déroulède, Barrès, Syveton, and Léon Bourgeois, the notion of France as the outpost of civilization beating back the barbarian race became a "fact," or rather an article of faith adhered to in the teeth of evidence. "One is a barbarian by birth," said François Combes at the University of Bordeaux in 1870. "Germany is always such to us who are the bulwark of the Latin races." (*Les Invasions,* 7.) Sixty years later Maurras was still harping on the same note. "The three historic centers of civilization are Athens, Rome, and Paris. All the rest are only satellites." (*Gauls, Germans, and Latins,* 1926, 30.) But whereas the racial basis of this belief consists for Maurras in the adjunction of Roman order to Celtic vigor and brilliancy, the racial components of culture differ widely in other writers. Adrien Mithouard, for example, thinks the region known as the Ile de France the cradle of what is truly French because it remained free of Roman influence.

However serviceable this creed of anti-barbarism, it presented difficulties which well-informed men, though prejudiced, were obliged to perceive. The Germans of the nineteenth century were not going about dressed in skins, living in huts, and plundering their neighbors for subsistence from day to day. Germany had an imposing cultural past. Mozart,[2] Beethoven, Lessing, Goethe, Schiller, could not be completely overlooked, except by ignorant or single-track minds. To this difficulty there were two solutions. One was to say that the greatness of these men is spurious, that German poetry "reeks of death and disease," and that Beethoven's music "arouses vague thoughts and harmful desires and corresponds to no reality." The other was to grant the genuineness of the art, but to demonstrate that it was due almost entirely to French influence. It was easy to pick out Goethe's French masters—he acknowledges them himself—and it was convenient to forget that he acknowledges other masters belonging to other nations including his own.

In any case, both solutions leave France, as the modern representative of the Latin race, the standard-bearer of civilization; the race-fictions justify alike a political and a cultural animosity against the unteachable barbarian. They also provide a neat device for reinterpreting history. The fifty-odd invasions of Germany by Gauls or French that occurred between the fifth century B.C. and the nineteenth century A.D., and especially the brutal devastations of the Thirty Years' War and the wars of Louis XIV are written off to the account of civilizing the barbarian, whereas corresponding irruptions of Franks into Gaul or Germans into France are simply primitive vandalism.

The full beauty of this system does not appear, however, until one perceives its utility for fighting home battles as well as external quarrels. By setting in opposition the Latin "classical" civilization against the barbarian, it is possible for this type of French nationalist to empty the vials of contempt upon the

[2] It is curious how infrequently Mozart is mentioned by French nationalist writers among German geniuses to be accounted for on racial grounds. Is this due to the French look and sound of his name, not quite a rhyme to *beaux-arts* nor to *musard,* but easily made "French" just the same?

cosmopolitan France of the eighteenth century, the Revolution which came out of it, and the Romanticist flowering of culture that followed the Revolution. Madame de Staël, Chateaubriand, Hugo, Berlioz, Michelet, and their contemporaries are stigmatized as un-French, "enamored of foreign literatures," and cosmopolitan in outlook. They are accused of treason for having abandoned the great classical tradition, and of misrepresentation for having admired products of German thought and art. Generally, their "racial descent" is investigated and their mothers, brothers, or aunts held responsible for their sins. It never occurs to the accusers that the "classical" tradition was also based on an infatuation for foreign literatures—the Latin and Italian; or that to admire the works of Kant and Schiller is not to make oneself an accessory before the fact to whatever "atrocities" may have occurred in the Franco-Prussian War. But the process of tribal identification, the hallmark of the racist, necessarily holds all the members of a group responsible for the acts of a part, and extends the group in space and time to include all the ancestors and possible descendants of the "alien race."

In view of the imperialistic rivalry which existed between France and England during the same period, it may be asked why the same rationalized animus did not develop. The answer is that it did in some quarters, at least until the definite alignment of France with England following the Fashoda incident of 1898. The "racial connection" between England and France through the Celts and Normans did much to allay the tender susceptibilities of French racial nationalists. Again and again, Shakespeare is adopted by the French writers as "one of our own Celts": it is the stock reply to the Germans' *"Unser Shakespeare."* Besides, the movement toward Pan-Saxonism had not yet reached its height in England. Although English opinion was preponderantly on the side of Prussia in the Franco-Prussian War, the sympathy rested not so much on a feeling of kinship with the Germans as on traditional disapproval of the Bonapartes and a present distaste for Napoleon III's diplomacy. The scholarly Saxonism of Carlyle and Freeman was not irrational enough to sway the multitudes to a blind Germanism. There was still too much knowledge in the historians' utterances, and it took the simpler slogans of a Cecil Rhodes to entrench the idea of "We Anglo-Saxons."

In Germany, Bismarck's policy tended after 1880 to the conciliation of the French, lest continued frustration lead to a war of revenge. In his willingness to allow France her proper sphere of influence, Bismarck used the accepted dogmas of race to indicate the basis for his leniency: "Thanks to a stronger mixture of German blood, the French people is the most powerful of Romance nations. Therefore it can claim a right to a position of leading civilizing power in the Romance world, as well as outside Europe. If France wants to extend her base of operations in accordance with her interests, she can count on our noninterference and even on our support, if we are not harmed thereby. Express our view that, in the impending appointment of General Cialdini to Paris, we see little to disturb us in this approach of Italy to France, but rather the natural expression of Romance relationship." (Dispatch to Hohenlohe, Apr. 8, 1880; *Grosse Politik,* III, 395-96.)

The official press that took its tone from the Chancellor was balanced by a group of anti-French publicists whose views and tempers are on the whole identical with those of the nationalists across the Rhine, save for the reversal of the adjectives French and German. An excellent collection of their beliefs and grievances was made in 1916—again for a belligerent purpose—by W. W. Whitelock and published under the title *Modern Germany*. One extract is enough to indicate the tenor of the whole: "Only by utterly disregarding the deep-lying differences in the Anglo-Saxon and the Latin conceptions of democracy and the strong aesthetic and temperamental differences between the Anglo-Saxon and Romance peoples, can one conceive of Western civilization as identical with the democratic ideal of freedom, progress and humanity. . . . Despite the German's yearning for the sunny South, the Northern Gothic germ is in his blood. . . . This explains the fundamental dissimilarities between the Germans and the Latin races. . . . This finds ample expression in the present Kultur war and in the minds of many forms the basis for the charges of barbarism." (Professor Ernst Troeltsch, 66, 80.)

Neither in France nor in Germany did the mutual antagonism attached to race-words meet with any obstruction. The liberals and radicals of both countries were too often suspected of disloyalty to their homeland for them to risk compromising their internal policies by tilting against the Protean myth of race. Too often, also, liberals and socialists harbored race-prejudices of another sort. The liberal sublimated his race-antagonisms by discriminating against individual artists or thinkers. The socialist, compelled to love his European brothers, indulged in animus against the yellow or black proletarian who competed unfairly against him ten thousand miles away by accepting lower wages and longer hours.

As for the mass of unthinking readers, the idea of race in their news-fed anti-Germanism or anti-Slavism acted as a comforting drug in a period of greater and greater insecurity. Herd-responses were organized by interested groups while economic, even more than political, frustation found a vent in the wholesale insulting of "enemy" nations. By providing an inherent, unchanging ground for contempt, race served better than any other notion to relieve the fury of impotence. This was especially true in France, where national weakness and isolation remained a psychological fact until the dawning of the Anglo-French entente in the new century. That sense of collective inferiority and its compensatory animus suggest an unmistakable resemblance to twentieth-century Nazi race-propaganda. What France needed after 1871 was what Germany yearned for after the humiliating Treaty of Versailles—reassurance about her own importance in the world and a flattering faith that should place her once more on good terms with herself. In 1871

Renan had urged France to strengthen the hatred of the Slav for the German, but the "natural affinity" of "Celts" and "Slavs" did not bear fruit till the Franco-Russian alliance of 1891. Meantime racial pride contributed to the success of General Boulanger's dictatorship movement in the eighties. As Drumont, the Jew-baiter, put it, "We want an imperator, a master, a leader, but he must first win a battle against Germany." (*La Fin d'un Monde,* 317.) In hatred there was the sensation of strength. The reactionary novelist Bourget, writing for the commemoration of the historian Fustel de Coulanges, testifies that the man's importance lay in "having taught us to shake off the yoke of German thought." He destroyed "the idea of the Gallo-Romans being enslaved by Germany" and provided a "reassuring doctrine" to the young men of the 1870 generation. The fact that Fustel aimed at being a "scientific" historian and arrived at his conclusions by a different route from that of his nationalistic readers did not embarrass Bourget and his compeers. The need for race-solidarity and race-hatred swept all scruples aside. "Foreign," "alien," "outsider," are the words of opprobrium that come up most often in the general literature of the period 1870-1914. Xenophobia animated the conservative and reactionary ranks in all countries, and to such a degree that it forced the liberals and radicals also to disavow "foreign" influences. The curious thing is that not only were foreign things foreign to these fanatics of all complexions, but the things of which they disapproved at home became necessarily foreign too. The Dreyfus Affair in France was, among other things, the dramatized and internal manifestation of all this "thinking."

III

Cornelius Herz is a foreigner, a cosmopolite of hostile race, of German origin, whom the accident of being born in France cannot make French.

—BARRÈS

DISAPPOINTED IN THEIR tribal desire for glory, disappointed in their personal desire for leadership in France, and also generously distressed at the mediocrity and corruption incidental to a democratic republic, many intelligent persons born between 1860 and 1880 formed around the turn of the century the various groups known as *L'Action Française, La Ligue de la Patrie Française, La Ligue des Patriotes, La Ligue Latino-slave,* and others. The same groups published newspapers: *La Cocarde, La Gazette de France, La Revue du Monde Latin,* and *L'Action Française* itself, which together employed the best talents for political propaganda among the nationalist, Catholic, conservative, and royalist elements. Despite their small numbers they influenced a considerable body of opinion and attracted within their orbits on the issue of nation and race many writers and intellectuals who did not accept their political programs.

The principal racial argument of this contingent was expressed by Charles Maurras, the prime mover of the *Action Française.* France, he maintained, is governed by four "foreign nations"—the Jews, the Protestants, the Freemasons, and the métèques (i.e., resident foreigners, whether naturalized or not). (*Enquête sur la Monarchie,* xxii.) The result is that "true Frenchmen are strangers in their own home." These men, "molded by twenty centuries of a life shared in common," are unlike any others in the world, even though Celtic, Roman, and Greek elements were fused in the formation of their race. "Twenty centuries of life in common" sounds a little suspect coming from a royalist strong on the caste idea, but let that pass. The important point is Maurras's belief that "France existed before the Franks" and that "the Gallo-Roman type is the starting point and explanation of the French type." (*Gauls, German, and Latins,* 7.) From this thesis it follows that any German, Jewish, or other foreign blood (save only the Greek) is inassimilable and harmful. For example, Maurras's friend the poet Moréas, whose real name was Papadiamantopoulous, is thoroughly French, being a Greek, and can be the restorer of the true French tradition in poetry, but Rousseau, being a Protestant and a "lunatic from Geneva" is manifestly un-French.

This juggling with race-epithets to cover up nearer hatreds was not new in France. Anatole France, discussing politics at the turn of the century, complained that anti-Semitism and race-prejudice were as old in France as the monarchy itself. (*Opinions Sociales,* 62, 113, 116; and *Pref. to Speeches of Prime Minister Combes,* v.) The undignified incidents that occurred at the inauguration of the statues of Renan at Tréguier and of Vercingetorix at Clermont-Ferrand show the wide range of the animosities involved, before, during, and after the Dreyfus Affair.

The Dreyfus Affair or, as it was and is still known in France, simply *the* Affair, exhibited the full force of race-hysteria that we have come to associate with Nazi Germany. The only difference was that in France the anti-Semitic, anti-foreign, anti-Protestant group was not in control of the government and therefore could not give full vent to its persecuting mania. Better than any demonstration, the Affair shows the split between the two Frances and its role as both cause and result. It was anti-republicanism that gave to the racial superstition its driving force, and it was the democratic and republican parties that first yielded, then rallied, and finally checked the threatened proscriptions. As usual in French politics, the conflict was made vivid by the clash of personalities. Dreyfus was the least of them, an accidental hero-victim in a drama whose plot began before the first act. Drumont, the versatile journalist who wrote *La France Juive* and *La Fin d'un Monde,* led the racial-minded ultra-nationalists, including Léon Daudet, Maurras, the Army, the Royalists, and many Catholics who for a time forgot the orthodox commandment of universal fraternity to indulge in the sin of vindictiveness. On the other side, the novelists Zola and Anatole France, the republican historians headed by Monod and Aulard, Clemenceau and all the radicals and liberals claiming descent from 1848 or from Gambetta, fought for the maintenance of the Third Republic and the Rights of Man.

The evenness of the contest prolonged the "atrocities" which, though not remarkably bloody, were none the less cruel. The Affair did more than show the fundamental rift in the nation, it extended it by reaching down into the smaller units of social life: friendships, marriages, families, partnerships—every conceivable human relation felt the pressure. Everybody had to take sides. The issues being complex and often incompatible with one another, the idea of race came to the rescue. The hesitant was jockeyed into partisanship with an expostulation: "You can't be for the Jews!" Or a reputation was settled with, "We no longer see him: he's a Protestant and a Freemason." Protestantism and Freemasonry were the result of race just as in our day Marxism and internationalism were taken in Nazi Germany as a sign of "blood."

In this French civil war which lasted from 1898 to 1906, the race-arguments followed the usual pattern of generalizing without regard for consistency, the plausibility arising not from the facts but from a convention about them. For example: (a) the ills of France were due to the Jews; (b) the Jews were all Germans and sold French military secrets to the land whence they had got their names of Stein, Meyer, Reinach; but (c) many of the ills of France were due to big finance; (d) all financiers were Jews and all Jews were financiers; they chose the business because it appealed to their unscrupulous tendencies, among which was (e) their lack of national loyalty to any people; their preference for their own racial kin across the borders; their insatiable lust for gain. Of course (f) the Jews were the cause of all social unrest for they were indolent paupers plotting in ghettos. (g) All socialists were Jews and all Jews were socialists; they were an unstable, emotional, and neurotic race (h) which explained their being artists, especially musicians, and professional men. (i) In their latter capacity they were devoid of feeling, over-intellectualized, dry and dialectical, whence their preference for finance and socialism.

When occasion required, these same beliefs were drawn upon to characterize Protestants, atheists, Freemasons, and foreigners. If a notorious example was advanced to disprove the supposed rule—for example, of a rapacious Catholic banker or a "pure-blooded" socialist—the racist interpreter was not in the least fazed: "Race speaks through the instincts, hence that Catholic must be a Jew; that socialist must be a foreigner," and with a shrewd look of supernatural wisdom, "I'll wager that if you went back far enough you'd find one of his ancestors, who, etc."

Evolution had supplied the word "atavism" and it did yeoman service on these occasions. Even a calm and just man like Anatole Leroy-Beaulieu, in a course of lectures delivered in 1902 at the Ecole des Hautes Etudes for the very purpose of abating the seething hatreds, could not resist the temptation to speak of the "atavistic survivals" causing the present-day struggles. He suggested that anti-Semitism and race-doctrines were "a Teutonic product." To be sure, he blamed Renan for his Aryan-Semite distinction and went on to analyze with true insight the interplay of passions and grievances that moved the clashing groups in France; but he failed to connect the two sets of facts, not seeing that to call race-prejudice a Teutonic product does not explain it away. Blaming Renan is quite just, but why did anti-Semitism spread in Germany and why was Renan led to elaborate his theory? The problem has only been pushed back one step. Leroy-Beaulieu tried to solve it by referring race to environment and adopting Taine's language. (*Doctrines de Haine,* 9; 12-13.) Better than these explanations is his picture of the intricacy of race-prejudices during the Affair:

"What does the anti-Semite say? He says: France is Aryan; France is Christian. Down with the Jews! Down with the Semitic spirit which denationalizes the French spirit and destroys national unity.

"What does the anti-Protestant say? He says: France is Latin, France is Catholic. Down with the Huguenots and Protestants; down with the Germanic or Genevese spirit which mars the French spirit and destroys its unity.

"Lastly, what does the anti-clerical say? He says: Modern France is a daughter of the Revolution and of Free thought. Down with Rome and the Jesuits, down with the clericals and reactionaries who dare oppose the France of the past to the new France, and who prevent the modern French spirit from building anew the spiritual unity of the nation" (285-86).

On top of this intensified nationalism couched in racial terms, the Affair had graver results: it bred the conviction that the internal difficulties of France were due to the treasonable practices of Frenchmen who had sold out to the enemy. *"Vendu à l'ennemi"* has been in modern France as terrible a phrase as the famous cry of "Outlaw" during the Revolutionary period. The former means ostracism as surely as the second meant death.[3] Gobineau in the seventies had already sarcastically deplored the French tradition of "crying treason." It is not exclusively a French trait, for it is the urge in every human individual to find some external cause for his faults in order to relieve himself of responsibility for them. In France, the solid citizens were confident that "if only the foreigners could be annihilated" the Garden of Eden would bloom anew on Gallic soil. A witness before the High Court that retried Dreyfus declared in all seriousness that "true Frenchmen were in a minority in France," a belief inciting to violence through its corollary that the true Frenchmen must exterminate the false, in the ancient style of civil war and proscription, which we know today as Hitlerism, totalitarianism, and the police state.

How Hitlerism antedates Hitler must be already apparent. A closer look at race-discussions in the Germany of William II will confirm that fact.

[3] In this regard see the career of Joseph Caillaux after 1912 when his policy of conciliation with Germany became suspect in the eyes of nationalists.

Chapter IX

RACE AND THE NATIONALISTIC WARS: 1900-1914

1

Degenerescence is a physiological term altogether incapable of measuring the psychological value of a people.

—RICHARD DEHMEL, 1904

THE COMBINATION OF racism, militarism, and cultural nationalism that our generation thinks a Nazi invention existed at least thirty years before, in Imperial Germany. Made up of disparate elements borrowed from other nations—abundantly from France, as has been shown, it owed much also to English thought and to Germany's own past. Just as French racism can be traced back to the Renaissance through Boulainvilliers, Hotman, and Bodin, so German racial pretensions of a political character can be found in Conring in the middle of the seventeenth century.[1] In each case, the germ is small compared to the ravages of the disease.

Misunderstood Romanticism furnished to modern Germans

[1] *De habitu corporum Germanicorum.* See also J. Barzun, *The French Race,* 59-84.

the same elements for building up an aggressive nationalism as it did to the French. Accordingly, Herder, Kant, and Goethe often appear in German racial literature as the august sponsors of a vulgar animus. Wagner, Nietzsche, Chamberlain,[2] Paul de Lagarde (the pseudonym of Paul Bötticher, 1827-91), and William II stand as the nearer masters, while Gobineau's lively ghost plays in and out of tune with the new German racial song of the turn of the century. Its burden may be examined in an anonymous pamphlet of considerable popularity published in 1904 and entitled *The Kaiser, Culture, and Art: Considerations on the future of the German people, from the Papers of an Irresponsible.* Not all racists are so self-conscious or so honest in describing themselves. This particular one turned out to be George Fuchs, an educated man and a capable writer, who significantly betrays the same lack of assurance about Germany that France was displaying about her own culture at the same time. Fuchs envies England and wishes that the German people had the same cultural unity as the English—"not on an intellectual but on a popular plane, a shaping force appropriate to the genius of the race. . . . The influence on the instincts of the *masses* which English culture undoubtedly exerts, although the Anglo-Saxon masses are on the average cruder and less educated than the German, depends rather on this, that *the same creative power of the Race* appears as the determining principle in all matters and functions" (9-10). Theodore Roosevelt earns Fuchs's praise for seeing that American*ism* must precede American power. The adaptation of that principle to Germany means but one thing: war is the purchase price of Culture (13). Hence no disarmament, no internationalism, no humanitarianism. Race-connection rests on Blood, not language or sentiment, and outside the narrow circle of race no sympathies can survive.

[2] The "renegade Englishman's" *Foundations of the Nineteenth Century* (1890-91) has been so often attacked and quoted from, and it is so largely a compilation of ideas from Gobineau, Wagner, Renan, Drumont, and Lapouge, that no new paraphrase seems called for here.

"The Huguenots would never have become completely German, they would have remained among us a foreign body, like the Jews, had there been no Frankish blood in their veins and no Celtic blood in ours" (24).

Fuchs, it is clear, repudiates the notion of a pure race; indeed, he points out that Gobineau's use of the term has been discredited by research. But this disclaimer is largely Pickwickian. Fuchs follows the Gobinian and philological argument in his handling of the Aryan, Celtic, and other race-questions that affect the history of Rome, the French Revolution, and the nineteenth century (31). Like Gobineau he is anti-liberal, antirevolutionary, anti-modern. He has nothing but contempt for the modern man who is "without Race and without culture"; he scorns the fruits of machine civilization—"the telephone, telegraph, water-closet, electric light and modern music" (35). This combination of antipathies will seem familiar to those who have read Hitler's views on art posted in every German theater and concert hall, or who recall his Party Day speeches at Nürnberg in 1933.

As Fuchs proceeds he becomes more and more symbolic and mystical in his explanation of the workings of race. Race becomes Rhythm and "culture is nothing more than the most headlong (*rücksichtsloseste*) application of the Rhythm of one's own people-hood in all things" (17). Some aliens, like the Mendelssohns, "have caught the rhythm of our blood and are true race-fellows" (42) but generally it is impossible to "break into the magic of blood-rhythm," of which culture is the expression.

Fuchs's admiration of William II leads him to consider the German army as the true type of modern culture, and he reminds us on page after page that "every culture is bought with blood." Words from Goethe are pulled out of context to support the assertion that the future of the German people is on the sea; whereby both branches of the service are awarded their cultural certificate (88-89).

Culture, in its narrow sense of fine art, Fuchs deals with in a fashion observers of Nazi Germany will recognize: art must elevate and encourage, not depress and criticize. Social and economic questions cannot be solved, except through racial-rhythmic order and culture. Hence Jewish art or indeed any disintegrating art must be prohibited. War against the Naturalistic school of writers and all un-German modernism is the order of the day, and the statesmanlike William II disdains no means of propaganda, including the theater, to achieve this end. Science, of course, is for Fuchs no more international than art, and he misquotes Liebig's famous saying that science is 99 percent art, to conclude that Berlin, as the center of scientific civilization, is the first city in the world.

Fuchs was no originator. All one has to do is to read Paris for Berlin, to substitute *instinct* for *rhythm,* keeping the omnibus word *blood,* in order to recognize in this popular treatise the nth sample of the old dogma. Not that the old dogma was ever one clear-cut idea. If after reading Fuchs one turns to Heinrich Driesmans's *Cultural History of the Race-Instincts,*[3] for example, one discovers that the beginning of modern decadence dates from Goethe, who was no creator but a weakling. "Goethe's poetic art is an art of decline and dissolution." (I, 15.) Since Goethe's death, as Victor Hehn observes, German art has seen "the Jewish epoch—witty, cynical, undramatic, impotent." The usual denunciation of mediocrity, utilitarianism, and materialism follows, in the most approved Gobinian style—though with a shift in racial qualities. In Gobineau, art arises only from the contact of two or more races. In Driesmans, despite some hedging on the point (II, vii-viii), the Aryans are self-sufficient, artistically as well as in other ways. "The real difference between the Aryan and Jewish peoples," says Driesmans, "is that the former have a sense of form and the latter have not." (I, 23.)

[3] Leipzig, 1898-1901, 3 vols.

In the history of race-doctrines Driesmans occupies the place of transition between Nietzsche, Darwin, and Gobineau, on the one hand, and Freud,[4] Spengler, and Nazism, on the other. The poet Heine, reacting against the puritanism of his co-religionists, had divided mankind into Jews and Hellenes, according to temperament and not according to birth. Matthew Arnold had followed suit and Nietzsche had used the terms "Dionysian" and "Apollonian" to separate the creative-passionate from the critical-rational. Spengler classifies natures and cultures into Faustian and Apollonian. Driesmans reverts to Heine's dichotomy and calls the ascetic, fanatical, and the puritan type, Nazarenes. They share the author's contempt with the "brainless Celts." The latter's conquest by the Franks, who were "German with something Asiatic in them," made of them "a people of acrobats, musicians, brokers, and comedians." (II, 10.) Historical examples are ready to hand: the rape of Helen shows a Semitic trait typical of Aryan-Semite relations, and on a nearby page Richelieu is maltreated for being a Gaul and a mountebank—the same Richelieu that Ludwig Woltmann, the "political anthropologist," was shortly to extol as a great German in a book full of similar discoveries, *The Germans in France*.

The desire to connect one's own race to the ancient Greeks, already seen in Maurras and other French self-praising racists, also moves Driesmans, who discovers in the Athenians a Nordic folk. Their racial hatred of the Spartans (puritanical Nazarenes) is a test of their superiority, as is the fact that they "gave an art-form to their acquired sensuality." Under Hitler the historians of culture changed their minds about the relative merits of sensuality and asceticism, but writing in 1904 Driesmans was still under the influence of Nietzsche.

Since France was the Celtic enemy to be feared, Driesmans eruditely reviewed French history on the lines that Boulainvilliers had laid down exactly two hundred years before—a

[4] See Driesmans, I, 176 ff., and II, vi, where art is shown as the sublimation of the sex-impulse.

witness to the enduring power of ideas. But the German overreaches himself in a piece of unconscious humor worth recording. Having just said apropos of Richelieu's "clowning" that the true German is serious (*ernsthaft*), he now wishes to claim some lighter virtues as well. "Irony," he says gravely, "self-mockery, are deep-grained Aryan and especially German traits." *"Solche Selbst-ironie ist arisch, urarisch."* (II, 22.) The Celts, having the faults of inferior persons, are a social menace. Their "mobility," sense of inferiority (and presumably lack of *urarisch Selbst-ironie*), make them revolutionaries, liberal and democratic anarchists. They are the makers of the modern destructive literature, notably of the socialist novel. Daudet (Père), Zola, and Maupassant are the counterparts of Racine and Corneille. No better proof of the Celtic-Nordic race-compound in the French people could be found than the significant type of tragicomedy produced by Molière and Maupassant. Shakespeare, on the other hand, was ever *"ein Germane von Grund aus . . . echt Sächsisch."* (II, 47-8.) Yet the capacity to give form to his inspiration and to become a great artist was not in his nature. Was this because "Saxon" betokens low-German or because Shakespeare was born in England? Driesmans tells us many things in his cultural history but not that; he merely asks rhetorically: "What dramatist or plastic artist has Low Germany, Holland, or England ever produced?"

The Germany of William II was willing to make the query a challenge to England and to extend it to France and Russia if need be. A handful of socialists and poets alone tried to go against the stream of official and national arrogance. The Kaiser himself subsidized Chamberlain's book for wide distribution, read Fuchs and Gobineau, and set the fashion of what might be called the scientifically justified pride of race.

II

Briand=Brandt.

—WOLTMANN

THE EMPERORS, politicians, and littérateurs who used race as a weapon in their private or public game during the era of nationalism had an easier time than their predecessors, for they did not have to rely on their own inventions or researches. The contemporary schools of thought furnished a ready-made article that, with a few alterations here and there, fitted almost as well as the previous custom-made doctrines. Among those schools of thought, two can be picked out as pre-eminent—anthroposociology and group-psychology.

The "science" of anthroposociology flourished in France, England, and Germany between the eighties and the First World War as still another movement of reaction against socialism and democracy. Its chief exponents were G. Vacher de Lapouge and Henri Muffang in France, Lucien Chalumeau in Switzerland, C. C. Closson in the United States, O. Ammon, L. Gumplowicz, and (with certain differences in politics) Ludwig Woltmann in Germany. The groundwork of the science was the familiar craniometry, and its superstructure was a mass of historical, aesthetic, and social judgments more or less ably propped up by the usual type of research. The anthroposociologists recognized Gobineau as their master, Darwin as their prophet, and Paul Broca as their mainstay.

From Gobineau they derived the idea that race explains all social and cultural phenomena; from Darwin they borrowed the notion that the natural selection of fit types ensures the continuance of the best possible race, despite the doubt that Darwin casts on the permanence of races and species. In point of fact, no doubts of any kind disturbed the anthroposociologists. They believed in evolution as well as in fixed races. They distinguished those races by skull-measurements, following the technique made familiar by Broca; and they arrived at a subdivision of the whites into three races: *Homo Europaeus,* dolichocephalic, tall, and blond—the "ideal Englishman"; *Homo Alpinus,* brachycephalic, shorter than *Homo Europaeus,* and dark—the Turk or Auvergnat; *Homo Mediterraneus,* dolichocephalic, of varying stature, and dark—the Neapolitan or Andalusian. The *Homo Europaeus* is of course the Aryan, who is the fated conqueror of all other races from earliest times. He is the pushing, active, brainy element that builds our modern industrial enterprises and creates our cities. Cranial statistics derived from city and country have a great importance for the anthroposociologists. Lapouge in Montpellier, Beddoe in England, Muffang in Northern France, Ammon in Baden, Nicolucci and Sergi in Italy, Broca and Collignon in Paris had assiduously gathered figures which were used to show that the city operated a natural selection upon the population by attracting to it all the energetic dolichos and leaving the brachys behind. The usual inaccuracy prevails in the use of the terms "dolicho" and "brachy." Ranging from 62 to 98, the indexes are grouped by each author according to his fancy. We find, for example, in Ammon[5] that in Milan the index 83.8 represents dolichocephalism compared to the country's 84.3; whereas in Freiburg and Karlsruhe 83.5 is the rural brachycephalic index opposed to 81.8-81.2 for the urban dolichos; and in the regions north, south, and east of Paris, the rural index averages between 82.6 and 83.1. The dolichos of one place are cranially identical with the brachys of another. The color of the hair plays a very secondary role in this complicated subject. Indeed, the "scientists" themselves were the first to discredit hair-pigmentation, chiefly because it upset their generalizations. Yet they were compelled to take note of it whenever they wished to differentiate an Aryan from a Mediterranean. This seesawing of opinion is only one of the wonders of the new science.

The sociological part of the discipline comes in with what the American practitioner, C. C. Closson, called Ammon's Law, though its elements are already found in Lapouge and in Gobineau. Stated in cranial terms, it asserts that the class struggle is nothing but an unconscious race-struggle between the Brachys—

[5] *Anthroposociol.*, 22 ff.

an old, conservative, pacific, and reflective people—and the Dolichos—new, restless, and adventurous. The outcome of the struggle is not in doubt, for as we know from earliest times the tall blonds are destined to own the world. In spite of this law, the anthroposociologists betray great anxiety lest that ownership be contested by the short brunets. To be sure, race is supreme and its effects are unavoidable, but . . . but we must do something quickly or the Unconquerable Race will be wiped off the face of the earth. So Lapouge fears that the "eugenics," the Aryan cream of the population, will be diluted out of existence; Ammon speaks gravely of a possible *Aryanendämmerung,* the twilight of the Aryans, which would come not from their individual but from their numerical weakness.

The same absurdities obtain in these writers' political views. That socialism and democracy should be their common enemies is no matter for surprise. The majority of educated men during the period were overwhelmed by disgust for the leveling down, the ugliness, and the confusion resulting from industrialism and political democracy, and these perceptions seemed to lead to only two alternatives—reaction or revolution. Revolution meant trying to organize, to educate, to abolish in a better system the formless and hopeless proletarian masses. Reaction could take many forms. In France Royalism was only one remedy; in Europe at large social Darwinism and anthroposociology were similar solutions. Both proclaimed the essential fitness of whatever survived. Yet the presence of natural forces regulating the social system did not seem to save it from revolutionary upheaval. Strangely enough, the brachys were accused by the anthroposociologists of being both an old conservative, unimaginative race of slaves and the chief makers of revolution. They were held to be feeble individualists anxious for a paternalistic state that would relieve them of responsibility while robbing them of freedom. And to achieve it they would upset the present order. Hence it is logical that Ammon should admire Bismarck for his anti-socialist legislation, but how can he condone his paternalism? Carlyle's neo-feudalism commends itself to the anthroposociologists because it requires an aristocracy of birth, and Darwin's free-for-all state of nature, seen through Herbert Spencer's eyeglass, is their ideal society; but still they complain of the staying power of the brachys, of their assimilation and weakening of the dolichos. Moreover, the name of the revolutionist race varies at every turn. Driesmans blames the Celto-Mongols, Chamberlain the Jews, Lapouge the *Homo Alpinus*. That same revolutionist race is praised by Woltmann as pure German, but if we look on Deniker's map, the *Homo Alpinus* is the reactionary Breton, the Chouan of La Vendée who fought for God and King in 1793.

The reader may be excused for losing the thread of the argument, wondering just what these race-ridden "scientists" really mean and want. That no talent should be wasted is no doubt one of their noblest aims, but their suggestions for securing that end are absurd. Is not democracy one form of the free-for-all that they advocate? Ammon calls mathematics to his aid and demonstrates by the law of combinations that if in respect of any human faculty the best is twelve times superior to the poorest, and if eight faculty-groups are involved in the individual make-up, then there is only one superior man among 429,981, 686 people. Fascinated by this exact figure, Ammon overlooks the improbable consequence that there would be only 3.5 "superior" men existing in the world. He argues further that the availability of qualities in men is even rarer than his figures allow, for the chance of many great gifts concurring in the same person is much less. The formula, we should be glad to know, is: $y=Yh^2x^2$, and we are referred to Galton—a comparative racist of the Spencerian school—for the comforting thought that no true genius is misappreciated, genius being what survives and flourishes in a Darwinian world. To make a practical use of these computations, according to Ammon, is simple: the vote ought to be given according to the probable occurrence of genius; less cryptically put, nine million moderately gifted Germans should be empowered to select 400 men out of the best 2,728. It ought not, says this new Lycurgus, to be difficult.

When it comes to historical retrospects, the anthroposociologists are subject to the usual infirmities of the historians and politicians. The anthroposociological use of Celt, Gaul, Aryan, and Frank continues arbitrary and serves to prove points which jibe with no later or earlier generalizations. For Ammon the French Gauls are dolicho Aryans and the French Celts are a branch of the Aryan race and therefore dolichocephalic (*Ibid.,* 31 n.). In Southern France, he tells us elsewhere, the dolicho element comes from the Aryan Franks, Burgundians, and Celts, and not from the Mediterranean race, which is also dolichocephalic but not so tall and quite dark (22). The rest of Europe is similarly peopled out of hand by our author, who relies now on Beddoe, now on Lapouge, now on Houzé, without seeing that a compilation of originally inconsistent nomenclatures can only give a medley of futile assertions.

Nevertheless, the "results" obtained by anthroposociology permeated the contemporary literature of social philosophy. All but two or three[6] of the "pure" anthropologists accepted the work of Ammon and Lapouge. It was favorably reviewed in the leading scientific and other journals. The non-anthropological sociologists, Tarde, Durkheim, and Fouillée, used their results. In the one year 1896 no less than thirty works on, or of, anthroposociology appeared in Paris. (*Rev. Ec. Anthrop.,* 1899, 250.) The doctrine, being completely elastic, served everybody. For example, it was urged against feminism that women and children are more dolichocephalic than men. Hence the inadvisability of woman suffrage, on the ground that since apes and Negroes are dolicho the possession of a long skull shows an "atavism" to savagery. (*Fouillée, Psych.,* 124.) Against urbanization, protective tariffs, and socialization; against philanthropy, pacifism, and a conciliatory diplomacy; against modern

[6] Principally Virchow, Manouvrier, and Quatrefages.

art and exotic art (Negro and Japanese), the certitudes of anthroposociology were good ammunition.

At the same time, the intricacies of anthroposociology repelled a good many general readers, who went to other sources for the satisfaction of the same emotional needs. Several schools of sociology competed for public assent, among them the *Science Sociale* expounded by the Anglomaniacs Henri de Tourville and Edmond Demolins; and the psychological sociology of Gabriel Tarde and Gustave LeBon. Tarde's system, the most popular in France and Europe around 1900, represents a compromise method of dealing with the race-doctrine. As an expert in mass psychology, Tarde was inclined to accept the idea of race for the group and to deny it for the individual. According to him, Gobineau, Taine, Renan, Ammon, and Lapouge have been right to stress the importance of race, but they have misunderstood its function. (*Grande Revue,* Nov. 1, 1900.) Their "profound views are misapplied when they seek to define the mental limits of the individual by his physiological type or to predict the possibilities of the group: "They believed there was a narrow path of opportunities for each race, whereas these are on the contrary infinite; they confused the incapacity of certain races to invent with that of adapting the inventions of others. The awakening of the Far East has disproved this narrow belief." (*Ibid.,* 321.)

Tarde combats Lapouge and Ammon in the dolicho-brachy realm by citing examples, a method that always leaves the opposition unscathed, for all examples can be discounted as exceptions or simply challenged in point of fact. But Tarde shows no desire to dispute race as an overlay upon the facts, as a superstition. Between the extremes of cold and warm climate, he believes, there is for each race a point of highest impressionability of minds. Race and stature are factors in "sociability," and the resulting "inter-mental" action, so important in explaining social phenomena, is therefore "a function of the race-constant" (305 ff.). Despite his inability to correlate genius with "purity of blood," he asserts that "the Latins are less patient, though better artisans than the Anglo-Saxons" (328). In other words, the habit of race-thinking persists under his verbal casting-off. Race appears again in his notion that certain groups of men are inventive and others imitative, as if the quality were an ingredient always to be found in stated quantity in particular places, and some men were inventive in all they do, never imitative. In truth, Tarde's judgments on the Far East and the Latins and Anglo-Saxons shows that he is engaged simply in erecting recent history into axioms: Japan gets westernized—clearly an imitative race; England exports more pig iron than the rest of the world, quite so: the Anglo-Saxons are a patient race; France still leads in handicraft and luxury products, no wonder: the Latins are such fine artisans (327-30).

On the whole, Tarde winds up as an internationalist. The "families of the great Aryan race" show a wide diversity of talents and achievements, but they have all done their bit. "The locomotive is the handiwork of all the human races together." He advocates a European entente, else there will be a torrent of blood, which will overwhelm conquerors and conquered in one ultimate destruction. Plenty of "races of prey" still exist, so let selection make for balance and diversity, not uniformity of type.

Not long after this pronouncement, in May, 1901, Tarde spoke at Bordeaux on the mooted decadence of the Latin races.[7] The air was heavy with suspicion of English hegemony and remembered hate of Germany's "crime of 1870." Tarde reviewed and refuted the usual alarmist accounts of Latin inferiority: Catholicism, communalism, classical studies, backward industry, and racial blood-mixture. He cheered up the "Latins" assembled before him by telling them that their individualistic military genius would surely triumph in a war with organized masses, and added in the next breath that encroaching socialism would be more favorable than its opposite

[7] *Sur la Prétendue décadence des races latines.*

to the ever-revolutionary Latin temperament. He foresaw decisive conflict in Asia and Africa to settle "whether the Germanic or the Latin genius will put its seal upon the world," and he opined that these two great races would continue to alternate in shaping the history of the world as they had done in the past.

These reassurances, which Guizot or Victor Hugo might have subscribed to eighty years earlier, show that the march of mind on certain questions resembles operatic marches: much tramping and no advance. The reason in this instance is clear. Tarde was really making a political speech at a moment of national crisis, a speech intended to counteract reactionary alarms and to allay national fears by boosting, as Renan had done thirty years before, the French alliance with the "Russian colossus."

Tarde's rival for influence on the prewar generation was Gustave LeBon, whose *Lois psychologiques de l'évolution des peuples* (1894) was in its fourteenth edition in 1919. To LeBon race is the substratum of history, and success is the Darwinian measure of racial superiority. He admires the Anglo-Saxon, whose "strength of character enables a bare 60,000 of them to keep under the yoke 250 million Hindus, many of whom are at least their equals intellectually, and some of whom surpass them immensely in artistic taste and depth of philosophical insight" (59). LeBon, who had started as a craniologist, was convinced that the Latin blood was decadent; but that the mixture of races and the part played in modern democracies by the crowd had more to do with the course of national history than pure race. Yet when war came, his earlier reservations fell away from him and he spoke with all the authority of age and learning on the "ethnic hatreds" and the "too many mental differences that keep certain races from understanding each other. Man belongs first of all to a race, and the barbarian cannot get rid of his mentality." (*Premières conséq. de la guerre,* 2, 5, 11, 15.)

These statements represented no very great change of mind to one who had been used to describing the evolution of peoples as if nations were solid geological strata. In other words, despite his earlier disclaimers and distinctions, LeBon was like the rest a habitual race-thinker. For it cannot be too often repeated that it is the *form* of race-thinking and not the contents of a given theory that makes it the superstition which is the object of this study. Before seeing in the copious war literature the most varied contents poured into that same mold, one more tendency of the early 1900's must be briefly recapitulated, for it spurred on or rationalized the particular alignment of nations that fought the war of 1914: the Anglo-French entente was preceded in France by a wave of Anglomania.

Between 1870 and 1900 the feeling of inferiority of the "Latins" was so acute that toward the end of that period the question was no longer whether but *why* they were inferior to the Anglo-Saxons. The writings of Edmond Demolins and of the group that rallied around the *Science Sociale* movement gave the answer by preaching economic and political liberalism and education *à l'anglaise*. This propaganda paraded as usual under the banner of a new science; Demolins's conclusions were "social chemistry." Since 1789, he said, France had been ruined by an ever-increasing state paternalism. No independence, initiative, or freedom of action was possible under the French school and governmental systems. Together they had made the race timid, sheeplike, indolent—and the Anglo-Saxon had won the world away from her. Demolins's criterion of greatness was colonial power and his panacea the establishment of boys' schools with compulsory cricket and rugby.[8]

His criticisms actually echoed the widespread dissatisfaction of the French with their government and their school system. Matthew Arnold might admire French secondary schools and urge the English to study them as a model, but to a part of the French elite the system seemed antiquated, narrow, unpractical, and destructive of imagination. With the disaffection felt by half

[8] The famous *Ecole des Roches* was founded by Demolins to put his theory into practice.

of France toward the Third Republic Demolins and his group had a natural affinity. Their propaganda offered as social science, with tables, footnotes, and historical parallels of doubtful accuracy, was very convincing to readers already in agreement with the conclusions.

Demolins's use of race goes with his division of all peoples into communal-minded and individual-minded. At times he "explains" that difference by climate and geography in the classic manner; elsewhere the communal weakness is simply Celtic; in still other places, the governmental structure is to blame. Demolins is a malcontent who is not quite sure where the shoe pinches, who would like to try going barefoot but is not certain that an amputation of the legs is not the real solution. But about *the* Anglo-Saxon, Demolins, who has seen him under happy circumstances in England, is quite sure. The Anglo-Saxon is the Englishman of the middle and upper classes, the far-flung colonizer, and also, apparently, every citizen of the United States, excepting the Irish, who are communal Celts. Demolins sees the rugged individualism of this "type" without seeing its ragged counterpart. No slums, no misery, no economic struggle come into Demolins's picture. Only the successful Anglo-Saxon "Struggle-for-lifers" whom the Latins must acknowledge as masters can serve as pattern for modern man. That paragon is a familiar figure in the pages of Kipling. He possesses the advantage of a public school education, a sojourn in India, county connections, a turn for machinery, and an ideal domestic life. Obviously, Demolins's romancing about the Anglo-Saxon is dictated by his displeasure with France. Germany he dismisses with the remark that the Prussians are a half-Oriental people and that socialism and militarism will take care of the German menace by undermining the nation. France need not fear the other side of the Rhine, it is the other side of the Channel that spells decline to the French unless they copy their natural superiors.

How the "Latins" came to ally themselves with the "Anglo-

Saxons" against the "Teutons" is a subject that touches racism at only one point, namely, where Latin decadence ceased to exist by the magic of military understandings with England, Russia, and Italy. Anglomania of the *Science Sociale* brand was ready to clasp as blood brothers the superior race on whom the Latins should model themselves, and the union was made easier by the loss of some English prestige in the Boer War. Sergi, Ferrero, and more sanely, Colajanni, reveal the relation of Italy to this racial and national maneuvering. Similarly, the division within each nation between the superior Aryan and the revolutionary brachycephalic could be healed over by an appeal to Gallo-Roman unity against the irreducible barbaric race—*La Nation contre la Race,* as Suarès put it in 1916. The English were again taken aboard as Celts, and race-convictions survived unscathed the mental chaos of the four years 1914-18.

III

Fling down thy gauntlet to the Huns
And roar the challenge from thy guns.

—HENRY TIMROD,
Ode to Carolina, 1862

For all we have and are,
For all our children's fate,
Stand up and meet the war,
The Hun is at the gate!

—KIPLING, 1914

FOR PEOPLE WHO had been measuring skulls and scanning features as a means of discovering the alien race, the War of Nations must have been an especially severe blow. Race and Nation had never been wholly comfortable in each other's company, mainly because internal politics split nations in half while race united people living under different flags. Hence the Sacred Union which was invoked to bind together in every warring nation the socialists, the Jews, the round-skulls, and the other "inferior" types, split all the supposed races at the frontier and called for a revaluation of all the race-values.

Fortunately, the shock of mobilization, despite all the previous talk of war, was so great that the rearrangement of race-ideas was swift and smooth. Only as regards England and Germany did the reversal of commonplace beliefs bring pause to some. H. W. Nevinson writing from Berlin in August, 1914, wistfully described the regiments going to the front: "Finely-built and well-trained fellows they are, of a stock so much like our own at its best." (*Daily News,* Aug. 10, 1914.) At that point, in England and America, Russia rather than Germany was seen as the destroyer of civilization, and the pan-Saxon, anti-Slav idea of Rhodes and Kipling died hard.

No such regrets were felt between Germany and Russia or Germany and France. The course of racial propaganda in these countries precluded even cultural amity, and the intellectuals on all sides lost no time before insulting each other over the frontiers. In the Tsar's empire, five decades of strife on the question of westernization had ingrained the notion of an inviolable "Russian soul" which no other people could comprehend or combine with. The novels of Tolstoy and Dostoevsky reinforced the idea, and the great drive toward pan-Slavism inflamed the Russians and the Balkan nations to racial hatred of both the Germans and the subject nationalities within Russia.

In Germany, the belief in Russian barbarism was as strong as was in France the belief in German barbarism. To the French, the Germans were an Oriental people—Mongols, said Suarès,[9] adding, "Bismarck and Li Hung Chang are a pair of old twins." (*La Nation contre la Race,* 1916, I, 105.) Against France, Germany had ready to hand all the anti-French, anti-Celtic, anti-Latin writings of Chamberlain, Bötticher, Gobineau, Wagner, and others. These matched the accusation of German barbarism

[9] The pseudonym of Yves Scantrel, a cultured and sensitive critic, whose works command to this day the admiration of a choice following.

with the counteraccusation of French frivolity, sensuality, and decadence. Germany gloried in barbarism as strength and youthful vigor, and felt superiority in possessing science and discipline, which the French attacked as materialism and lack of imagination. For trained publicists it was not difficult to make virtues and vices change with each new situation. When Italy threw in her lot with the Allies, there was an abrupt cessation of Italian boasts that Northern Italy was Germanic as far back as the Lombards, and the French pressed to their bosom another Latin sister. The war of words accompanied every phase of the death-struggle—Magyars, Rumanians, Serbs, Kurds, Turks—all nationalities and would-be nationalities used race-slogans to maintain anger at fever heat. A detailed survey of this brawling would be equally tedious and useless, since wartime racism is only an intensification of the normal thing and can easily be appreciated from typical fragments. The pattern of noncombatant behavior during nationalistic wars, first standardized in France in 1870, was improved upon in 1914 and extended to all the belligerents.

In general, England and France came together to condemn the German race by adopting one mode of thought compatible with their own differences of race. Among the high-class professional men of the allied countries, the "necessary lying" took the form of writing histories about the enemy nation to prove that *German* (no longer Anglo-Saxon or Nordic) art, manners, and morals revealed a brutish and barbaric race.

It was repeatedly asserted that the philosophy congenital to the Germans was the glorification of the ego and the justification of force. Kant, Fichte, Hegel, and Nietzsche were the exemplars of this mode of thought and Bismarck was indignantly condemned for giving it practical application. This condemnation by France would have had a great deal more weight had the same writers not simultaneously extolled Napoleon, Stendhal, and Barrès—all proponents of the cult of energy and sacred egoism—and if they had not shown gratitude to Richelieu and

Sully for their policy of "ruining Germany." "Naïve" is no word for the discovery that Frederick the Great was a liar and a land-grabber, and "disingenuous" rises to the lips when it is assumed that government and conquest had been a courteous parlor game until the German race took a hand in it, centuries after the glorious Gallo-Roman tradition which includes Caesar, Machiavelli, and Talleyrand. English historians should have known better, but they did not refrain from chorusing the same opinions compounded of race-fictions and national hatred. With few exceptions, the publicists and readers who had accepted Cecil Rhodes's mystic imperialism that was "of Race and not of Empire" and who had approved the grant of fifteen Rhodes scholarships to Germany "for the peace of the world," now accepted with complacent indignation the "historical fact" that "the Germans are still what they were fifteen centuries ago, the barbarians who raided our ancestors, and destroyed the civilization of the Roman Empire." (A. H. Sayce, London *Times,* Dec. 22, 1914.) "Our ancestors" had suddenly changed from the Saxon raiders of Kemble, Green, and Stubbs to their formerly despised victims.

In treating of art, the same blindness served the same purpose. People worried whether "Leibniz, Goethe and other German geniuses were more human than German or more German than human. It is from this point of view that it is not a matter of indifference to find out what race Beethoven belongs to." (Maurras, *L'art Français et les barbares,* 85.) Such childishness can be laid to the account of wartime panic, but it must not be forgotten that the words carried meaning and satisfied emotions because they called up familiar ideas. Repetition diminishes strangeness and what we recognize we accept without question because it is already a part of ourselves. By being drilled into thinking for nearly a hundred years that the Germans were a barbaric race, the French in the end came to believe in the reality of racial abstractions. And these were eagerly borrowed by the English to replace their no longer tenable forms of the same superstition. At the same time, for some the sudden shock of abstract hate turning real caused dismay. *"On croyait se connaître!"* cried René Lote querulously. Behold! The catastrophic events so often predicted had come to pass.

Understanding was not promoted then or for the future by the torrent of publications that issued from French, German, and English presses on the race and Kultur of the enemy. The popularity of these obscurantist compilations is perhaps one of the worst results of war hysteria, for it inevitably lowers the standard of intellectual honesty by substituting for it a standard of political utility that is irrelevant and inimical to culture.

Still, it would be wrong to suppose that hatred was the only motive behind so much bad writing. There were many who wished to ennoble the conflict and make it something more than the traditional quarrel between France and Germany. For those, the Allies represented the civilized West and Central Europe the amorphous East. As Easterners, the Germans were Mongols; when the Bulgarians joined the Central Powers, they became Mongols, too, and the Yellow Peril became explicitly identical with the German peril and the socialist peril. The author of these suggestions, André Suarès, was by no means an isolated voice. His views were echoed or paralleled by such notables as Claude Farrère, Bergson, Babelon, Massis, Bainville, Allier, Louis Bertrand, Barre, Barrès, Bordeaux, Broermann, Dimier, Jean Finot,[10] Gaston Gaillard, C. Jullian, LeBon, Lange, Lavisse, Mauclair, Muret, Mithouard, F. Masson, Picot, Julien Rovère, Seillière, Schuré, and Spiess. Incomplete as it is, the list suggests the diversity of tendencies united behind the broad range of anti-Germanism during the war.

What emerges pathetically from the articles, pamphlets, and books by these writers is the yearning for some kind of idealism

[10] The author of an earlier book against race-prejudice, Jean Finot contradicted many of his previous assertions in *Civilisés contre Allemands,* 1915.

to cover the appalling reality of the struggle. That is what Suarès is seeking for when he distinguishes the French nation from the German race, "Race is matter, nation is spirit." (*La Nation contre la Race,* I, 15.) This idea was perhaps difficult to popularize in just these words. In practice it proved easier simply to identify the Allies with civilization in the usual manner, or to contrast Celtic goodness (despite the Celts' human sacrifices) with the harsh cult of Thor and Wodin. The cruelty of the East was often mentioned, but it had to be qualified in order to allow for the presence of Russia on the side of the Allies. At that point "Celticism shakes hands with the Slavic soul above the oppressive pan-Germanism." (Schuré, *L'âme celtique,* xvi.) Or else East and West are reversed, as in Marc Saunier's *Origines secrètes de la guerre,* where the conflict turns out to be the struggle between the pacific Hindu (Aryan) civilization and the crude habits of the Celts (Germans). (*Revue Hebdomadaire,* July 27, 1918, 454 n.) For many, including the diplomat Gérard and the anthropologist Perrier, the War was the "reawakening of the Latin races" after a period of eclipse at the hands of Germanism (*Revue Hebdomadaire,* Nov. 4, 1916, 7; 29-46); while for one casuistical disciple of Gobineau, the War was a conflict between the True Germanism of France and the barbaric Teutonism of Germany. (Spiess, *Impérialismes,* 1917, x.)

The preoccupation with the national and cultural aspects of race during the War might be thought to have killed all interest in the "science" of race. To a certain extent this is true, though Suarès, Sageret, and others still argued the question of skulls and the color of Goethe's hair. (Suarès, I, 101.) It was left once more to French genius to discover under the pressure of emergency a new application of "science" to race-discrimination. This discovery, made by one Dr. Edgar Bérillon, is recorded in the Bulletin of the Society of Medicine of Paris (June 25, 1915) and expanded in the reports of the French Association for the Advancement of Science (Feb. 4, 1917). Incredulity on reading it must yield to authority. Besides being published by these journals, Dr. Bérillon occupied important medical positions and was officially subsidized to lecture all over France on the subject of his researches. His discovery is that the German race suffers from polychesia (excessive defecation) and bromidrosis (body odor). These diseases are the result of intemperance and lead to degenerescence and unnatural crimes. Their advantage to the enemy in wartime is that they serve to detect infallibly the spies of German race masquerading in France as Alsatians. By means of these criteria the doctor was able to discover such a spy in his own service and to bring him to book. The doctor confirmed his views by urinalysis which led to the further discovery that German urine contains 20 percent non-uric nitrogen as against 15 percent for other races. Moreover, the large intestine of the German race is about nine feet longer than normal, a test that unfortunately requires an autopsy. When any of these abnormalities and diseases occur in France, they are generally found to accompany a German cast of countenance.

The physician, whose ideas have not been followed up since the War but whose methods are characteristic, combined them with the well-established systems of race-thinking. The War occurred, said he, because the true Germans are blond dolichos, whereas the leaders in France, England, and Italy are brachycephalic. "In other words, it is the age-old struggle of the Celts and Germans." (*Assoc. Fçse. Avanc. Sci.,* Feb. 4, 1917, 11.) Since Bérillon believed that "race is not an idea of the mind, but an entity" and that among races there is superiority and degenerescence, he suggested the establishment of a new science called ethnochemistry, for he was sure that "chemically and physiologically there is more difference between the French and the Germans than between a Senegalese and a Zulu." A blood-count might provide good criteria, since French blood "is superior in point of globular richness." (*Ibid.,* 26, 27.)

The date of this theory is not so remote as to warrant a condescending smile. It was only a matter of a few years before science reached the official (though temporary) faith in blood-testing established in national institutes and eugenic clinics under Hitler's Ministry of Public Enlightenment.

Chapter X

RACISM BETWEEN THE WARS

1

Lastly we have learnt something that I shall mention straight out: the ability to hate. Whoever cannot hate is not a Man, and History is made by Men.

—SPENGLER on the Political Duties of German Youth, 1924

THE VIOLENT USE of race-thinking in Nazi Germany has obscured and confused more truths than the obvious ones visible on the surface. In the first place, as the previous chapters have tried to show, race-thinking is more universal and deep-seated than any one doctrine of race, however fanatical its proponents. But in addition it is a mistake to think that the German leaders invented any part of their race-system. It is a mistake to think that they forced it upon an educated elite to whom the notion of race was new and repellent. Finally, it is a mistake to think that Nazi Germany adopted a single and consistent race-creed. At least three divergent race-beliefs, all built on ideas antedating the advent of the Nazis to power, inspired the vast literature on race that Germany read under Hitler. The first is the anti-Semitic, anti-Marxist prejudice of the nineteenth-century pro-Aryans. It was the official dogma because of its obvious political utility. Caught up in it were the culturally convenient Nordic

Myth and a mixture of puritanism and pagan religiosity. The second race doctrine was a compound of natural science, philology, and historiography. It was also official but not practical (although required for study in the schools[1]), for it found six European races present in Germany, difficult to differentiate and not determinant of special political views. The third official system was part of the propaganda emanating from the Ministry of Agriculture. It was designed to make the peasants proud of their race and more productive. It denied most of the postulates of the Nordic hero-worship and exalted the racial virtues of tenacity and endurance at the expense of the warlike and adventurous. Its chief proponent was Walther Darré and its practical intention is self-evident.

In the first (Aryan-Nordic) stream of thought, many elements mingled which were best summed up in Alfred Rosenberg's *Mythus der* 20*ten Jahrhunderts* (1920). A popular idealism, grounded in all the self-sacrificing impulses, was appealed to for the establishment of a "complete culture." Every trait or quality that could possibly help Germany as a nation in her precarious postwar condition was glorified as the exclusive appanage of the *Nordisch-deutscher*. A verbose mysticism clung to the Soul of the Race, the Unity of Being, and the Racial Ideal of Beauty. The diverse origins of these uplifting ideas were recognized by the makers of the *Mythus*. A. Moeller van den Bruck (1876-1925), the coiner of the phrase *Third Reich* and a devotee of Prussian racial superiority, was, together with Julius Langbehn,[2] the chief immediate forerunner. The older ones are Gobineau, Nietzsche, Chamberlain, and Paul de Lagarde.[3]

[1] It is required in all teaching establishments, regardless of the subject taught. For example, the Mary Wigman School of the Dance in Dresden had to examine all candidates for diplomas, whether they were Germans or foreigners, in the *Rassenkunde des deutschen Volkes*.

[2] The author of *Rembrandt as Educator* (1913), a cultural and racial critique of prewar socialism modeled after Nietzsche's *Schopenhauer as Educator*.

[3] On Lagarde, Langbehn, and van den Bruck, see Fritz Stern, *The Politics of Cultural Despair*, Berkeley, 1961.

To be sure, the popular idealism just referred to does not go very well with the aristocratic ideas of these earlier men, but in its literature National Socialism was, for domestic purposes, social, popular, democratic. In its external relations, the whole people claims superiority over all others: each democrat is an aristocrat. Such is the marvel of race: it is a common ground for national cooperation and cultural autarky, and also an inexhaustible source of pride.

Again, the mystical inalienability of race does not comport with the clumsy practices of "race-hygiene," but the two were forced to exist side by side. It was propaganda and not race-instinct that made German women for a time stop smoking and powdering, though theory said that blood expresses itself as much in behavior as in art.

Behind the anti-Marxist side of Aryanism there were of course the scattered hints to be found in Gobineau. Hence it was appropriate to find these expanded in a life of him by Franz Hahne dated 1924. Hahne called for a high-minded Führer who, "raising himself above the Marxist Party clichés, will know how to create an order without harm to the economic needs and necessities of the times and who will satisfy the majority." (*Gobineau, Ein Lebensbild,* 72.) Gobinism and satisfying the majority are strangely mated here, but they aptly illustrate the simple purpose and twisted scholarship of Nazi racism.

Hahne was also concerned with the pre-eminence of the tall blonds, but he did not say how it should be secured. That was the task of the hygienists. The social science of eugenics also was an old idea. It goes back to the theorizings of Ammon, Muffang, and Vacher de Lapouge, who in the nineties had talked knowingly of social selection. Alfred Ploetz then invented the term "Race-Hygiene," and other German writers subsequently attempted to give it practical meaning. Ranging all the way from public health and baby-prizes to the sterilization or extermination of one's opponents, the word covers many intentions, most of them tyrannical or fraudulent. The literal notion of "blood-testing" to determine race, which was tried for a time by the many race-hygiene museums and institutes for biological research in Germany, was finally repudiated by Professor Leffler of the Racial-Political Bureau. The question usually arose out of the "problem" of blood transfusions between "Aryans" and "Semites." Before the official pronouncement, "Semitic" doctors were reported to have been penalized or sent to concentration camps for using their own blood to save an "Aryan" patient. The theory of such punishments rested on a mental confusion due, in the words of Dr. Leffler, "to the figurative use of the word 'blood' in the sense of heredity." (*N.Y. Times,* Oct. 20, 1935.)

As for the descriptive account of the various races that form the German people, Dr. Hans F. K. Günther, Professor of Social Anthropology at Jena, had a virtual monopoly of the books presenting these facts. He did not abuse the privilege that monopoly confers. One could buy, according to one's purse, a large Günther in two volumes, several sizes of smaller ones in a single volume, an abstract of fifty pages, and even an outline of sixteen pages for a few pfennigs. Günther's six races were the Nordic, Westic, Ostic (Alpine), Dinarian, East Baltic, and Falic. They were sharply distinguished by the comparison of fifteen characteristics ranging from stature to carriage, which latter may be quiet, stiff, lively, or controlled. The Jews were described as "not belonging to the German people" but they were not a race so much as a people composed of several races. However, "a certain something, difficult to describe, is common to almost all Jews." (*Kurzer Abriss,* 5-6.) After this almost tolerant account—which would prove once more, if there were need, that two official race-doctrines can coexist despite flagrant contradictions—the author gave a full historical, psychological, and cultural explication of each of his six races, and concluded that the German people has particularly cherished and manifested the Nordic blood-heritage, at no time more so than in the New Germany.

The Minister of Agriculture, Walther Darré, was, despite his French name, an ardent Nordicist, though of a peculiar cast. He saw Nordics wherever he found the admirable qualities of the husbandman; for instance, if Plutarch may be trusted, Cato was a Nordic. Although Darré made no pretense at writing scientific works, he took issue with Dr. Kynast and other German racists who thought that only warlike noblemen could be Nordic heroes. On the contrary, said Darré, the peasantry is the key to the understanding of the Nordic race; for to be a peasant is to be free, to understand handiwork, to be successful at it, and "thereby to possess a feeling for the organic interplay of forces in Work as a Whole." (*Bauerntum als Lebensquell der Nord. Rasse,* 1928, 3rd ed., 1933, 279.) The historic criterion of race, as between Nordics and Semites, is the Pig—a sacred domestic animal for the former and shunned by the latter because it represents the antithesis of nomadic desert life (239).

Darré at one time joined hands with the eugenists and advocated polygamy for the sake of producing from selected Nordic German women the best possible breed. Such a policy was difficult to carry out in a still individualistic world, and in a country where the thinkers on these issues were as disunited as elsewhere; where Nietzsche, who wanted Jewish-Prussian Supermen, and Chamberlain, who believed the physiological basis of race negligible, were equally heeded; where Max Wieser called Günther's researches "card-index pedantry" and where L. F. Clauss preferred the blue-eyed Berbers of North Africa among whom he lived to all the degenerate races of Europe.

Practical as it may seem, race-propaganda is in the end unmanageable. Many, indeed most, of the books on the Nazis' recommended lists and shelves antedated 1933 and were therefore full of unorthodox views. The staggering catalogue of the Munich publishing firm of J. F. Lehmann, which had taken the lead in issuing books on race since the First World War, supports the same conclusion. Even at the height of National Socialist unity Brownshirts and Blackshirts, as well as private persons, entertained the most divergent views. On the Semitic question, notably, it was not uncommon to find racial distinctions being made in favor of the "German" as against the "Baltic" Jews.

In that same period of postwar anxiety, the great majority of German books and articles dealing with race concerned themselves with its cultural manifestations. "Race in the Liberal Arts,"[4] "Art and Race,"[5] "Speech and People,"[6] "Race and Soul,"[7] "Race and Spirit,"[8] "Nordic Thinking"[9]—these titles disclose an uneasiness of mind. The erudition and judgment found in these works, side by side with ill-digested science or rank prejudice, makes their perusal distressing. But it is their insistence on certain topics that gives away their emotional starting point: philosophy, natural science, and music belong wholly to Germany; they are domains won by its genius. What else is to be expected? The German race is the culture-maker par excellence. Ludwig Woltmann, a prewar racist who edited the *Politisch-Anthropologische Revue* and wrote *The Germans in Italy* and *The Germans in France,* had shown the way to this conclusion with his studies of musical heredity.[10] After the War, Richard Eichenauer pursued this line and in his *Musik und Rasse* (1932) furnished a racial interpretation of the great composers' work. The "Western soul" appears as "form" in the greatest musical masterpieces and is conspicuously absent from the works of "Semitic souls" like Mendelssohn and Mahler.

[4] By L. Schemann, 1928.
[5] By P. Schultze-Naumburg, 1928.
[6] By Fritz Stroh, 1932.
[7] Two books by that title: one by L. F. Clauss, 1926; the other by Max Wieser, 1933.
[8 and 9] By Franz Weidenreich, 1932.
[10] He found that among 4,067 musicians only about 20% had unusual parents or forebears, and on these he based his conclusions about racial transmission. The other 3,270 are "isolated cases."

Bizet gives trouble, for *Carmen* is "a high point in Western music" and Eichenauer has ascertained that the composer had blue eyes and blond hair, yet finds that he may have had a Jewish mother. Rossini is another bad case. He is clearly not "Western" (i.e., Nordic) but in the *Barber of Seville* "one believes that one finds traces of the *westisch* racial spirit, though rather as a result of the subject." (254-55 and n.)

For more than a dozen years the monthly magazine *Die Musik* was given over to similarly profound discoveries. Articles entitled: *"Richard Wagner as Announcer of the Aryan World,"*[11] *"Home-feeling and Foreignness in Music,"*[12] *"Richard Wagner and Germanism"*[13] furnished a hypnotizing reiteration of the words "blood, race, spirit, German, Nordic, Aryan." Aside from this identity in the refrain there was nothing but inconsistency in the sentiments about music and musicians, a state of things paralleled in other periodicals dealing with the other arts, history, philosophy, the physical sciences, and mathematics.

If one turns to the political speeches of the German leaders for a race-doctrine and asks which of the three official theories and which of the several cultural racialisms emerges as dominant, there is no clear-cut answer. The leaders big and little are not of one mind, and race remains purely a means to rally popular feeling behind something simple and obvious. Race in Germany was a means to give back to the German people a feeling of self-respect after the national humiliation at Versailles and since. Inevitably, giving self-respect meant giving a sense of superiority, as well as the chance for live persecution. And it has its uses also for concealing political vendettas. To state these facts is not to condone them: it is to show the further vice of thought attached to race in its function as a cloak to coarser

[11] By Fr. Baser.
[12] By Brockt: Schönberg, Hindemith, Weill (all moderns) are foreigners.
[13] By Fr. Panzer.

passions. What emerges therefore from the speeches of Hitler and Goebbels is that race, culture, and political action have been welded together into an instrument for national uplift. When the French used the same means after 1870 they called it *redressement* and praised the intellectuals who gave them biased lectures or histories to raise their depressed spirits. The case was identical, if the relative magnitudes of the two wars are kept in mind. The compound of race, culture, and political purpose is indeed quite natural. Hitler says: "At all times, social philosophies have conditioned not only the trend of politics, but also the aspect of cultural life." (*On Culture,* Party Day, 1933.) This insistence on culture is nothing but a roundabout justification of power. The "race" is great because it produces certain kinds of thoughts, machines, or art-forms and these warrant, nay, demand, the use of force to make the world notice and adopt them. Such was the old prewar *Kultur,* even the *Kulturkampf* of Bismarck and certainly the Anglo-Saxonism of Cecil Rhodes, the White Man's Burden of Kipling, the French *mission civilisatrice,* and all other Manifest Destinies. In Nazi Germany the device carried the added burden of making acceptable a dictatorship at home. The economic crisis made anti-Semitism as "useful" as it had been in France during the Dreyfus Affair. For all purposes, the chief value of race-worship is that it stimulates group conceit after paralyzing the critical faculties. Perhaps too much nonsense has already been quoted to show the abdication of reason in race propaganda, but a choice example by which to remember Nazi theory is to be found in Czech-Jochberg's popular *History Seen National-Socialistically* (1933). It is the caption beneath the head of the Venus of Melos, opposite page 16, which reads: "A typical Nordic Woman's Head."[14]

[14] The cream of the jest lies in the fact that the Venus dates from the Hellenistic period, when Greek art was probably "semitized" by an influx of artists from Asia Minor.

II

The superior race must reject the inferior or, mixing with it, or even living alongside of it, degenerate itself.

–KARL PEARSON on *National Life from the Standpoint of Science*

FAR FROM DIMINISHING the amount of race-thinking and race-antagonism in other parts of the world, the German use of race tended to encourage the habit elsewhere. Indignation at the persecution of Jews and liberals and the shaking of fists at Gobineau by certain critics accomplished little. Refutations of German racism generally consisted in a denial that the Nordic race was superior or that the Aryan was the only pure race. The idea of race itself was seldom called into question by the opponents or the victims of the persecutions. On the contrary, racial pride was often stiffened by the onslaught, and related needs of group consciousness played into the hands of racists everywhere. The "idealism" of the First World War had made both sides feel the inhumanity, the alienness, the racial difference of the other side. After the War the habits thus engendered led to cults of energy as well as to the revulsions of pacifism. Asserting the utility of war was for some a way of reassuring themselves that the four years of bloodshed had been justified. In this pathetic situation the rise of Mussolini and Hitler finds another psychological explanation. Their reliance on racism is equally logical. Race-thinking and race-prejudice strengthen the warlike attitude of groups. Sir Arthur Keith said as much in his Boyle lecture at Oxford in 1919. The War was barely over and the university undergraduates might reasonably have expected more peaceful counsels from the dean of British anthropologists, Hunterian Professor at the Royal College of Surgeons, and internationally known writer on science. But only the familiar passions and prejudices enlivened his discourse. Referring to the foundation of the lectureship, he said with amused condescension that for Robert Boyle and his contemporaries there were no race-problems. He then set out on a historical merry-go-round to show that race-antipathy has proved "experimentally successful" as a method of government in "Saxon America." He talked familiarly of "British or Nordic stock," the "North Sea breed," and the "usual Saxon sense of race-discrimination." With no great prophetic insight he said that the chief racial problem on the Continent is that of the Jews, and he found it convenient to discern in modern England "pure types" of Celt, Iberian, Saxon, and the rest. Gobineau addressing an Oxonian audience might have been wittier or more vehement, he could not have outdone Sir Arthur in extravagant applications of the race-principle. Nor did this lecture prove to be an irresponsible sally into unfamiliar territory. Sir Arthur proved himself a second and even third offender, with his Rectorial address to the students of Aberdeen on the "Place of Prejudice in Modern Civilization" (1931) and in his book *Ethnos, or the Problem of Race.* In both, war is advocated as desirable for the evolution of the race, of the "great race," in the best style of Bernhardi, Keyserling, or Benito Mussolini.

The earlier of Keith's speeches coincided with the activities of the second Ku Klux Klan in the United States, which proclaimed anew that the "Nordic Protestants" are the noblest and fittest race alive and that pure blood and race are the guarantees of a great civilization. "The Klan," said Imperial Wizard Evans, ". . . does believe in white supremacy. It believes that never in the history of the world has a mongrel civilization endured." (*Lit. Digest,* Feb. 5, 1921.) The Klan was anti-Japanese in the Northwest, anti-Negro in the South, and against foreigners, radicals, and Catholics everywhere else. This combination of antagonisms is not new, nor is the flatulence of the race-doctrine, but its popularity after the War is characteristic of an era of suspicion, insecurity, and explosive touchiness thinly veneered with talk of heroism and self-sacrifice.

The Peace Conference, with its colossal problem of exacting a victory and appeasing hungry nationalities, still further vulgarized the notion of race. Every self-determining population had a race-problem—had two or three race-problems—to be settled by gerrymandering or aggression. The right to self-determination was itself often grounded on the fact of being a "separate race" in the manner of the Albanians already cited. The conflicts of race and nationality were therefore conflicts of terminology fed by territorial greed, and not, as is often thought, the natural conflict of two non-congruent entities.

The special position of Germany as the chief defeated power, together with the historical importance of Prussia in the Germanies, accounts for the strength and seeming unity of racism there in the postwar period. The pre-Hitler growth of race-thinking may have been stimulated by the influx of Polish and Russian Jews after 1918, but that local factor is trivial when compared with those having historical and psychological roots. The real diversity of race-doctrines is the best proof of this, as was also the mounting tide of race-propaganda in Sweden, Finland, Rumania, Czechoslovakia, Holland, Italy, France, England, the Baltic countries, Turkey, Persia, Mexico, and the United States. The truth of the matter is that in the modern world real or supposed feuds apparently cannot be carried on in their own terms. Race has become the accepted form of gloss for simple hatred, as a few final examples will show.

In England during the thirties, Sir Oswald Mosley's anti-Semitism proved a merely imitative outburst of racism, but the controversy between militarists like Major Yeats-Brown and pacifists like Beverley Nichols and Sir Norman Angell was more important and it brought up the bogey of race at every turn. It was the Major's fear that if we forget race we shall perish culturally and nationally; we shall perhaps "save our skins but lose our souls. That is the price we have to pay for a deracialized world." There was in fact little danger of that so long as respected writers such as A. H. Sayce continued to "teach" race in connection with other subjects. Bringing out a new edition of his *Races of the Old Testament* in 1925, Sayce wrote: "Thirty-four years have passed since the first edition of my book was published but I find little to alter in it. Perhaps this means that ethnological science has not advanced so rapidly as some of the other historical sciences; but it may be that the main facts had been already acquired once for all." (*Pref.*, June, 1925.)

The book continues to deal in orbital indexes, prognathism, pigmentation, higher and lower races, and their mental qualities: "Prominent jaws imply the development of physical strength and appetite at the expense of the intellectual faculties" (30). Nine years later another scientist, Sir Grafton Elliott-Smith, addressing as Chairman the International Congress of Anthropology and Ethnology, said while fingering a skull found near the Thames: ". . . at the present time it is of the greatest importance that anthropologists should reach some consensus of opinion on such problems as may be used to justify or excuse political action. If our discussions do nothing more, it will be a definite gain if we can impress upon politicians some respect for anthropological truth and the generally admitted knowledge of the facts of race and culture."

The London *Times,* in commenting on the assertion, nearly simultaneous with the Congress, of Sir John Simon's Aryan purity, made an ironic and gloomy forecast: ". . . race is merely one of many equally valid ways of establishing affinity. . . . The instinct for separatism is too deep-seated ever to be at a loss for a means of expressing itself. In the expanding scale, when frontiers have fallen out of fashion, it can fasten on still untried combinations of race, language, or creed; in the diminishing—and then the cycle of history will have made a full turn—it can rediscover the indisputable affinities of clans, totems and matriarchal descent." (Sept. 1, 1934.)

In a nearby column Professor Flinders Petrie was carrying on the old cultural-scientific fight against anti-Semitism, by using archaeology and likening Jews and Englishmen as "mixed races" against which "pure races" have little chance. This was but the old liberal appeasement at work; and as we know, pointing out the advantages of "mixed ancestry" leaves the race-superstition just where it was for the next system-maker to make use of.

Thus Lothrop Stoddard, who had cried wolf when the Yellow Peril was fashionable, published in the United States a revised version of his program of racial fears, admitting his former error and committing it again with improved details. It would be unjust to say that he was out of touch with the times, when one could read of a Southern governor's electioneering appeal to his constituents' race-prejudice and discover in the Republican presidential platform of 1928 a guarded reference to the perilous subject. The Harlem riots, the growth of overt anti-Semitism, the printed attacks on the Roosevelt administration as the "Ju-deal," the continued hardships imposed by the Immigration Law upon individuals of certain races, the increasing reliance on race-explanations in cultural matters—all these signs warranted the belief that race-thinking had a promising future in the United States, and that the creation of a "new race" out of the melting pot, which Woodrow Wilson and others foresaw in 1917, had either failed to take place or failed to produce that unity of mind which our best experts on race tell us is one of its infallible tests.

In France, the various traditions of race-thinking continued as before. The postwar boom in Gobinism was described on an earlier page. In addition, the nationalist cult of the "French race" benefited from the new emotion of the worship of the dead heroes of the War. True, the old quarrel of German versus Gaul no longer worked as an explanation of internal politics. Three wars against the Germans in less than a century had made that impossible, but the position formulated by Maurice Barrès in his Integral Nationalism still stood as the bulwark of conservatism against internationalist opinion. The fervor and completeness of its expression gave it an enduring hold on half the intelligent youth of France, all the more so because, like many nationalists, Barrès began his intellectual and political career as a kind of socialist. In his early work race remains largely undefined, but he uses it freely to account for many things—notably for Bakunin's anarchism, due to the Slavs' backward race. From this type of cliché Barrès soon proceeded to a system of prejudices combining politics and art. In novels and travel books, which have something of Stendhal's passion for crime, danger, and vivid color, Barrès proclaimed himself a "passionate Mediterranean." His cult of the Ego was nothing but the fierce sensitive individualism of Gobineau or Nietzsche with Soil- and Ancestor-worship superimposed upon it. The First World War confirmed him in a mystical collectivism, a deification of the "soil and its dead," as a spiritual refuge. "One hopes for nothing save from that inner music transmitted with their blood by the dead of our race." The strength and obscurity of this mysticism surpass anything that the Germans or the Anglo-Saxonists have conceived upon the common sentiment of patriotism. Between the wars Barrès continued to make disciples. Echoes of his thought resounded everywhere: "The energy of France is the resources of the race." (Bainville.) The planting of a tree symbolic of the Latin race at Monterrey but in soil taken from France and to be watered with water from Paris, was recorded in moderate newspapers as "an idea not without grandeur." Scientists, historians, artists, and miscellaneous writers continued to proclaim their faith in the soil, the eternal life of the nation, and the sacredness of the Occidental heritage, with a kind of arrogant shrillness indicative of acute nationalistic fear. An academician soberly described the fatherland as "an association on the same soil of the living with the dead and those to be born . . . : we are ourselves only when we are penetrated, saturated by the traditions of our race." (Bordeaux.)

How far the "soil" extends and how it is the same are questions these racists do not answer. We have no inkling either who our sacred dead ancestors are—do they include, for the French Catholics, the dead terrorists of the French Revolution?

For the Protestants, the soldiery who massacred them in the St. Bartholomew and the *dragonnades?* Do they include, for the Bretons, the Southern "blues" who came under Hoche to shoot them down? But although the fundamentals of the creed are, like most articles of faith, diplomatically vague, the results are tangible and expedient. First and foremost, a policy of France to the French; second, a hatred and suspicion of aliens, and lastly a preference for some special corner of France where the "race" is, so to speak, more racial than national. Hence an adherence to the movement of decentralization known in France as regionalism, analogous to the American States' Rights. Particularly strong in Lorraine, this type of racial nationalism has been created in large measure by the French statesmen and writers from that region. Barrès himself points out how the "exasperation of this race face to face with the Germanic race" has produced the energetic nationalists of his time—Funck-Brentano (a Luxemburger), Louis Madelin, Emile Hinzelin, Ernest Babelon, Georges Ducrocq. He might have completed the list by adding Poincaré. These men, aided by circumstance, created a movement that has gone beyond their special pleading and their local or temporary influence.

With the example of Nazi Germany before them, the younger French patriots, fed on the writings of Barrès and others, tended to develop a sentimental regard for the anti-Semitism of the Dreyfus period. Writing in 1934 about Drumont, the author of *Jewish France,* a well-known columnist deplored the fact that Drumont's articles had not been collected. The critic expressed profound respect for the violent anti-Semite and referred to his work as "bearing witness to a past which is not so past as all that." (Jules Véran in *Comœdia,* Apr., 1934.) In another periodical, *Atlantis,* space was given to race-theories of the most diverse and fantastic make-up, which somehow conveyed a claim of Aryan race-supremacy for France under the slogan *Ex Occidente Lux.* (Seventh Year, No. 49, Sept.-Oct., 1933.)

Characteristically, the Stavisky scandal of 1934 generated a slight but unmistakable wave of anti-Semitism and xenophobia. Another flock of articles appeared on Gobineau. Two plays, one German and one French, dealt with the race-problem, and newspapers, both in Paris and in the important towns, gave space to articles, reports of lectures, and even presidential messages on France's Latin, Roman, Gallic, "hyperborean," or racially unique civilization.[15] While the frankly fascist "Francistes" adopted the Germanic double-edged ax or *francisque* as their symbol, the more numerous youths of the *Croix de Feu* who participated in the February riots of 1934 made no secret of their racial antipathies, despite their leaders' caution to avoid resemblances with Hitlerism. For them just the same, French communism, Moscow, and Germany form one "Oriental" peril, while the "Anglo-Saxon" policy of the Balance of Power in Europe expresses a racial tendency which the "Latins" must be on guard against. Between 1934 and 1936, when Léon Blum's premiership brought forth a fresh batch of the old politico-racial arguments, these feelings no doubt fluctuated, but these variations do not alter the fact that when passions flare up over some event of internal or foreign politics, the long tradition of race-thinking in France is ready to give the passions form and direction. The nature and motives of race-thinking are as constant and tireless as the tides of the Ocean.

III

Every biologist knows that intelligence is inherited, energy is inherited, insanity is inherited, emotional possibilities are inherited, a man's inner character is inherited.

—A. E. WIGGAM in *The New Decalogue of Science*

[15] In the course of many conversations in France with a great variety of persons—from university and professional men to civil servants, business and working men—the writer found race-beliefs to be quasi-universal. In most cases, the subject of race was spontaneously offered as an explanation, a reason, a justification of unrelated matters, by an interlocutor entirely ignorant of the writer's curiosity on the subject. [Note written in 1936.]

ALTHOUGH RACE-THINKING is not new in essence or purpose, the "facts" it exploits are renewed from time to time. Tacitus and Boulainvilliers, Montesquieu and Bishop Stubbs, were content with historical research and climate theories. Then came the "biological revolution" and race-thinkers pinned their hopes on anatomy, while philologists made race subsist on linguistic roots. The twentieth century also has made its contribution, in keeping with its new interests and powers. One need only refer to social (including criminal) statistics, to experiments in genetics and medicine, and to the renaissance of descriptive anthropology. These last two sciences will receive ampler treatment in the next chapter. Here a few words are in order on statistics in general and biologico-physical science in particular. The growing use of so-called intelligence tests gave rise, especially in the United States, to statistical studies for determining the relative capacities of selected groups. Nathaniel D. Hirsch in his study of *Natio-Racial Mental Differences* (1926) reported on several earlier studies which tended to show that nationalities of superior intelligence are "largely Nordic" (240-42). Hirsch conducted tests to disprove these results and, finding that the tests showed "no connection between intelligence and the possession of Nordic blood," concluded that "differences in intelligence are National or Natio-racial, not Racial" (308-9). In spite of this fine-drawn distinction, the author continued to speak of "the Natio-racial Frenchman," "the formation of the Natio-race in Germany" and the "biological blend of . . . three races," giving exact indications for each of mental and other capacities. As in the controversies of the anthroposociologists, the new science of intelligence testing is adapted to proving or disproving the superior intelligence of the Nordic race. The existence of that race Mr. Hirsch took for granted, like his opponents.

Biological research on race-problems followed two avenues of which the first was the correlation of race and disease. The "incidence" of cancer, arthritis, asthma, and other widespread ailments among various groups has been studied in the hope of discovering a particular racial susceptibility to one or other of them. It has long been a popular as well as a medical supposition that the Jews were especially subject to nervous disorders.[16] The difficulty with a racial division of diseases, which would naturally imply some chemical or physiological difference in the structure of the human beings composing the race, is that the medical statistician has to argue in a circle to prove his theory. He takes the Jews or the Eskimos as a starting point, finds some degree of correlation between membership in the group and a certain disease, and offers the correlation as a test of common race. The point to be proved—and it has never been done—is that no other factor save that of race causes the susceptibility to (let us say) arthritis. But since arthritis would be, in that event, the only positive test of race so far produced, all that could be said would be that arthritics are a race. If the ailment chosen were housemaid's knee, no one would associate it indissolubly with the Irish (Celtic) race but would ascribe it to occupation. It is equally probable that the different incidences of the chief diseases are due to social or environmental factors that are concealed by the initial grouping of Irish, Nordic, Negro, or Jew.

The second line of modern biological research into race is that of body chemistry. Over a hundred years ago the French physician Chevreul had suggested that each race must present chemical differences. It was then (1824) the day of five-race classification according to the color of the skin, so that the hypothesis, involving the chemical fact of pigmentation, had plausibility. When skull-shape replaced pigmentation as the test

[16] In nineteenth-century France alone Le Dantec, Charcot, Foville, Boudin, Chervin, and Bérard paid more than passing attention to "race-diseases." Driesmans, on the contrary, was rationalizing current superstitions when he said that the three signs of the German race were ease of infection by contagious disease, depressive nervous ailments, and a tendency to suicide. (*Die Kelten,* III, 75.) See also Sofer (1909), Bauer (1924), Beneke (1878), Draper (1930), Keith (1930).

and when the climate theory of the sun-darkened skins of Negroes and Indians was discarded, chemical explanations went by the board. They have returned in the form of new ideas about diet, but with inconclusive results. Some lead to the extinction of the race-issue altogether, as we shall see in the next chapter, but all depend for their validity on the evolutionary transmission of acquired characteristics, which brings back to the science of genetics the whole question of the meaning of race.

At the opposite pole from chemical or environmental interpretation is that provided by several psychoanalysts. Nothing like a race-system is to be found in the works of Freud himself, except for a suggestion that the growth of certain race-animosities is due to "narcissism in respect of minor differences,"[17] but in the writings of several other analysts, notably Dr. Beatrice Hinkle of New York, mental patterns and race are often interchangeable terms. Says Dr. Hinkle: "If the author [the French mathematician, Henri Poincaré] had substituted the *introvert type* for the 'Latin temperament' then there would be no difficulty in his reconciling the French thought with Hebrew blood and German training, for they all belong to the introvert type of thought, while the Anglo-Saxon belongs to the characteristic extravert type.

"It is to introverted Germany that we must go for the highest development of abstract philosophical and idealistic thinking. True to type, in this realm her masculine principle finds its expression, and when, departing from her natural field, she assumes the extraverted mode of aggressive action, she must of necessity produce an overdetermined behavior and be doomed to failure when matched against an equally strong and naturally extraverted power. It is only forty years ago that one of her greatest statesmen spoke of her scornfully as a nation of philosophers, poets, and dreamers. It is this natural Germany that corresponds to the simple introvert type as described. If our

[17] *Civilization and Its Discontents,* 1930, 90.

world had been one in which philosophy, science, and poetry were held in equal regard with trade, commerce, and machinery, Germany might have continued to use her own functions in the realm for which they are fitted and have found her path to power along lines where her supremacy could hold unchallenged. Then the history of the world would have been differently written." (*The Re-Creating of the Individual,* 1923, 196-197.)[18]

Dr. Hinkle perpetrates the old fallacy of taking the groups—German, Latin, Anglo-Saxon—for granted and ascribing the mental habits of individuals, loosely grouped as introvert and extravert, to the whole unsorted mass, the generalizing process itself giving a kind of verisimilitude to the two unconnected ends of the argument.

Still another type of analysis straddling the mental and physical factors, and called by its originator the Method of voice-analysis (*Stimmanalysemethode*), was brought forth in Estonia in 1929. Dr. Willy E. Peters, director of the Phonetics Laboratory of the University of Tartu (Dorpat), embodied his researches in three papers dealing with the racial type of Mussolini, Tolstoy, Hjalmar Branting, and Graf Zeppelin. Dr. Peters used gramophone disks and the Miller phonodeik to record the curve of the speech-melody, and analyzed syllable by syllable the "shape" of a text averaging seven lines of print. In so doing he discovered an "east-falling and a west-rising inflection," taking care first to allow for the effect of the language, syntax, or oratorical device that might overlay the racial inflection with accidentals. Short biographical sketches and mental portraits completed the classification of the four men. Melodically speaking, they fall into two groups—the *staccato-energetic* (Mussolini) type and the *legato-nervous-depressive* (Tolstoy) type.

Several other typologies could be mentioned. They come and

[18] See also Dr. Philip S. Graven: "Case Study of a Negro," *Psychoanal. Rev.,* April, 1930.

go and return, for the urge to divide mankind into fixed types and races is evidently endless. Each attempt only illustrates anew how race-groupings have been shaped not by nature but by the mode of thought or the stage of mechanical efficiency that mankind valued at the moment. The history of these attempts confirms the statement found near the beginning of this book that race-theories occur in the minds of men for an ulterior purpose which, once set in motion, suggests an infinite series of possible systems, more and more complex as civilization expands, more and more abstract as the changing standards of morality demand an ever more intellectual rationalization for the concealment of primitive aggressiveness and snobbery.

Chapter XI

RACE: THE MODERN SUPERSTITION

I

Ancient Maxim: *Nihil humanum a me alienum puto.*
Modern Version: *Nothing alien is human to me.*

IF THE READER'S PATIENCE has not been exhausted by the description of 150 years of race-thinking, sketchy as that description is when compared with the full record, he may like to feel that in reading this chapter his turn has come to criticize. For practical purposes, both reader and author are now in possession of the same facts, and it is the author's business to recapitulate in orderly form his previous and necessarily disconnected objections. The reader, on his side, is probably full of questions: Has there not been at times a confusion between race-beliefs and merely national pride? Have not the fanatics of race been indiscriminately lumped with writers only occasionally guilty of using race-epithets? Cannot one reject theories of Nordic superiority without being forced to consider Negroes and white men as belonging to the same race? Since the contradictions of many erring minds do not in themselves preclude the possibility that some later system will be true, is it legitimate to deny the existence of race? Even granting that fixed races cannot be found, are there not genuine divisions of mankind into broad groups, proved to be distinct by the work of reputable modern scientists? Does not indeed the common aspect of "national character" reveal tangible differences that have an environmental basis and a cultural significance? Lastly, does not the mere fact of racial belief create the very distinctions spoken of by the racists? In other words, can an intellectual process get rid of the social, economic, political, and cultural facts behind the emotions of race?

These questions not only express a proper skepticism, but they require an answer as being the very questions that started the author on his original quest. They can best be dealt with by setting down the conclusions that the search has led to. First, a brief review of the ground covered will permit a summary of the major objections to race; these will be followed by positive remarks to take care of the question of national differences; next and last, the views of modern anthropology and genetics about physical differences will bring our enterprise to a close.

Starting with the political uses of the Nordic Myth, historically evident since Tacitus, and the climate theory of racial differences, which is even older, the course of the argument early established as the basis of all race-thinking the assumption of a fixed relation between the physical and the moral nature of groups of men. A short account of anthropology showed how the notions of species, variety, and heredity bore upon the idea of race, regardless of its ulterior motives. Conversely, the history of linguistics revealed how the words "Celtic, Aryan, and Semitic" have provided politicians and scientists with another mold into which to cast their race-ideas, at the very time when the forces of Nationalism, Evolution, Sociology, Imperialism, and Militarism made race-beliefs needful, authoritative, and picturesque.

At no point in the narrative did the author consciously describe or discuss race-theories from the point of view of any party, religion, or system.[1] Apart from the emphasis on France, designed to prove the greater by the less, whatever impression of bias may result from the apportionment of space among the several ideas, races, or authors presented is accidental and must be laid to faulty composition rather than to tendentious choice. As for the blanket denial that races exist until it is proved that they do, this must be ascribed not so much to a desire for singularity or paradox as to an effort to regain the naïve, hospitable open-mindedness that must have existed before the first race hypothesis was conceived by the human mind. William James somewhere counsels us for the sake of truth to look at unfamiliar things as if they were familiar and at familiar things as if they were unfamiliar. To deny race after an examination of the major theories in the field is to follow both halves of James's precept at once. It is to look on all human beings as substantially alike until their radical differences have been established beyond doubt; and it is also to force oneself to think as if White, Aryan, Mongoloid, and brachycephalic were words for things as remote from direct perception as Syphilitic, Arthritic, and Diabetic—three words that might just as readily be used to divide mankind into distinct groups. By so forcing oneself to await proofs of racial differences, one puts the burden where it really belongs, namely, on the racial historian, scientist, or art-critic, and one is able to apply the ordinary rules of logic and

[1] The racist critic might like to find an "explanation" of this skeptical stand in a book by Francisque Michel, the friend of Mérimée, on *The Accursed Races in France and Spain* (Paris, 1847). The work describes the inferior position of certain presumed Goths, light-haired and blue-eyed, in Southwestern France, the home of my remote ancestors. On p. 107 of Vol. I, it is said that "in the town of Barzun, there were only two inhabitants belonging to this caste. . . . They have left only one daughter who, though afflicted with goiter, enjoys as great respect and consideration as the other inhabitants." Although I have never set foot in the town of Barzun and my traceable forebears left it well over a hundred years ago, it must be clear to any racist that the spirit of tolerance for other "races," so unusual in that part of France, has been transmitted in the blood.

inference to the theories presented, instead of enthusiastically or lazily jumping to a congenial or merely familiar conclusion.

This attitude also explains the refusal to differentiate in this book between makers of race-systems and casual users of race-adjectives, for if race is conceded to be a dangerous superstition, the latter are no more excusable than the former. The judges and divines who readily burned a witch because everybody knew that witches were a menace are not to be excused on the ground that they never wrote treatises describing the signs and causes of witchcraft. Is the analogy thought too strong? We judge our neighbors, we incite others to war, we promote or dismiss our inferiors, we damn an author, we accept or reject as immigrants and as voting citizens persons whose "race" is the ostensible ground of discrimination. Witch-burning was certainly crude and barbaric, but it lies open to doubt whether concentration camps and the stirring up of hatred and violence are such obvious proofs of greater enlightenment.

These practical applications of race-thinking will remind the reader that this study has not given any account of a particular race-prejudice in its concrete manifestations. Material interests have been only alluded to as furthering the vogue of race-ideas. The reason for this omission is twofold. There are, in the first place, numerous works that deal with the economic, social, and political realities of current race-antagonisms, whether in Poland, in South Africa, in the Southern states, or in Spain before the expulsion of the Moors. The advantage in forgoing actualities and treating of race generally as a mode of thought was precisely to show that it had always been a practical device and that its forms are reducible to a common pattern. In the modern world race-thinking uses history, it uses philology, it uses anthropology to cover up realities that should be dealt with in their own terms.

The writer, when he has been rash enough to speak his thoughts to casual acquaintances, has often been interrupted by questions of the common type: How would you like your sister to marry a Negro? Or: do you mean to say you think an Eskimo is your intellectual equal?[2] These bland flatteries are beside the point. No argument has ever been advanced by any reasonable man against the fact of differences among men. The whole argument is about what differences exist and how they are to be gauged. Philosophically speaking, there is nothing within the scope of this book to prevent a man from hating his neighbor, from abhorring mixed marriages, or from disliking swarthy complexions. The objection that is made is to the validity of the reasons offered for hating and killing. The demonstration is meant to show up the confusion of the moral issues involved. It is impossible to fight the real forces behind race-hatreds until they have been uncovered by the general recognition that race-theories are pretexts—unconscious hypocrisy or willful camouflage. Lynching requires perhaps no very great courage, but a man who came to see that he participated in lynchings for sadistic fun, for releasing anger, or for expressing fear would be more deserving of respect and more amenable to reform than one who justified himself with the self-righteous conviction that the Negroes are a subhuman race akin to the apes. The problems of colored populations, of immigration and miscegenation, of anti-Semitism and national hatred are not problems about a natural fact called race: they are problems of social life, of economic status, of educational policy, and of political organization. The presence of the race-idea creates an additional problem which it has been the purpose of this history to elucidate. Each individual can work upon his own mental habits as he chooses, but the helpful formula runs roughly as follows:

Those human beings who have not lost their pigmentation are simply more clearly marked than others for discrimination; they wear a uniform that they cannot take off, but they are not alone

[2] More formal utterances of the same kind are not wanting: "Would any amount of training ever make the *average* Chinese as good a boatman as the *average* Eskimo, or could the average Eskimo by any possibility be as careful and patient a farmer as the Chinese?" (Ellsworth Huntington in *The Pulse of Progress.*)

in their plight. Others have eyes, noses, skulls, or ways of speech that distinguish them in a rough-and-ready way and make them bear all the faults or all the virtues supposedly inherent in the group to which they are said to belong. Those faults and those virtues are themselves social in origin. We remember the "Jew" or the "Irishman"[3] who stepped on our toes without apologizing where we forget a dozen others not so striking to our dull and hasty senses. Among the Hottentots a white man is similarly noticeable and alien, while those among our fellow whites who have offended us but have escaped classification have done so only by the accident of inconspicuousness. For all we know, the forgotten "Nordics" who have been rude to us were all tagged with invisible characteristics—say, stomach ulcers—and were working off their physiological irritation on our person. Striking differences are far from being proved significant differences, but they are the tokens whereby group antagonisms perpetuate themselves like Kentucky feuds; and in time they create the very inferiority or degradation in one group which the other originally assumed to exist. In Nature there are, to use the words of Buffon and Lamarck, no genera; there are only individuals until we class them arbitrarily according to particular criteria for particular purposes, as when we choose men of a certain stature to be policemen. Such a classification means something because it means only one thing.

By extension, the same reasoning invalidates all the comparisons, crude or complicated, between the mentality of, say, the Eskimos and the Western Europeans. Obviously, an Eskimo who could not write or read these lines could thrive in an environment where the writer would promptly starve and freeze to death. More universally put, the achievements of intelligence and adaptive power are incommensurable. This is equally true of persons and of groups. There are no standards of truly gen-

[3] The difference between the anti-Jewish prejudice in New York and the anti-Irish-Catholic prejudices in Boston is both an example and a proof of the social and economic bases of race-feeling.

eral intelligence, the so-called intelligence tests being only, in the eyes of their makers, tests of special techniques, such as book-learning, visual imagination, and so forth. With present methods, furthermore, there is no way of knowing a group except by rough sampling and no way of measuring the value of the ends sought by diverse cultural groups. What is true of intercultural comparisons is all the more true of the inter-racial comparisons attempted by art-critics and philosophers concerning two artists or statesmen of the same tradition. For that tradition itself is not one thing but many. This diversity of traditions naturally brings up the question of "national" as against "racial" differences. Are the falsehoods of race possibly the truths of nationality? Before giving an answer, the objections to race are here listed and labeled as an aid to further reflection.

OBJECTIONS

1. *General Inconsistency*. Whether any one race-theory be true or not, the fact that there exists no agreement whatever about race-terminology, its application, or its proofs, puts all the theories to date beyond the reach of scientific verification. Inconsistency is the rule both between any two systems and within any one. Some anthropological congresses have disclosed and discussed as many as 100 races.

2. *Pretense of Materialism*. The idea of race can start from two premises: either that a given physique produces a given type of mind or that a given type of mind presupposes some hidden physical similarity. Granting a connection for the sake of argument, there is always a gap left by the racist between the physical fact and its mental concomitant. Proof of material causation is not shown in either of the two possible ways:

I. It is not shown that wherever sign A occurs (let us say, a dolichocephalic skull), result B (the quality of initiative) is present, and that wherever A is absent B also is absent.

II. It is not shown that even though we may not know what the physical factor at work is, whenever several signs A, B, C, D, the quality X also is present. For example, that the Germans, a loose term involving signs A, B, C, D, are the only people who are distinguished in the world of science.

3. *Circular Argument*. Race-theories of whatever kind all lead to a point where the proponent drops his pretense of scientific analysis and begs the question. He says in effect: the Nordic race is a group apart; it is the greatest race. Why? Just look at its triumphs, look at Columbus, Nelson, Shakespeare, Edison—all Nordics. But what made these men great? The racial something that they had in common. Now, how do you know they were Nordics? Simply by the definition of Nordic race, that is, English, North American, energetic, inventive.

4. *Elusiveness*. No system of race-belief stays within its original limits. If it is a historical system, it drags in science or pseudo-science; if it is scientific, it leans on historical or pseudo-historical facts; if philological, it relies on the other two disciplines. The proofs of any system are proofs only by assuming the truth of other "facts," themselves assumed in a field beyond the one where the investigator originally bade you look.

5. *Statistical Fallacy*. A race is by hypothesis a group of individuals, and the distinguishing characteristics of the group must be those characteristics by which they differ from other groups of exactly the same composition save in that one respect; that is to say, men's skulls from one group must not be compared with women's skulls from another. Age, diet, and occupation ought also to be common to both groups if the racial difference between them is to appear clearly and indisputably. It is obvious that the number of relevant facts about men in society is much

too great to permit so exact a grouping of qualities for comparison. Even rough approximation is not generally attempted, and if achieved would still expose the results to the objection that a distinguished statistician has raised against his own craft: "Statistical methods are only necessary in so far as experiment fails to attain its ideal . . . they are to the experimenter a warning of failure." (G. Udny Yule, *Brit. Jour. Psych.,* XII, 106.)

6. *Fallacy of Exception.* Accustomed as we are to approximate rules, we readily accept the answer of "Exception!" when we can point to one or more individuals who do not fit the definition given by the systematic racist. It is generally overlooked that if race is an unchanging factor which marks human beings distinctively, it cannot break down at any point. An individual may vary from the cultural pattern, for he may have been reared in isolation or become a rebel. But how can the one thing that is transmissible by way of generation fail to be transmitted? It is as if a human being were born oviparous through "exception" to the rule that says men are viviparous vertebrates.

7. *Duplicity of Motives.* Very few works dealing with race can be cleared of the charge that they were inspired and brought to completion for some other motive than the discovery of race-divisions. In the light of so many admissions by the authors themselves that if they prove their race-contention, then some other conclusion of the greatest importance follows, it can be said that race-theories are motivated by ulterior interests and not by curiosity, which in turn explains the slovenliness, inaccuracy, and illogic of virtually every system.

8. *Rhetorical Devices.* Although all discourse is compelled by the limitations of language to use images and analogies, the mystical nature of race-belief forces its apostles to use figurative language literally. *Mein Blut spricht* is a typical metaphor the literal application of which, as we have seen, leads men to war and donors of blood for transfusion to jail. Terms like "melanized" or "mongoloid" or even "the blending of races" are also

metaphorical expressions that sound plausible only when we do not insist that they raise in the mind definite pictures of human events. Race-theories are not only bad science; they are bad poetry.

9. *Tautology.* In discussions of culture the use of race-epithets does not add to an understanding of the question in hand, but rather dismisses it. To write that "Martin Luther is the incarnation of the instinct of his race" (Montégut) is to leave one's reader in the dark. Even a treatise explaining what the author means by race would not bring additional information about Luther's life and work, since the only reason Luther is spoken of at all is that he diverged from the common run of his compatriots. The critic, by invoking the vague characteristics of the mass, does not get nearer to his subject but further away from it. Race does not cover cultural facts, it covers them up.

10. *Predestination and Obscurantism.* The upshot of race-thinking is that by offering us the mystery of heredity as an explanation it diverts our attention from the social and intellectual factors that make up personality. Race interpretations presuppose that from the moment of conception *and by conception alone,* the nature and mind of an individual are predestined. The thousand incidents and accidents composing a life are mere footnotes to a text that was written *ab ovo.* In such a world, eugenics must replace education and physical culture must take precedence over social reform. Writing in a philosophical journal at the turn of the century Topinard doubted whether "reason and education ought to try to interfere with the products of natural evolution." (*The Monist,* 1897, II, 600.) But obviously, if race is all-powerful, tampering with it is impossible; which negates evolution by making the nature of man an essence carried intact and intangible within the bodies of the living and expressing no more and no less than it was prehistorically fated to do.

11. *Absolutism.* In the realm of politics, science, and philo-

sophic materialism, race stands as an absolute, a first cause, an unmoved mover. In the familiar world of shifting appearances, race satisfies man's demand for certainty by providing a single, simple, and adequate cause for a great variety of large and complex events. On the one hand, race appeals to those who find discomfort in relativity—hence its charm for fascists; on the other, it appeals to all the lovers of teleology and straight determinism—hence its use by communists in the form of the absolute class-myth.[4] The bourgeois and the capitalist become genetic entities that engage in necessary strife apart from immediate desires.

12. *Utopianism.* The irony of race-theories is that they arise almost invariably from a desire to mold others' action toward the good rather than to explain facts. From Tacitus to Gobineau the great racial ideas have come from disappointed men. In Germany, where race-thinking became official doctrine for a decade, the surrender to folly originated in despair. Van den Bruck wrote *The Third Reich* at the lowest ebb of national egoism and killed himself before the materializing of his pathetic appeal. Rosenberg and Darré illustrate the same point: racism is an alternative to madness for educated men balked in what they consider their legitimate ambitions. It is a faith rooted in the consciousness of worth and confirmed by the Tertullian principle of *Certum est quia impossible.*

II

I used to flatter myself on guessing at people's nationality by their faces and, as a rule, I guessed aright. This faded, crumpled, vaporous beauty, I conceived, was a German . . .

—HENRY JAMES in *Eugene Pickering*

[4] See Frederick L. Schuman's excellent comparison of race and class in *The Nazi Dictatorship* (115) and Margaret Schlauch's substitution of class for national determinism in linguistics. (*Marxian Quarterly, Science and Society,* I, No. 1.)

HENRY JAMES's pastime of guessing at nationality is so universal and, as he hints, so flattering to one's detective powers, that it supplies an obvious line of retreat for those whose outer works of racial beliefs have been destroyed. A whole library of books by respected writers such as Brownell, Madariaga, and Pittard endeavors to show that nationality, not race, is the factor making for similarity within large groups. In popular and educated conversation nothing is more common than references to the American type, the average Frenchman, and other abstractions of the sort, which cultivated people know to be rough approximations, but which they none the less use in thought and speech as if they were exact and definite. A noteworthy fact about these ideas is that they usually apply to foreigners. When a man familiar with the history of his own nation attempts to draw up the characteristics of the national type, he generally finds it difficult in direct proportion to the amount and vividness of his knowledge. James Truslow Adams admitted as much when the *New York Times Magazine* asked him to discover the American type. The headline-writer, presumably not the historian, was disappointed but candid:

AN OBSERVER FINDS IT DIFFICULT, IN THIS LAND OF VARIED REGIONS AND PEOPLES, TO SET DOWN CHARACTERISTICS, RACIAL OR OTHERWISE, THAT ARE REPRESENTATIVE AND DISTINCTIVE.[5]

We are at once in the midst of our problem: there are, not only in the United States but everywhere, "varied regions and peoples" and an observer who deserves the name finds it "difficult to set down distinctive characteristics." It may be objected that, on the contrary, there are perfectly plain national and regional characters, that a New Englander is not like a Virginian or an Irishman like a Hungarian. Who could deny the differences that occur to the mind when comparing a Virginian and a

[5] May 19, 1935.

Vermonter? No one, but the rebuttal is perhaps as stiff a poser, namely, how exact is the correspondence between the things that readily occur to the eye or the mind and the reality of life? The question is, in fact, a tangle of separate questions. First, are the differences that we "at once think of" differences that apply to all members of each group? Second, are those differences greater than those existing within each group? Third, what are the group differences traceable to—heredity, occupation, income, or environment? Fourth, does the word "environment" mean soil and climate only, or does it include custom and tradition? Adequate answers would require the analysis of a multitude of examples and a body of information that belongs to a neglected branch of study—the Psychology of Traveling. To develop it here is impossible, but a few suggestions can be made on the topic "What Can a Man Believe About Large Groups."

Granted that a German and a Frenchman differ, at least as soon as we have been told which is which, let us see what is reasonable to assume. Our first impulse is to suppose that they differ fundamentally, but common sense bids us take stock of certain outward matters, chiefly clothing, tricks of speech, and social behavior, traceable to a certain environment. That environment generally is more local than it seems, that is to say, it is a regional, an occupational, a social, or a class environment. On this point the Marxists are right to insist, and by the same token they are wrong to transform their perception into a totalitarian absolute. The proof that local environment is a truer index than the national is that we are apt to mistake the "class" of a foreigner much more than that of a compatriot, even when we know to what nationality the foreigner belongs. The same conclusion can be reached from the opposite side: what do we mean by a Frenchman? Is it anybody born in France, be it in Brittany or Dauphiné, Paris or Marseille? Are such varied types more nearly alike than they are like Englishmen and Italians? Racists of a physiological turn of mind answer No. National-minded racists say Yes. The decision ultimately rests on a quantitative judgment of human traits. Is a French country doctor *more* like a French peasant than he is like a German country doctor? One may doubt whether such a question has any meaning. For it is foolish to suppose that a man is ever all of a piece, always honest or always scientific—and hence always a doctor or a German. As soon as we probe these superficial aggregates of character we are trying to weigh imponderables, which is an arbitrary business at best.

Again, consider the extreme nationalist in France and in Germany. The objects of their love and hatred are of course precisely opposite. The one hates Germany; the other hates France. But the thinking process, the language, and the activity of both men are precisely alike. Should we not postulate a Chauvinist Race cutting across other classifications and differing markedly from the Cosmopolitan Race? It is clear that a cosmopolitan race does not exist, but that in all nations there are cosmopolites, who over the centuries have established a cosmopolitan tradition. In things not of the mind there are similar traditions or habits that shape and mark the individual. Eating peas with a knife doubtless runs in families. It is the sum of these habits and traditions that forms individual or regional character. What must be found out, then, about a nation or an individual is not the single epithet that Chekhov was looking for to embrace the whole mass, but the sum of traditions that constitute the culture of the group or the man. As individuals of the Western world we belong in various ways to hundreds or thousands of traditions. Some of them are national and are acquired through language, ritual, and history; some of them are regional and rest on economic, social, and dialectal peculiarities; others are still more limited and come from education, family background, and one's own unique experiences. It is, once more, an oversimplification and a denial of the infinite plasticity of the human mind to suppose that once a man's birthplace or income or forebears have been ascertained he has been sufficiently explored and stands before us like a fully answered riddle.

At the same time, the conditions of modern life make men act more and more in collective units, in large anonymous groups that merge individualities out of existence. Nationalism and democracy are but two manifestations of this tendency, and Mérimée was right when he said that racial history was the democratic form of dynastic history. But in order to know what we are talking about when describing groups, we must take the same precautions as when talking about a single person. Large groups are always forming and re-forming out of different constituents. Unseen forces change so-called national characters and national purposes. In the eighteenth century, the Germans were a dreamy and philosophical lot—so we are told; fifty years later they are practical industrialists and conquerors. In the sixteenth century, the English were regarded by Continentals as extravagant and ungovernable; in the nineteenth, they had become dull, repressed, and a law-abiding nation of shopkeepers. If history and criticism pretend to enlighten us by using national epithets, these must be circumstantial about time, place, and persons. The French nation in August, 1914, can be treated as a unified group because a certain emotion was uppermost and compelling. By 1917, that unity had dissipated: mutiny and defeatism were in the air. In times of peace, workers or employers or university professors unite for a while on particular issues, permitting temporary generalizations. But all statements based on national or professional classifications are always misleading. Even in constituted bodies that poll their members—a legislature or a medical association—there are always minorities of whom what is true is the exact opposite of the majority truth. Minorities may be overlooked in practical affairs, but in critical judgments, in histories, in anything resembling a desire to know, the recording of divergence is the third dimension necessary to a lifelike portrayal. The urge is strong to speak of groups as if their actions formed an indivisible whole, and it is hard to be sure which of the infinite number of differences are significant, but usually that discovery is the point of the investigation, as when Napoleon III consulted his prefects to find out whether France was ready for war with Prussia. More than half said no: he disregarded them in favor of the other, more congenial view, and so put himself back into the state of ignorance from which he had tried to lift himself by asking. The same error is committed in any assumption of unanimity.

If the notion of culture, of various and variable traditions is accepted, and a clear picture kept in mind of what the make-up of a man or a group includes, there are still obstacles to sane judgment of a foreign nation or a social class. The first lies in our personal error—our unfamiliarity with the foreign language, our misinterpretation of social usages, the small range of our observations, too often bearing on shopkeepers and hotel proprietors rather than on the motley millions who form the people about whom we talk so glibly. The second consists in the presence of ready-made formulas. The mind tends to see only what has been pointed out to it, and a theatrical tradition has accustomed us to feel that one good trait implies every good trait and conversely. Between these two aberrations, it is extraordinarily difficult to keep, as it were, a painter's eye on the object. That is why observers of national traits so often fall back on race and so often ascribe to nationality all the biological attributes that they have just denied in repudiating racial explanations. Says André Siegfried: "The personality of a nation is a striking thing. A people lives, behaves, and reacts like an organism, and, when highly civilized, like an individual." (*New York Times Magazine,* July 24, 1932.)

Political scientists such as Siegfried are not alone in saying that the modern nations are races. Critics of literature and the arts also are fond of nation-race epithets. And here again, whatever may be the intention, the result is not greater understanding but reduction of light and evasion of the problem. In a civilization where high art matters to many people, this ultimate type of racism means a serious loss of perception and enjoyment. Let us illustrate it by taking a cue from Havelock Ellis and considering George Bernard Shaw with the aid of race and nationality. Our subject is a wit, an Irishman, and a socialist. What easier than to explain his wit by the axiom that "all Irishmen are witty" (despite the equally profound belief in dumb Irishmen) and his socialism by a reference to the economic miseries of Ireland. Nothing has been explained, but the mind is somehow satisfied about Shaw's make-up because he has heard of Irish wit and Irish poverty and because nation-race explanations are familiar.

Now suppose the reader does not stop thinking where the critic stops but goes on to recall a few other commonplaces, in equally good standing; for example, that the Irish are Celts and that the Celts are melancholy, unpractical, and passionate individualists. Shaw is none of these things. Then let another gifted Irishman be brought into the discussion, say William Butler Yeats, a poet, a theosophist, and a temperament that changed from dreamy to tough-minded during a long life. Where are the common effects of race and nationality? The racial-national classification has broken down, powerless as it is to embrace divergent cultural and individual truths. Taking refuge in environmental influences is of no avail, for Irish poverty is agricultural poverty, and just as we know all about Celtic melancholy so we "know" that peasants are individualistic and reactionary. Shaw therefore could not possibly be a socialist if he were "really and truly" an Irishman. Shall we throw out Shaw as untypical? Why not throw out Yeats? Full of melancholy dreams, how could he become a political realist? Or must we enlarge our definition of racial "Irish" to include both? But there may be still other exceptions which will strain our definition beyond endurance. This suggests that we should become not more general but more particular. We should study Yeats, examine the facts of Shaw's life as a Protestant Dubliner with a particular background, a particular mother and father, a particular history *of his own*.

Going one step further, let us ask whether the class mind is a truer index to personality than the racial mind. Shaw's thought, his political activity, and his art are all permeated by his socialist convictions; but his income, his outward behavior, and 90 percent of his social contacts are bourgeois and capitalist. To call him either a bourgeois mind or a revolutionary mind without further qualification is patently absurd. Yet we are not dealing with a Dr. Jekyll and Mr. Hyde, but with a public person who was held to greater consistency than the average and whose ideas were conditioned like others by his environment. That environment was roughly the same as that which acted upon the mind of a Prime Minister, say Stanley Baldwin. Yet the two men reached diametrically opposed political faiths. Subject to the same London environment they had only citizenship and perhaps a few historical symbols in common. Their accents and their clothes were not the same, their diets were not alike, for Shaw was a vegetarian—this last trait reminding us of physiology and of the need to glance at what may be, according to science, tenable ways of grouping human beings.

III

Was ever Tartar fierce and cruel
Upon the strength of water gruel?
But who can stand his fire and force
When first he rides, then eats his horse!

—SAMUEL BUTLER, *Hudibras*

ALL RACIAL GROUPINGS according to fixed factors, such as skull or pigmentation, having failed to bring order out of chaos, certain men of science who seem free from political prejudice have recaptured the humility of the true investigator and begun again to survey the supposed facts of race. They have ceased to look for a single cause of diversity in human beings and have studied instead the variables of environment and heredity.

Environment in this new sense is no longer a force determined by the degree of latitude and expressible as Northern or Southern, but a complex of separate agents among which, owing to its direct connection with the formation of the adult body, diet seems the most important.

Diet affects the characteristics associated with race in three ways—stature, coloring, and shape of skull. An interesting statistical fact peculiar to the United States first revealed the connection between diet and physique. It was found that the children born in the United States of Southern European immigrants tended to be taller than their parents. If the Sicilian "race" were one of nature's constants, then these changes of physique would not occur. But if the effect of diet is tentatively assumed capable of producing the change, then a new line of investigation is opened. Determining whether it is the abundance of milk or vitamins or a difference in the water supply on this continent that "causes" the physical modification is laborious but fruitful. Statistics also show a difference in the height of those peoples that subsist on rice and those that eat meat. A general hypothesis can be drawn that if the food eaten produces more energy than the body requires, the surplus is stored in the form of bone or tissue, with a consequent alteration of bodily appearance. The relation of the jaw to the size of the skull being normally constant, it follows that changes in the size of the jaw through diet must affect the size of the skull. Whether or not acquired characteristics are transmitted, diet may account at least in part for the variations in one of the so-called racial characteristics.

Color depends upon a more involved process by no means fully understood. It appears as if the salt content in the system bore some relation to pigmentation by hastening or retarding the deposit of color pigment under the skin, which is in all peoples transparent. Light and heat are known within common experience to affect color, but the exact conditions that produce a given degree of color or its permanence has not been determined. Professor John M. Nelson of Columbia University, who specialized in enzymes, isolated the principal catalytic agent of pigmentation, called Tyrosinase. Dr. Mark Graubard went on to find out whether the enzyme exists in the chromosomes of dark-colored insects. The evidence turned up is still inconclusive as to the reasons for the existence of variously pigmented races. All that a layman should retain on the color question is an open mind, grasping only the capital fact that color is not a single characteristic but a component of variables as yet unnumbered and unanalyzed.

Both diet and the chemistry of pigmentation raise the problem of hereditary transmission which our first chapter declared to be central to any tenable theory of race. Two groups of scientists, both of which discard the hypothesis of race, have attacked the problem. The anthropologists—chiefly Franz Boas, R. H. Lowie, A. A. Goldenweiser, and Alfred L. Kroeber—have, by a comparative and descriptive study of primitive and civilized peoples, arrived at a new formulation of the fact of bodily similarity. That formulation answers not so much the question, "What is transmitted?" but "Who are transmitted?" Thus the presence in Ireland of many persons with blue eyes and black hair discloses not the criteria of the Irish race, but the existence of a "population" in the genetic sense. It happens by the convergence of genes through intermarriage that these particular traits repeat often enough to become striking. But they are neither fixed nor certain of transmission, the genes that "carry" traits being only predisposing factors which require environmental support.

The race-theorists who believed in the infallibility of "blood" never stopped to examine whether the offspring of parents that they dubbed Nordic inevitably showed the same Nordic symptoms. Yet ordinary observation shows how dissimilar blood relatives can look—and act—despite recurrent likenesses from generation to generation. This simple truth inspired Thomas Hardy's verse, which could serve as a caution to racists:

> I am the family face;
> Flesh perishes, I live on,
> Projecting trait and trace
> Through time to times anon,
> And leaping from place to place
> Over oblivion.[6]

The distinction between a race and a family or population presents a double aspect. First, it excludes any causal connection between a genetic line and a cultural pattern. For culture takes hold of the next generation entirely, whereas the members of that generation do not reproduce their parents' features, even with slight modifications. Second, it throws back upon the student of genetics the difficult problem of predicting morphological likeness. For example, had the Great Elector of Prussia wanted his tall grenadiers to procreate a fresh generation of tall grenadiers for his royal successor, he would have had a harder time arranging for it than Hitler and Darré seemed to think. In the words of Boas: "The existence of diverse genetic lines is clearly proved by family resemblance between parents and children and between brothers and sisters. It is necessary to determine the degree of genetic complexity in a population. Obviously, if all families were genetically alike and uninfluenced by outer circumstances, there would be no family resemblances because for any one member of a family, one of another family might be substituted. In a closely inbred population something of that kind may be expected, but no such case is known in which an identity of family lines, such as is nearly attained in pure breeds of domesticated animals, is found."

The geneticist on whom has fallen the burden of research as a result of substituting population for race, attacks the problem

[6] *Moments of Vision.*

from the opposite side. In dealing with genes he becomes aware of the complexities of bodily reproduction. As H. S. Jennings of Johns Hopkins pointed out, there is no such thing as a unit-carrier of characters. "At least 50 genes must work together to produce a single feature such as red eye" in the fruit fly. The racist's hope of physical predestination fails again: "Characters are not inherited at all; certain material which will produce a particular character under certain conditions is inherited."

The master of modern genetics, T. H. Morgan, indicates the relevance of his findings to social problems and his statement seems definitive: "If within each human social group the geneticist finds it impossible to discover with any reasonable certainty the genetic basis of behavior, the problems must seem extraordinarily difficult when groups are contrasted with each other where the differences are obviously connected not only with material advantages and disadvantages resulting from location, climate, soil and mineral wealth, but with traditions, customs, religious taboos, conventions and prejudices." (*Evolution and Genetics,* 207.)[7]

Race-thinking was called at the close of our first chapter a superstition, that is, according to Webster, "a belief, an act, or a practice . . . regarded as irrational, idle or injurious." The truth or falsity of this appellation is not to be measured by the amount of illustrative evidence so far presented in this book or in the appendix and bibliography still to come. It lies rather in the inherent vice of the reasoning embodied in the very idea of Race. As John Stuart Mill said over a century ago: "Of all vulgar modes of escaping from the consideration of the effect of social and moral influences on the human mind, the most vulgar is that of attributing the diversities of conduct and character to inherent natural differences." (*Princ. of Polit. Econ.,* I, 390.)

[7] To these remarks written in 1936-37, much could be added today, and notably some paragraphs about the intricacies of blood groups, classifications based (at last) on actual blood, and which also fail to coincide with the common criteria of race.

In that calm statement is condensed the nature and danger of the error. It is a vulgar error, not only because it thrives and is abroad among the people, often unaware of itself, but always charged with hatred and hypocrisy; it is also and above all a vulgar error because it denies individual diversity, scouts the complexity of cause and effect, scorns the intellect, and ultimately bars Mind from the universe of created things.

Appendix

RACE-THINKING: A BRIEF ANTHOLOGY

THE FOLLOWING EXCERPTS have been chosen to illustrate the extremes and the commonplaces of race-thinking. The excuse for the repetitiousness lies in the spectacle of distinguished minds entertaining the vulgar error or vulgar minds giving birth to extraordinary notions. The headings used to break up the sequence are, like the theories they cover, neither exact, nor logical, nor mutually exclusive.

NOTABLES

Cecil Rhodes (*c. 1900*)

The furtherance of the English Empire for the bringing of the whole uncivilized world under British rule, for the recovery of the United States, for the making of the Anglo-Saxon race but one empire—what a dream! But yet it is probable. It is a possible. (*Last Will and Testament,* 33.)

Briand on Locarno policy (*c. 1926*)

I am a Celt: it needed the imagination of a Celt to attempt this foreign policy. (Quoted from Louis Piérard, Socialist Deputy from Mons and an intimate of Briand, by Emile Buré and reported in *l'Echo de Paris,* Dec. 4, 1933, with the comment: "If one recalls that Lloyd George was also a Celt, one will be forced to admit that the Celts deserve the gratitude of the Germans.")

Louis Blanc (*1872*)

It is the energetic development of soul and spirit that makes the races strong and it is the strong races that make great peoples. (*Discours,* Nov. 25, 1872.)

Bernard Shaw (*1928*)

The Nordic race beloved of North America and German "blonde beasts" may be a romantic fiction; but when we speak of a Nordic temperament and a Latin temperament we are indicating facts which distinguish the north from the south of Europe as they distinguish the north from the south of America; and these facts may deadlock or greatly hamper Geneva until it recognizes that the Federation of the World will come before the Parliament of Man, which can hardly be realized until Man becomes a much less miscellaneous lot than he is at present. (*What I Really Wrote About the War,* 363.)

Charles Darwin (*1871*)

There is, however, no doubt that the various races, when carefully compared and measured, differ much from each other—as in the texture of the hair, the relative proportions of all parts of the body, the capacity of the lungs, the form and capacity of the skull and even in the convolutions of the brain. (*The Descent of Man,* VII, 167.)

Karl Marx (*c. 1880*)

This does not prevent the same economic basis from showing infinite variations and gradations in its appearance, even though its principal conditions are everywhere the same. This is due to innumerable outside circumstances, natural environment, race peculiarities, outside historical influences, and so forth, all of which must be ascertained by careful analysis. (*Capital,* III, 919.)

Maurice Barrès (*1894*)

According to race, Hegelianism produces special combinations. It produced Proudhon in France . . . Max Stirner and the sacred law of egotism in Germany. . . . In an absolute Marxist state, the influence of race, occupation and climate would soon regain their power. (*De Hegel aux Cantines du Nord,* 26.)

T. H. Huxley (1894)

The criminal law . . . prevents the propagation of hereditary criminal tendencies; and the poor-law, in so far as it separates married couples whose destitution arises from hereditary defects of character, are doubtless selective agents operating in favor of the non-criminal and the more effective members of society. (*Evolution and Ethics,* 38.)

Galton (1869)

The Negro race is some two grades below our own [the Anglo-Saxon]. (*Hereditary Genius,* 327.)

Paul Broca (1873)

Buffon, for lack of precise data, was unable to raise his thinking to the notion of race. (*Mém.,* II, 415.)

Chateaubriand (1833)

Charlemagne had the Germans' natural taste for music. (*Anal. Hist. de France,* 38.)

Balzac (1846)

This strange alliance seemed to be the result of a strong will acting ceaselessly on a weak character, on that inconsistency peculiar to the Slavs which, while it gives them heroic courage in battle, also accounts for their incredible disorder in conduct—a moral flabbiness whose causes ought to interest the physiologists, for physiologists are to politics what entomologists are to agriculture. (*La Cousine Bette,* 71.)

Taine (1890)

Manifestly, he [Napoleon] is neither a Frenchman nor a man of the eighteenth century. He belongs to another race and another century. . . . Italian he was, by extraction and by blood. (*Régime Moderne,* I, 5-6.)

Henry James (1900)

With his diminutive stature and his perpendicular spirit, his flushed face, expressive protuberant eyes, high peremptory voice . . . he reminded me of the gentry who figure in the revolutions of his native land. If he was not a fierce little Jacobin he ought to have been, for I am sure there were many men of his pattern on the Committee of Public Safety. (*A Little Tour in France,* 202-3.)

George Meredith (1875)

Mr. Romfrey entertained no profound fellow-feeling for the Negro and except as the representative of a certain amount of working power commonly requiring the whip to wind it up, he inclined to despise the black spot in the creation. . . . (*Beauchamp's Career,* 86.)

John Livingston Lowes (1936)

Moreover, this same simple and sensuous quality shows itself in another way—in the inexpugnable racial tendency of the Hebrew mind to express not only emotions, but ideas, in apt and telling imagery. (*Essays in Appreciation,* 9.)

Henry Fairfield Osborn (1924)

The Northern races, as is well known to anthropologists, include all those peoples which originally occupied the western plateau of Asia and traversed Northern Europe, certainly as early as 12,000 B.C. . . . They invaded the countries to the South, not only as conquerors but as contributors of strong moral and intellectual elements to more or less decadent civilizations. Through the Nordic tide which flowed into Italy came the ancestors of Raphael, Leonardo da Vinci, Galileo, Titian; also according to Günther, of Giotto, Donatello, Botticelli, Andrea del Sarto, Petrarch and Tasso. . . . Columbus from his portraits and from busts, authentic or not, was clearly of Nordic ancestry. Kossuth was a Calvinist and of noble family, and there is a presumption in favor of his being a Nordic; Kosciusko and Pulaski were members of a Polish nobility which at that time was largely Nordic. Coligny, Colbert, Richelieu, Lafayette, and Rochambeau, beyond all question were of French (Norman) Nordic nobility, and in modern France we observe that two of the leaders in the recent great struggle, Joffre and Foch, are both Nordic, while Clemenceau and Poincaré are of Alpine blood. France includes among her great artists Rodin, of Nordic origin; among her leading literary men, Lamartine, Racine, Anatole France, all Nordics. The intellectual influence of the Northern race is also apparent in Spain where it appears in her greatest man of letters, Cervantes; also in Portugal in the poet-hero Camoëns, whose ancestors were Gothic. Of the fighting stock of Italy, Napoleon, although born in Corsica, was descended from the old Lombard nobility, of Nordic origin, and it is probable that Garibaldi with his

Teutonic name was largely of Northern stock. . . . (*N.Y. Times,* Apr. 8, 1924.)

Samuel Butler (1879)

Priggism, or whatever the substantive is, is as essentially a Teutonic vice as holiness is a Semitic characteristic. (*Alps and Sanctuaries,* 142.)

Léon Daudet (1921)

The work of the Semite is revolution, the overthrow of the autochthonous by the nomads. (On Edouard Drumont, *Revue Universelle,* Jan. 1, 1921, 28.)

Rudyard Kipling (c. 1900)

The Gaul, ever an artist, breaks enclosure to study the morale, at the present day, of the British sailorman. (Quoted in Fowler, *The King's English,* 43.)

D. B. Wyndham Lewis (1928)

The Gauls and Latins have ever been indifferent alike to loud noises and strong smells. (*François Villon,* 40.)

Emerson (1856)

Again, as if to intensate the influences that are not of race, what we think of when we talk of English traits really narrows itself to a small district. (*English Traits,* vi.)

Roheim and Freud (1932)

With Freud's *Totem and Taboo* a new science has come into being. . . . "We sometimes call it psychoanalytical anthropology, but we all believe it will be the only anthropology of the future." (Roheim, *Internat. Jour. Psychoanal.,* 1932, 6.)

Malvina Hoffman and Chicago Field Museum (1930-36)

Have proposition to make, do you care to consider it. Racial types to be modelled while travelling round the world.—*Field Museum.*

The sculptress accepted and contributed to the Hall of Man, among other racial types: the Nordic type, the Elusive Alpine, a Study of Mixed Type, and a Symbolic Group portraying the White, Yellow, and Black Races, with "each figure holding the weapon by which the race has defended its own boundaries." (Malvina Hoffman, *Heads and Tales,* 1, 6, 161, 135, 334.)

Oscar Wilde (*1895*)

Dear Duchess, and how is the Duke? Brain still weak, I suppose? Well, that is only to be expected, is it not? His good father was just the same. There is nothing like race, is there?

"MYSTICS"

Baron Ernest Seillière (*1902-11*)

The mysticism of race, which has played almost no part in France . . . (*Les Mystiques du Néo-Romantisme,* iii.)

No doubt he [Charles de Villers] has, as a Lorrainer, a little German blood in his veins, but he has less of it than Mme de Staël. (*Revue de Paris,* Oct. 1, 1902, 599.)

Edgar Quinet (*1831*)

The power of new ideas in the Germanies, so unfathomable and so incorporeal . . . arises to confront us like the very genius of a race, . . . of that Germanic race . . . which is beginning to enter modern history like a flood . . . and which is only awaiting its opportunity. (*France et Allemagne,* 22-24.)

Emile Faguet (*1895-1906*)

Race is the consciousness of self attaching to institutions, religion, climate, customs, mores, history and language. (*Revue Latine,* Oct. 25, 1906, 590.)

The barbarian is, after all, of the same race as the Roman and the Greek. He is our cousin. The Yellow man, the Black man, is not in the least our cousin. . . .

Will there be a renaissance, a white soul under a yellow skin? (*Jour. des Débats,* July 25, 1895, soir.)

Berl (*1900*)

Religions are not merely doctrines, they are races. (*Grande Revue,* Oct. 1, 1900, 7.)

W. T. Stead (*1902*)

The English-speaking race stood to Mr. Rhodes for all that the Catholic church stood to Ignatius Loyola. (*Last Will and Testament,* 63.)

Vacher de Lapouge (*1899*)

What makes an individual act is the legion of his ancestors buried in the earth. (*L'Aryen: Son Rôle Social,* 350-51.)

LeBon (*1912*)

Race plays a mighty rôle in revolutions . . . mixed breeds are ungovernable. . . . The soul of the race is the strongest braking power upon social upheaval. (*La Révol. Française et la Psychol. des Révol.,* 53, 68.)

Marius-Ary Leblond (*1933*)

If it is the study of French History that guided him [Hanotaux] to politics and in his foreign policies, it is the spiritual contemplation of the Mediterranean that inspired his wisdom. It differs, however, from that of the ancient Greeks . . . he remained therefore above all a great African with a missionary soul. (*Eclaireur de Nice,* Nov. 19, 1933.)

Alex Small (*1933*)

At the risk of appearing to be seeking sunshine in cucumbers, I find something more in Hitlerism than can be described in any formulas. After the program has been defined—a program which has in it something for everyone—remains the impression that the essential has not been touched. It looks like a new religion, one which has not yet made its doctrine rigid. (*Paris Chicago-Tribune,* Sept. 11, 1933.)

MEN OF SCIENCE

J. Laumonier (*1885*)

Around the positive notion of race must revolve the explanation of historical events. . . . That notion is physiological and psychological; we owe it to the school of Broca. (*Revue Scient.,* July, 112.)

Sigmund Freud (*1930*)

Neither was it an unaccountable chance that the dream of German world-dominion evoked a complementary movement towards anti-semitism; and it is quite intelligible that the attempt to establish a new communistic type of culture in Russia should find psychological support in the persecution of the bourgeois. One only wonders, however, how the Soviets will manage when they have exterminated their bourgeois entirely. (*Civilization and Its Discontents,* 91.)

Lapouge (1899)

Good observers among gynecologists claim they can recognize the race of a woman merely by examining her genital organs. (*L'Aryen,* 30.)

Cénas (1897)

The so-called "apron" of the Hottentot women is in no way peculiar to that race. The protuberance of the *labia minora* is more frequent among the whites than it is generally admitted. It occurs in one out of seven patients examined, to a length of 4 or 5 cms., which is the length of the Bushman apron. (*Assoc. Française Avanc. Sci.,* 1897, II, 708.)

Chalumeau (1896)

The less strength an occupation requires, the more it appeals to tall men. (*Influence de la taille . . .* 1896, 15.)

Souffret (1892)

Would the Australian in Europe ever become German, Slav, Celt or Latin? (*De la Disparité . . . des races,* 9.)

C. S. Myers (1909)

The racial differences that exist in reaction-times are largely the outcome of similar psychological factors, determined by habits of life and possibly by some obscure racial tendency to react rather in the sensorial than in the muscular fashion or vice versa. (*A Textbook of Experimental Psychology,* 307.)

Rochet (1895)

With such a norm [the beau ideal derived from an "anthropology of the fine arts"] the races would be easy to study and compare. (*Mém. Soc. d'Anthrop. Paris,* Feb. 21, 1895.)

Driesmans (c. 1900)

Whoever wishes to work in this field [race-learning] must for the greater part rely on the living aspects of things as well as on his own feelings; he must at the same time see in the dark and make his way in it. (*Die Kelten,* Vol. III, xi.)

A. de Candolle (*1873*)

If Israel peopled all Europe, there would be no more wars, but a very civilized people with excellent qualities and very bearable faults. Science and art would be highly advanced. . . . But the children of the Greeks or Latins, Celts, Slavs or Huns would exterminate them. (*Hist. des Sci. et des Savants,* 405.)

Gaillard (*1913*)

History is explained far better by the idea of race than by the idea of nation. . . . The blond type is an anthropological type possessing the most remarkable qualities and it has served as the finest model in the great periods of plastic art. . . . The blond beauty of Mme d'Etampes did not care for the art of Benvenuto Cellini and no doubt preferred that of Jean Goujon. . . . Only recently have brunettes been placed in the same rank of beauty as the blonds. Formerly the blonds were always sought after, a sexual attraction due to the greater generative qualities of the Nordic races. (*Bull. Soc. Anthrop.,* Oct. 16, 1913, 589-95.)

Chavée (*1873*)

. . . the native or acquired difficulty among the Germans of getting the nervous centres of the *medulla oblongata* to carry out the orders of the cerebral centres regarding syllabic sound-production—they say *Fa* and *Pa* for *Va* and *Ba*—is a pathological fact still observable in our own day. (*Bull. Soc. Anthrop.,* 1873, 505.)

Nadaillac (*c. 1885*)

All races are not equally fruitful. Climate, social, economic, biological conditions play a part as yet not scientifically defined. . . . It can be said in general that the Latin races, the French race in particular, are less fecund than the Slavic and Anglo-Saxon races. For us it is a matter of indisputable inferiority. (*Affaibliss. de la natalité en France,* 71-72.)

LITTERATEURS

Jean Lorrain (*c. 1900*)

One must cut loose from individuals and fall in love with a race. (*M. de Phocas, A Novel.*)

On Barbey d'Aurevilly (1885)

The ancestors of Barbey d'Aurevilly wielded the enormous and heavy two-bladed axe of the Franks. (*Rev. du Monde Latin,* 1885, 209.)

T. H. Huxley (1879)

The energetic Greek might find fierce joys in a world in which "strife is father and king" but the old Aryan spirit was subdued to quietism in the Indian sage. (*Evolution and Ethics,* 54.)

On Jesus Christ (1933)

The name of Galilee does seem of Gallic origin. Christ was Galilean, was he then a Gaul? There is in this an argument highly in favor of Celticism. (Paul Lecour, *Atlantis,* Sept.-Oct., 1933.)

On Renan (1885-1900)

Renan . . . is the Breton coming to grips with the Gascon, which explains his versatility from dreaminess to irony. (Fouillée, *Tempérament et caractère,* 340-44.)

It is enough to remember that M. Renan is Breton to see that his imagination comes to him from his race. (Bourget, *Essais de Psychol. Contemp.,* 46-47.)

Imagine the temperament of a believer, a contemplative being, grown in the mists on the coast of Brittany. . . . He comes to Paris . . . bringing the devout dream of his race and of the milieu where he grew. (Zola, *Le Roman Expérimental,* 70-71.)

It is a timid race, reserved and living within itself, dull in appearance but possessing profound feelings and carrying into its religious instincts an adorable delicacy. . . . This delicacy which characterizes the Celtic race . . . is equally removed from the rhetoric of feeling too common among the Latin races and from the purposeful naïveté of the Germans. (Renan, *Poésie des races celtiques,* 7.)

On Tolstoy (1894)

Where one can discover the man who is truly not of the same blood as ourselves is in the idea he has of beauty and art. In him [Tolstoy], an Asiatic impervious to sense-impressions, the plastic sense does not exist, the beauty of form does not touch him. . . . In spite of steam, electricity and the newspaper press, the races maintain—all arguments to the contrary notwithstanding—an almost complete autonomy of feeling, sensation and idea. (M. Spronck, *Jour. des Débats,* June 11, 1894, soir.)

On Meredith (1905)

George Meredith . . . had the serious sympathy of the psychologist for every variety of souls and races. (E. Legouis, *Revue Germanique,* Jan., 1905, 408.)

On Mistral (1931)

. . . whereas Mistral brings us the elements of a harmonious system, of a rational whole rooted in the Latin earth, in the earth of France. (F. J. Desthieux, *Heures Perdues,* V, 1931, 129.)

Jean Richepin (c. 1910)

Before the Aryas, who tilled the soil
There lived Turanians, the wandering killers.
. . . and though I live in France
No Gaul am I, nor Latin. My bones
Are small, yellow my skin, copper my eyes;
I have a rider's stance and full contempt for laws.
(*La Chanson du Sang.*)

By and About Bourget (1894-1921)

Paul Bourget has opened the way to the symbolist spirit, Wagnerian, Tolstoyian and Ibsenite, which may be great indeed, but not very French, and which on our soil seems dubious and unhealthy. (P. Lalo, *Jour. des Débats,* June 9, 1894, soir.) One must exacerbate one's national sensibility by contact with other nations. . . . The naïve Gallo-Roman with his simple but generous rationalism . . . against the tentacular Germany with the hard mentality of a predatory race . . . [illustrate] the law of reciprocal national incompatibility. (P. Bourget, *L'âme étrangère, Illustr.,* June 11, 1921, 546-47.)

On Sidney Dark's The Jew Today *(1934)*

Another fact that Mr. Dark very much minimizes is the importance of race. . . . In any environment the Jew, even if unorthodox, even if a Christian, remains a Jew. He is a Semite, even as a Chinaman is a Chinaman; physical characteristics are allied to mental and emotional characteristics, in men, as in horses and dogs. (Sir John Squire in London *Sunday Times,* Jan. 28, 1934.)

On Enesco (1937)

The listener felt it as explicable background of Enesco's achievement which is so indubitably of his soil and race. (Olin Downes, *New York Times,* Feb. 8, 1937.)

German Writers' Guild (*1934*)

The German Writers' Guild is convinced that in the present perilous situation of Western civilization no new intellectual order can be created, no literature can spring from such dissolute elements, no style can be formed, no historical rôle can be expected from this part of the world, if the idea of Fatherland, considered as a genealogical fact, moral heritage, and language mysticism, does not become the dominant idea and controlling factor of the future. (Hans Johst, President, and Gottfried Benn, Vice-president.)

PATRIOTS

Pirenne on Belgium (*1900-26*)

Like our soil, which has been formed by the deposits of rivers coming from France and Germany, our national culture is a kind of syncretism wherein we find the genius of two races mixed together and modified by each other. (Henri Pirenne, *History of Belgium*, 3rd ed., I, 11.)

On Anglo-Saxon virtue (*1932*)

An appeal for the city-wide revival of the "Anglo-Saxon principles of virtue" was made by Magistrate Michael A. Ford in a hearing on the sale of twenty-six allegedly obscene magazines. (*New York Herald Tribune*, Apr. 3, 1932.)

Montégut (*1857-77*)

The French people is the only one that has no race instinct. Never did this feeling have any influence in France. (Emile Montégut, *Libres Opinions*, 35.) Although he [Michelet] has not in the same degree as Thierry a feeling for the genius of race. . . . (*Ibid.*, p. 65.) Caesar's idea of democracy . . . was revived eighteen centuries later by a man of Italian race who had the secret of it in his blood. (*Ibid.*, 2nd ed., 315.)

Jullian (*1922*)

Writers of remarkable intelligence will write "we are Romans with Julius Caesar." The followers of Romanticism and their heirs protest: "We are Gauls formed by the Druids." The recent discoveries of the Ligurian period have made the fanatics of innovation exclaim: "Avaunt, ye Gauls and Romans, we are Ligurians." (*De la Gaule à la France*, 1922, 83.) France is something of greater worth than Latin or German, namely Gauls. . . . What they once were they have remained by virtue of race; I mean the character transmitted at birth. (*Ibid.,* 152, 172.)

Suarès (1916-17)

A race in history is no doubt the more or less intact remains of a race in nature. (André Suarès, *La Nation contre la Race,* 1916-17, I, 101.) France . . . is not a race, but a nation and a *nation is a person.* (*Ibid.,* II, 8.) Whether there are races or not in natural history, there are races in history and history recognizes them (13). A race is the idea entertained by the men who boast of belonging to it. . . . A race is the opposite of a nation, for a nation is a spirit (14). The danger of the Germans is that they are a race and not a people (16). A race is the corporeal form of a nation. . . . The forest primeval, that is the race (20).

A Socialist on Race (1903)

For this task of nationalism, science is invoked. Theories are made about the shape of the skull or the pronunciation of vowels and consonants. Ammon, Spencer, Lapouge and Lombroso are called upon, between two orisons at the Sacré-Cœur and Notre-Dame de Lourdes. (Eug. Fournière, *La Petite République Socialiste,* July 29, 1903.)

Faguet (1895)

The yellow and black perils will smother our race and destroy our civilization. (*Jour. des Débats,* July 25, 1895.)

Schuré on Gobineau (1904-15)

Decidedly, France is beginning to do Gobineau justice. . . . The Aryan idea sheds a new light on history and might lead to perfecting the race through intellectual and social selection. (*Précurseurs et Révoltés,* 1904, 283-85.)

There is a portion of truth in the idea of the dominant characteristic of the human races, of certain effects of crossbreeding, and of the danger resulting from excessive mixture. (*Revue Polit. et Litt.,* Nov. 1915, 558.)

The Latin World (1882-85)

To the Latins the Latin world. The Latin idea is not political pan-Latinism, but that of cooperation in the ethnic competition, the struggle between the two Indo-European groups of advanced races. (Motto and Plan of the *Revue du Monde Latin,* founded Dec., 1882, by Baron Charles de Tourtoulon.)

The Mulatto Race (*1923*)

Ashamed of my race?
And of what race am I?
I am many in one.
Through my veins there flows the blood
of Red Man, Black Man, Briton, Celt and Scot
In warring clash and tumultuous riot.

(Joseph S. Cotter, *The Mulatto and His Critics,* 1923.)

Abbé Gratry (*c. 1850*)

My family, the race of Adam, the race of the Children of God. . . . [Father Gratry advocating a crusade against the Turks in magazine *La Paix.*] (*Pages Choisies,* 258.)

Hermann Oncken (*1915*)

The antipathy to the Germans . . . makes the Slavs more deeply conscious of racial antagonisms than ourselves. (*Modern Germany,* 503.)

General Marjoulet (*1934*)

Would Gaul have benefited more by being less Latin, or a little more Hellenic, or exclusively Gallic . . . ? Modest Gallo-Roman as I am, I cannot help thinking that the affinities of Gaul to the Athenian Republic did not need—God forbid!—to be accentuated. (*Eclaireur de Nice,* Jan. 22, 1934.)

A recent French History (*1932*)

Since Roman days, our head has been Roman while our soul remained Celtic. (Emille Saillens, *French History,* 1932, 19.)

Isaac Blümchen (*1913-14*)

Some try to maintain that there are no human races, that a Spaniard or an Eskimo, a Jap, a Norwegian, a Kaffir or a Sicilian, a Patagonian are beings of the same species, with the same faculties, with the same physiology, mentality and sensibility. That theory is a gross absurdity. (*Le droit de la race supérieure* and *A Nous la France,* 54.)

PRO AND CON

Spinoza

If anyone wishes to maintain that the Jews . . . have been chosen by God for ever, I will not gainsay him if he will admit that this choice, whether temporary or eternal, has no regard, in so far as it is peculiar to the Jews, to aught but dominion and physical advantage (for by such alone can one nation be distinguished from another), whereas in regard to intellect and true virtue, every nation is on a par with the rest, and God has not in these respects chosen one people rather than another. (Ratner, *Philos. of Spinoza,* 70.)

On the book God Among the Germans *(1934)*

The study is based on a thorough discussion of German folk consciousness and points out how Hitler's power is possible through the peculiar race mysticism of his people. Rooted in the Teutonic temperament, this movement has been growing since the ignominious defeat of Versailles, particularly in the unparalleled organization of youth, and has been greatly augmented by Alfred Rosenberg's philosophy of Nordic supremacy. (Paul H. Douglas, quoted in publishers' advertisement.)

Two botanists on the Pines (1914)

There are also species—and this is equally important for the systematizer as for the physiologist—which adapt themselves so completely to changing conditions of moisture that their extreme forms seem to belong to different species. (Schimper quoted on the title page of George Russell Shaw's *Genus Pinus.*)

Bagehot (1869)

It may be answered that in this there is nothing new . . . that when a philosopher cannot account for anything in any other manner, he boldly ascribes it to an occult quality in some race. (*Physics & Politics,* 2.)

Tenney Frank on the Roman Empire (1916)

. . . But it is offered in the hope that a more thorough study of the race question may be made in conjunction with economic and political questions before any attempt is made finally to estimate the factors at work in the change of temper of Imperial Rome. (*American Historical Review,* July, 1916, 708.)

Jules Sageret (1919)

There is no psychology of the races because there is no psychology *tout court.* (*Revue du Mois,* June 15, 1919, 163.)

Simar (1920) and Hovelacque (1875)

The doctrine of race finds few adherents in France. (Simar, *Etude Crit. sur la doctr. des races,* 246.)

It is antiquated to speak of dolicho-Celts and mongoloid Basques and other such fine Germanic inventions, though in truth they were made in Paris. (Hovelacque, *Langues, Races, Nationalités,* 12.)

Franz Werfel (1932)

The petty bourgeois . . . yearns for "Nordification" or "Latinity"; he concerns himself with Anthropology to prove that his race surpasses all others, though it is well known that the European is a fearful mixture, compared to which any village cur is a pedigreed race-specimen. . . . All this means an impious and sinful hypostatizing of the body into a single Godhead and conceals behind inflated verbiage the dismal despair of lost souls and sick minds. (Vienna, *Neue Freie Presse,* March 5, 1932.)

Watson Davis on the Advance of Science (1934)

There is no doubt that the anthropological topic most widely debated in recent months is a topic that has little or no scientific meaning. This is the burning question: Who is a Nordic and how important is it to be one . . . ?

Nordicism was evolved as a theory years ago. Dr. K. Holler, well-known German eugenist, credits a Frenchman and a German with awakening the movement in Germany. The Frenchman, Prince Gobineau (*sic*), obtained little recognition in his own country, when his work on the inequality of human races was translated into German about the turn of the century (*sic*). At about the same time, Houston Stewart Chamberlain's [the German?] *Foundations of the Nineteenth Century* appeared and exercised a profound effect on German thought. (Watson Davis, ed., *The Advance of Science,* chapter on *Living Races,* 350 seq., Chemical Foundation Publication.)

The movement of race betterment by sterilization was started by a group of forward-looking persons who considered the enormous improvement in races of plants and animals. . . . These people saw no reason why similar methods should not be adopted for the improvement of the human race. (*Ibid.,* 275.)

Ruth Benedict (1929)

Anthropology has no encouragement to offer to those who would trust our spiritual achievements to the automatic perpetuation of any selected hereditary germ plasms. (*Century Magazine,* April, 1929.)

University of Chicago (1936)

The department of anthropology of the University of Chicago approves the suggestion made recently by Dr. I. Zollschan of Carlsbad that the League of Nations call an international conference of scientists to enlighten the world on the question of race. (*New York Times,* Apr. 27, 1936.)

BIBLIOGRAPHICAL NOTES

THE FOLLOWING LIST of books is designed to supplement those mentioned in the text. Any selection from the vast literature cannot help being arbitrary, but that which follows will, it is hoped, serve to illustrate once more the endemic and allotropic character of race-thinking.

CHAPTER I

Few works exist in any language on the general problem of race-thinking as it has been posed in these pages, but several previous attempts contain valuable views and an abundance of facts. First in lines comes Th. Simar, with his *Etude Critique sur la formation de la doctrine des races,* Bruxelles, 1922. It is scholarly, but often unphilosophical, anti-German, and inclined to underrate grossly the influence of French ideas on race. Jean Finot, *Le préjugé des races,*[1]

[1] All French titles have Paris as their place of publication unless otherwise specified.

For bibliographical suggestions to span the time elapsed since the first edition of this book, see the Unesco volume *Race and Science,* N.Y., 1961.

1906, is critical but limited. The same holds true of A. Firmin, *De l'Egalité des races humaines,* 1885, designed to vindicate the Negro "race" to which the author "belongs." F. H. Hankins's excellent work on the *Racial Basis of Civilization,* N.Y., 1926, is concerned chiefly with the Nordic-Aryan idea and deals with it historically and biologically. Eugene Pittard, *Race and History,* N.Y., 1926, is a well-written critique of race-doctrines marred by the belief that nationality accounts for most of the so-called racial traits. The point of view of the present study is admirably expressed in short compass by George A. Dorsey in C. A. Beard's *Whither Mankind,* N.Y., 229-63, but without historical background or description of the ramifications of race-thinking in the arts and sciences. A satire of the Nordic idea was included by Hilaire Belloc in his *Short Talks with the Dead,* Kensington, 1926. More recently Huxley and Haddon in *We Europeans,* N.Y., 1936, have attempted a refutation of racism, though with a desire to salvage some of the elements of the thinking they condemn by ascribing too much to local hereditary influences.

For contemporary evidences of systematic race-thinking, the *New York Times Index* since the year 1930 furnishes under the heading "Race" some notable and curious specimens of the usual varieties of racism. The *American Journal of Sociology* provides still more refined examples, of the kind made respectable by the worthy intention of studying cultures. See also Clark Wissler, *Man and Culture,* N.Y., 1923, and Salvador de Madariaga, "Do the Gods Prefer Blonds?", *Forum,* Nov., 1929. The purely intellectual use of race-divisions continues in such works as Hirsch's *Genius and Creative Intelligence,* Cambridge, 1931, and M. T. McClure's *Greek Genius and Race-Mixture* in Vol. III of *Studies in the History of Ideas.*

The student of race must also consult the proponents of Eugenics (e.g., Charles W. Gould, *America, A Family Matter,* N.Y., 1922) and follow with the critique by Raymond Pearl in the *American Mercury* for November, 1927. The color-problem dealt with in the old terms can be found in J. H. Curle's *Our Testing Time,* N.Y., 1926, as well as in the reissue of Lothrop Stoddard's classic, *The Rising Tide of Color Against White Supremacy* (1920). Lastly, the *Transactions of the American Philological Association,* XXIX and *passim,* show the persistence of the alliance between race-thinking and linguistics. Similar foreign publications in these fields are listed under Chapter X.

CHAPTER II

To the historians cited in the text should be added C. C. Fauriel, Trognon, Raynouard, and Ozanam, all of whose studies of Gauls and Germans brought them into contact with the race-question in France. Echoes of it are also found in the works of the radicals and socialists: Considérant, Cabet, Leroux, Louis Blanc, and in most of the well-known Romanticist writers—Vigny (see *Cinq Mars* and the *Journal*), Victor Hugo (*Han d'Islande* and *Le Rhin*), Balzac (*La Princesse de Cadignan, Catherine de Médicis, Maître Cornélius*), Mérimée (*Notes d'un Voyage*), Dumas (*Gaule et France*), Lamartine (Preface to *Fatella*).

The lack of interest in historical origins during the French Revolution is shown by the burning of archives and by such pamphlets as Cérutti's *Mémoire pour le peuple français;* Guich's *Origines Gauloises,* 1801; de Sade's *Histoire de la Nation Française;* the *Abrégé de l'Histoire . . . à l'usage de l'Ecole Royale Militaire;* Dupuis's *Histoire des Révolutions de France;* as well as anonymous works such as *Montesquieu Bon François* and *La Résurrection des Gaulois,* which show that the intertwining of race and French history was not limited to either cranks or highbrows.

To the list of names associated with the new Saxonism in the English-speaking world should be added Sir Walter Scott (opening chapter of *Ivanhoe*), J. L. Motley, Bronson Alcott, and the prolific lexicographer, Archbishop Trench. For a full bibliography on the development of the ideas of Tacitus in France to 1789, see J. Barzun, *The French Race,* N.Y., 1932, 260-70.

CHAPTER III

For the state of anthropology before the days of craniometry it is advisable to read Blumenbach, Cuvier, Buffon, and other notables, but sidelights of great interest are to be found in William Lawrence's *Lectures on Comparative Anatomy,* London, 1819; in the works of Charles White, *An Account of the Regular Gradation in Man,* 1799, and *Of Six Tall Grenadiers,* 1799; in Desmoulins's *Histoire Naturelle des Races Humaines,* 1826; and in J. J. d'Omalius d'Halloy's *Des Races Humaines,* 1845.

Hollard, Virey, Bory St. Vincent, and Humboldt likewise dealt with language, facial angles, and the question of man's place in the animal kingdom. Flourens summed up in 1847 the debt anthropology owed to Blumenbach and made some interesting comments on others in the field (*Mém. Institut,* XXI, I). In the United States John Campbell's *Negromania,* Phila., 1851, attempted to refute those who believed in the equality of races and quoted liberally from a score of contemporary scientists to prove the point.

The standard work on the French Idéologue philosophers is François Picavet, *Les Idéologues,* 1891, to be supplemented by L. Halphen, *L'Histoire en France depuis Cent Ans,* 1914. On the relation of biology and anthropology to religion and scientific dogma, see Walter Scheidt, *Allgemeine Rassenkunde,* München, 1925, and Eric Nordenskiöld, *The History of Biology,* N.Y., 1936. Balzac, *Avant-Propos* to the *Comédie Humaine,* 1842, shows the interest educated men took in the question of evolution as presented in the debate between Cuvier and Geoffroy Saint-Hilaire. Samuel Butler, *Evolution Old and New,* London, 1879, reviews the history of the theory in a fashion more scholarly and critical than does the Historical Sketch in Darwin's *Origin of Species,* 3rd ed., 1860 ff.

CHAPTER IV

The list of books and articles by and about Gobineau has lately grown to such an extent that only a general notion of the literature can be given. The most recent French issues of Gobineau's works, with their publishers, are the *Gobineau-Prokesch Correspondence,* Plon, 1933; *La Fleur d'Or,* Grasset, 1928; *Etudes Critiques,* Kra, 1927; *Ce qui se passe en Asie* and *l'Instinct révolutionnaire en France,* Cahiers Libres, 1928; *L'œuvre de M. de Stendhal,* Champion, 1926; *Nicolas Belavoir,* NRF, 1927. In Germany, Schemann's editions of the posthumous works in French and the translations begun in 1924 and published by the new *Verein* at Leipzig must be consulted, together with Schemann's *Quellen.* The works of Gobineau's supposed precursor, Dr. Gustav Klemm, are hard to find, but both the original essay entitled *Die Verbreitung der activen Menschenrasse ueber den Erdball,* Dresden, 1845, and the expanded history based upon it are to be found in that city, in the Sächsische Landsbibliothek. The essay alone was reproduced in 1906 in the *Politisch-Anthropologische Revue.*

Among Gobineau's biographers, Faure-Biguet is the most recent and in some ways the best. Lange (1924) is very thorough but strongly anti-German, Robert Dreyfus (1905) and the Catholic Dufréchou (1907) are the fairest. Schemann is overenthusiastic and uncritical on the literary side, while Kretzer and Hahne fairly represent the uses of Gobinism in Germany. The *Bayreuther Blätter,* May 5, 1881, Nov. 11, 1882, and May 5, 1886, show the Wagnerians' attitude toward the Count, and Romain Rolland, *Jean Christophe,* IV, 129, expresses the internationalist view.

Other articles of interest are: Frollo, "Soyons Gobinistes" in *Le Petit-Parisien,* Aug. 4, 1904; Thérive, "Gobineau Poète," *Revue Universelle,* 1922; T. de Visan, "La morale de Gobineau," *Akademos,* March, 1909; Kretzer, "Nietzsche und Gobineau," *Frankfurter Zeitung,* July 22, 1902; A. Hallays, "Viollet-le-Duc et Gobineau," *Jour. des Débats,* Apr. 25, 1903; Faguet, "Le Gobinisme," *Revue Latine,* Oct. 25, 1906; A. Sorel, "Le Comte de Gobineau," *Le Temps,* Mar. 22, 1904; Barbey d'Aurevilly, "Le Renaissance," in *Les Œuvres et les Hommes;* for a Gobinian Bolshevist, see Bertreint in *La France Libre,* June 28, 1923, and for an anti-Gobineau Communist, Th. Balk in *Commune,* May and Dec., 1934. Gerald M. Spring has studied *The Vitalism of Count de Gobineau,* N.Y., 1932; Edda Riebe his ideas on eugenics in *Gobineau im Lichte der heutigen Rassenhygiene,* Göttingen, 1926, and Paul Souday his style in a number of articles published in *Le Temps* from 1913 to 1929, some of them reproduced in the two series of his *Livres du Temps.*

CHAPTER V

The use of race in literary and other criticism has been shown to be well-nigh universal, though systematic treatments are relatively few. The earliest seem to be: F. J. Fétis, "Classification des races humaines d'après leurs systèmes musicaux," *Bull. Soc. Anthrop.,* June 21, 1864; Ch. Rochet, "Une Anthropologie des Beaux Arts," *ibid.,* Feb. 21, 1895; Bourdin's studies on race and sculpture, *Acad. des Sci.,* 1866; César Daly's similar studies on architecture, 1875-78, the "evolutionary" studies of language, literature, war, marriage, and the fine arts in the various races published by Ch. J. M. Letourneau in the *Bibliothèque Anthropologique,* XV, 1894, and the *Bibliothèque de Philosophie Contemporaine,* 1890-1903.

Taine's works, as we know, are informed by the spirit of race-discrimination and an excellent summary of his judgments on cultural matters can be found in Quenelle Harrold's *Taine, Master Eclectic of the Nineteenth Century,* Columbia University Master's Thesis, 1932. An interesting discussion between Goethe and Zelter (*Briefwechsel,* II, Apr. 20, 1808) bears on the point.

More recent systematizers of race-thinking in the arts are Alois Riegl (*Gesammelte Aufsätze,* Vienna, 1929) and Heinrich Wölfflin, one of whose works has been translated into English as *Principles of Art History* (orig. pub. 1915). Herbert Read bases himself on the work of Thouless which purports to show differences in aesthetic perception among the several races; Siewers adopts *Schallanalyse* and the study of metric as a means of discrimination; Walter Rauschenberger (Frankfurt, 1932) applies obscure criteria to philosophical systems in order to find out whether they are Indo-Germanic or not. Between these and the older men just cited are some more casual users of race-criticism: Victor Bérard (*Pénélope et les Barons des Iles,* II), Odin, *Genèse des Grands Hommes* (1895), Lichtenberger (*Revue Germanique,* Jan., 1905), Gaston Paris (*Litt. Française au Moyen-Age*), Larroumet (*Encyclopédie de la Musique,* III, 1767), Van Gennep ("Le Rôle des Germains," *Rev. des Idées,* Feb. 15, 1906), Ricciotto Canudo (*Le Livre de l'Evolution,* 1908), Y. M. Goblet (*Revue de Paris,* Mar. 15, 1933), G. Poisson (*Atlantis,* Sept.-Oct., 1933), Eug. Broermann (*Le Rhin Gaulois,* 1918, and *Genèse Atlantique,* 1933).

CHAPTER VI

Racial aesthetics so frequently merges with Celticism and general philology that it is sometimes difficult to classify authors and their works. On the Aryan question it is useful to consult Isaac Taylor, *The Origin of the Aryans,* London, 1890, which gives the anthropological view of the earlier controversy. S. Reinach, *L'origine des Aryens,* is more skeptical, as is also Emile Houzé, *L'Aryen et l'anthroposociologie*. The latest summary in half a dozen pages of the modern ideas on the subject is F. Boas, *Aryans and Non-Aryans,* N.Y., 1934, dealing with the Jewish problem in Nazi Germany.

Going back to the Aryanism of the early nineteenth century, one must take in J. C. Prichard, *Researches into the Physical History of Mankind,* 5 vols., 1836-47, and the no less interesting *Eastern Origins of the Celtic Nations,* 1831. Poesche, *Die Arier* (1878), together with Penka, *Origines Ariacae* (1883) and *Herkunft der Arier* (1886), bridges the gap between the early philologists like Grimm, Bopp, Rémusat, and Pictet and the modern Aryanism qualified or condemned by Taylor and Reinach.

On the Jewish question a summary comparable to Leroy-Beaulieu's quoted in the text is Lombroso's *L'Antisemitismo et la scienza moderna,* Torino, 1894. *Early American Jews* by Lee M. Friedman, *The Jews of Germany* by Marvin Lowenthal, and an article by Montefiore on anti-Semitism in modern England in the *Hibbert Journal* (Jan., 1921), all reflect the desire to clarify the race-question within the terms set by modern prejudice, whereas the writings of Lewisohn and Moses Hess (e.g., Epilogue to *Rome and Jerusalem*) merely reinforce racial beliefs by shifting complimentary labels. Any number of works on Freemasonry, in English, French, and German, assert the connection between that movement and Jewish influences: they can be found in any general bibliography. Perhaps the most interesting is Nivodo, *La Franc-Maçonnerie en France.* B. Faÿ, *La Franc-Maçonnerie,* 1935, gives a different but no less partisan idea of its origins and activities.

Celticism has produced libraries of books and articles. *La Revue Celtique* is one source of material, Roget de Belloguet's excellent *Ethnogénie Gauloise,* 1858-68, is another. Though laboring under a profound belief in race, it combines Celticism, anthropology, and sound sense, and provides a critical analysis of the various streams of Celtic research. Renan's remarks on the Celts are to be found in his *Essais de Morale et de Critique,* 1860, and *Questions Contemporaines,* 1875. Raoul Allier and Pierre Lasserre have written on Renan and indicated modern indebtedness to him for his racial and other previsions. Napoleon III's *Histoire de Jules César,* prepared by several historians and military experts, appeared in Paris in 1865-66 and added to the French consciousness of Celtic and Roman origins. In England, Matthew Arnold wrote *On the Study of Celtic Literature,* 1867, and *Irish Essays* (1882), and participated in Celtic demonstrations similar to Renan's Celtic dinners, both movements being recorded in the current periodical literature.

A popular theory combining speech and race-divisions was that elaborated by Friedrich Müller of Vienna. His *Grundriss der Sprachwissenschaft,* 4 vols., 1880-84, divided mankind according to the texture of the hair and the supposedly correlated forms of speech. Haeckel adopted the theory in the later editions of his *Anthropogenie* (5th ed., 1903), which also led to the confusion of doctrines in Lefèvre, *Les races et les langues,* 1893.

CHAPTER VII

The Proceedings of the several anthropological congresses that met after 1867 give the best insight into the practices and results of craniometry. Some byways of anthropological thinking, however, can be indicated briefly. Bouglé related Anthropology and Democracy in an article under that title in the *Revue de Métaphysique et de Morale* for July, 1897, and again in the *Revue Philosophique,* Apr., 1900, under the title "La Sociologie biologique et le régime des castes." The *Dictionnaire des Sciences Anthropologiques,* 1894-95, furnishes the best sampling of the diverse theories on all branches of the subject, but one should also look up Thomas Wright's theory of the posthumous transformation of buried bones through the action of moisture in *The Athenaeum* for Feb. 25, 1861. Serres's notion about the shape of the heart in the colored and white races is reported in *Le Moniteur* for Feb. 3, 1855, after having been taught by the author in his course on comparative anatomy, while the differences found in the shape and texture of lice inhabiting different races of men are described by Murray in the *Transactions of the Royal Society of Edinburgh,* 1861, 567. The frequent references to the gradual approximation of the white "Yankee" to the American Indian type can be sampled in Laumonier (*Revue Scientifique,* July, 1885, 116), in Quatrefages (*Races Humaines,* 1887, *passim*), and in Fouillée (*Psychologie du Peuple Français,* 1898, 24).

Anthropological studies on particular geographical or anatomical regions are numberless. Bloch, like Cénas, wrote on the *labia minora* as a criterion of race, *Bull. Soc. Anthrop.,* 1898, 284; Durand de Gros studied the noble races in Aveyron, *ibid.,* 1879; Labit covered the Ardennes, *Avanc. des Sciences,* 1897; Atgier examined the conscripts in Vienne (France), *Soc. Anthrop.,* 1898; Mantegazza and Dr. Jacobus each published in 1900 ethnologies of sex; Richter related Nietzsche's doctrines to contemporary biological theories (Leipzig, 1903); Pulle and Sergi separately covered Italy in *Profilo-antropologico,* Florence, 1898, and *Le Origini,* Milan, 1909, respectively. Twentieth-century periodicals dealing with "scientific" anthropology are for France alone: *Encéphale, Anthropologie et Ethnographie, Revue d'Anthropologie, Anthropos,* and *Revue de l'Ecole d'Anthropologie.*

CHAPTERS VIII-IX

The easy transition from race to nationalism is seen in Blanqui's *La Patrie en Danger,* 1870; in Quatrefages's *La race prussienne,* 1871, showing the invaders of France to be barbaric Finns; and in the refutation signed A. B. in *Zeitschrift für Ethnologie,* Berlin,

1872. In the *Revue des Deux Mondes,* May 15, 1872, Fustel de Coulanges published his famous manifesto denying Germanic influences in the formation of France, and the following year Alexandre Bertrand was addressing to Paul Broca his "Lettres sur les Celtes, Gaulois et Francs," *Rev. d'Anthrop.,* Apr. 15-Oct. 15, 1873.

The feeling of decadence that spread over Europe in the nineties appears in Max Nordau's works, particularly *Degenerescence;* in Bazalgette (translator of Walt Whitman), *A quoi tient l'infériorité française?* (1900); Paul Adam, *Le Malaise du Monde Latin,* 1910; Alfred Berl, "Race et Nationalité," *Grande Revue,* Oct. 1, 1900.

Somewhat earlier the poets Strada (*Le Promethée de L'Avenir,* 1895) and Péladan (*La Décadence Latine,* 1895) had given varying interpretations of the race-problem in fictional form. The latter work was a sequence of fourteen novels, ending with the death of a pretender to the throne of France and emphasizing the epigraph of the series: *Finis Latinorum.* The Italian politician Colajanni, whose *Latins et Anglo-Saxons* was translated in 1905, and the Brazilian Felix Bocayuva (*Sur l'Arène: Latins et Anglo-Saxons,* 1928) continue the same tradition.

The more cheerful Pan-Saxonism is visible in Cecil Rhodes's *Last Will and Testament,* ed. W. T. Stead, 1902; Sidney Low in *Nineteenth Century* for May, 1902; Chamberlain's London speech of Nov. 11, 1895; Lord Beresford's "Future of the Anglo-Saxon Race," *North American Review,* Dec., 1900; an article in the *Alldeutsche Blätter* for Apr. 15, 1900, entitled "Die Romanen im XXten Jahrhunderts"; and Treitschke's *Politics,* Berlin, 1907.

Everywhere, judgments of culture and race followed standards of contemporary political power: Gehring's *Racial Contrasts, Graeco-Latins and Teutons,* N.Y., 1908, must be put side by side with Bramsen's *Rasse, Kultur, und Kunst,* Leipzig, 1905, and with George Edward Woodberry's lectures at the Lowell Institute on *Race Power in Literature,* 1903. Homer Lea, *The Day of the Saxon,* N.Y., 1912, and Madison Grant, *The Passing of the Great Race,* N.Y., 1916, usher in the era of fears for the white race. Novicow's *Avenir de la race blanche,* 1897, was more reassuring, but the question remained open until the War itself, as is shown by works like Boerschmann's *Allgemeine Gesetze bei dem Problem des Aufstiegs und des Niedergangs der Rasse,* Würzburg, 1914, the writings of Bernhardi (e.g., *Deutschland und der nächste Krieg,* Stuttgart, 1913), and of Nadaillac, Chambrun, Anold, Lapouge, and Demolins in France.

The War itself was viewed as a racial struggle by Gohier, *La race a parlé,* 1916; Chamberlain, *Deutsches Wesen,* München, 1916; S. Kennedy, *The Pan-Angles,* London, 1915; G. Ferrero, "Le Génie Latin," *Revue Hebdomadaire,* May 12, 1917; and many others. The conflict brought forth a useful lecture by James Bryce on *Race Sentiment as a Factor in History,* London, 1915, as well as a good deal of delving into the history of the Germanic Invasions. The typical use of Tacitus and the Nordic Myth is best exemplified by Eduard Norden's *Die Germanische Urgeschichte in Tacitus Germania,* 1920, written during the War for the avowed purpose of national and racial glorification. Its 520 large pages are devoted to anthropological and historical comments on the Roman historian's thirty pages of epigrammatic condensation.

CHAPTER X

For the National Socialist Literature, which is huge, it is best to begin with Rudolf Benze's *Wegweiser ins Dritte Reich,* Braunschweig, 1933, and to proceed with the bibliographies given in the works of Günther, Darré, Clauss, and Erbt (e.g., *Weltgeschichte auf rassischer Grundlage,* 1934). The catalogue of the firm of Lehmann in München, which publishes so many of the German works on race as well as Grant, Stoddard, and Henry Ford (*Der Internationale Jude,* 1921-22), also helps. As for the periodical literature, both learned and popular, it permits and requires no survey.

In modern France have appeared works of varying scope and merit that can be read in conjunction with those cited in Chapters I and X. M. M. Gorce, *La France au dessus des races,* 1934; Georges Montandon, *La Race, les races,* 1933, which tries to be enlightened about racism but sticks to somatic criteria; E. F. Fabre, *Le Choc suprême ou la Mêlée des races,* 1921, which deals with nationality and ought to be compared with Aug. Longnon, *Formation de la Nationalité Française,* 1922; Muret, *Le Crépuscule des nations blanches,* 1925, to be read at the same time as H. Massis, *Défense de l'Occident,* 1927. In novel form, Marius-Ary Leblond and Louis Bertrand continue the colonial and racist tradition of Paul Adam with *Le Miracle de la Race,* 1934, and *Le Sang des Races.* Malraux, *Tentation de l'Occident,* 1926, has many points in common with Mauclair's *L'Orient Vierge* which antedates it by a score of years. An ambitious critico-anthropological work by P. Abraham, *Créatures Chez Balzac,* 1922, deals with the physique and character of the fictional persons in the *Comédie Humaine* and exemplifies the method applied by Havelock Ellis in *British Genius*.

In English, the modern literature on race can be approached through the indexes to periodicals. The names of H. F. Osborn, H. J. Eckinrode, Ellsworth Huntington, W. McDougall, Langdon-Davies, Seton-Watson, E. M. East, A. E. Wiggam, Roland Dixon, and Lord Acton will suggest others whom they quote or from whom they borrow science, history, or philology according to the usual pattern.

CHAPTER XI

Titles to add to those cited for Chapter I should include these self-explanatory general works: *Anthropology and Modern Life* by Franz Boas, N.Y., 1928; *Diet and Race* by F. P. Armitage, London, 1922; "The Struggle of Races and Social Groups" by H. E. Barnes, *Journal of Race Development,* IX, 394, 1919; *The Negro in Chicago,* Chicago, 1922; *American Minority Peoples* by Donald Young, N.Y., 1931; *Race Differences* by Otto Klineberg, N.Y., 1935; "Racial Inequality" by W. O. Brown, *Journal of Negro History,* XVI, 43.

On the question of nationalities: Henri Hauser, *Principe et origine des nationalités,* 1916; W. D. Babington, *Fallacies of Race Theories as Applied to National Characteristics,* London, 1895; John Oakesmith, *Race and Nationality,* N.Y., 1919; Sageret, "La question des races et la science," *Revue du Mois,* June 15, 1919; and C. J. H. Hayes, *Historical Evolution of Modern Nationalism,* N.Y., 1931.

INDEX

(*The index to this edition was prepared by Virginia Xanthos Faggi*)